THE BEST
TAR HEEL
BARBECUE

Manteo to Murphy

This guidebook is a listing and critique of some of the best Tar Heel barbecue places Manteo to Murphy. Each critique of a restaurant in this book only reflects the tastes and opinions of the author.

Published by The Best Tar Heel Barbecue Manteo to Murphy, Inc.
http://www.tarheel-bbq.com

The Best Tar Heel Barbecue Manteo to Murphy
ISBN: 0-9722979-0-1

Suggested Retail: $14.95 plus tax

Illustrations and photos with text by the Author

Cover Photos:
Center photo - Brittny Austin, daughter of Kim Austin at Bubbas in Frisco - Author
Photo of mountains courtesy of NC Division of Tourism, Film and Sports Development

Foreword Photo:
Courtesy of Wake Forest University - Ken Bennett, photographer

Cover and Book Design:
Steve McCulloch
Raleigh, NC

Printed by Harperprints
One Industry Drive
Henderson, NC 27536
1-800-682-5948

Manufactured in the United States of America

Second Printing 2003

For the greatest gifts that God has given to me personally,
my children: Jim, Anna and Mary Elizabeth.

Acknowledgments

First and foremost I wish to express my love and appreciation to my children - Jim, Anna and Mary Elizabeth - for their continued support and encouragement while I was writing this book. The simple words "Dad we're so proud of you" kept me going many times when the mind was willing but the body was weak.

I also wish to express my thanks and appreciation to two young women in my law office, Jennifer Boorse and Amanda Tucker. These two served not only as office managers, paralegals, secretaries and good right and left hands but were also pressed into learning more about barbecue than they probably ever wanted to know. Thanks ladies.

I wish to thank my friends at Knollwood Baptist Church, the Forsyth County Courthouse and other places who continued to inquire month after month about the progress of the book. Their encouragement, along with my children and staff, sustained me through some very long hours for a period of approximately thirteen months.

Special thanks to Will and Deni McIntyre, my harbor pilots who guided me through the unfamiliar waters of self publishing a book.

Last, but certainly not least, I would like to thank the sponsor(s) that contributed in so many ways to making the second printing and future printings of this book possible. Their support has made possible this books continued strong run. My heartfelt thanks to Branch Banking & Trust Co. (BB&T), Richard "Dick" Ward, Executive Vice President and Marketing Manager and Ron Denny, Senior Vice President and Marketing Group Manager.

FRIENDS OF SPECIAL OLYMPICS NORTH CAROLINA

Table Of Contents

Foreword 13

Introduction 15

A Brief History of Tar Heel Barbecue 21

A Map of North Carolina 25

TAR HEEL BARBECUE PLACES

Section I: The Mountains: (See Top Quarter Tab)

   A Map of the Mountains 33

   Barbecue Inn, Asheville 35
   Mountain Smoke House Barbecue, Asheville 37
   Perry's BBQ, Black Mountain 39
   Old Hickory House, Brevard 41
   The Bar-B-Q Wagon, Bryson City 42
   Skeeter's BBQ House, Canton 43
   Carolina Smokehouse, Cashiers .45
   Craig's Barbecue, Cherokee 46
   The Cajun Pig, Chimney Rock 47
   Duncan's Barbecue, Chimney Rock 49
   Dillsboro Smokehouse, Dillsboro 50
   Sam's Country Cook-Out, Edneyville 51
   The Barbecue Shack, Etowah 52
   Fat Buddies Ribs and BBQ, Franklin 54
   Rib Country, Hayesville 56
   Butts on the Creek, Maggie Valley 58
   Herb's Pit BBQ, Murphy 60
   Green River BBQ, Saluda 62
   Smoky Mountain Grill and Lee's Barbecue, Sylva 64
   Eddie's Bar-B-Que, Waynesville 65

   NOTES 67

Section II: The Piedmont (See Second Quarter Tab)

A Map of the Piedmont 73

Log Cabin Barbecue, Albemarle 75
Whispering Pines Cafe, Albemarle 77
Speedy Lohr's BBQ of Arcadia, Arcadia 79
Pappy's Barbeque, Banner Elk 81
Bubba's Barbecue, Charlotte 84
Gary's Bar-B-Que, China Grove 86
Little Richard's Lexington Bar-B-Que, Clemmons 88
Troutman's Bar-B-Q, Concord 89
Bennett's Smokehouse and Saloon, Conover .92
The Hickory Log Barbecue, Forest City 94
R.O.'s Barbecue, Gastonia 95
M&K Barbecue and Country Cooking, Granite Quarry 96
Kepley's Bar-B-Q, High Point 98
Wallace Brother's BBQ, Lambsburg, VA 100
Hannah's Bar-B-Que, Lenoir 102
The Barbecue Center, Inc. Lexington 104
Jimmy's Barbecue, Lexington 106
Lexington Barbecue, Lexington 108
Bar-B-Que King, Lincolnton 111
Spear's BBQ & Grill, Linville Falls 112
Fuzzy's, Madison 115
Deano's Barbecue, Mocksville 117
Lancaster's BBQ, Mooresville 120
Timberwood's Family Restaurant, Morganton 122
Snappy Lunch, Mount Airy 124
Doc's Deli, North Wilkesboro 127
Arey's Barbecue, Rockwell 128
The Barbecue Place, Rutherfordton 130
Hendrix Barbeque, Salisbury 131
Richard's Bar-B-Q, Salisbury 132
Wink's Bar-B-Que, Salisbury 134
Alston Bridges Barbecue, Inc., Shelby 136
Bridges Barbecue Lodge, Shelby 138
Carolina Bar-B-Que, Statesville 140

Little Pigs Barbecue, Statesville 142

Scotz BBQ and Diner, Taylorsville 144

Stamey's Barbecue, Tyro 145

Smoky Mountain Barbecue, West Jefferson 147

Hill's Lexington Barbecue, Winston-Salem 149

Little Richard's Bar-B-Que, Winston-Salem 152

Hall's BBQ Restaurant, Yadkinville 154

NOTES 157

Section III: The Flatlands: (See Third Quarter Tab)

A Map of the Flatlands 165

Ralph's Barbecue, Angier 167

Henry James Barbecue, Asheboro 168

Hop's Bar-B-Q, Asheboro 170

Hamilton's Barbecue, Biscoe 171

Wells Pork Products, Burgaw 173

Hursey's Barbecue, Burlington 174

Bon's Bar-B-Q, Carrboro 177

Williamson's Barbecue and Seafood, Chadbourn 180

Allen & Son Barbecue, Chapel Hill 182

Farmhouse Barbecue, Clinton 184

Lewis Barbecue, Clinton 186

Southern Style BBQ and Chicken, Clinton 187

Ron's Barn, Coats 189

Bob's Barbecue, Creedmoor 190

Bud's Place, Cumnock 192

Ernie's Barbecue, Dunn 194

Bullock's Barbecue, Durham 195

Fuller's BBQ, Elizabethtown 199

Cape Fear Bar-B-Q and Chicken, Fayetteville 200

Chason's Famous Buffet, Fayetteville 201

McCall's Barbecue and Seafood, Goldsboro 203

Wilber's Barbecue, Goldsboro 205

Stamey's Barbecue, Greensboro 208

Evan's Famous Barbecue and Chicken, Henderson 211

Gary's Barbecue, Henderson 213

Nunnery-Freeman Barbecue, Henderson 213

Skipper's Forsyth Barbecue, Henderson 215

Knightdale Seafood and BBQ, Knightdale 217

Ken's Grill, LaGrange 219

General McArthur's Original Pig Pickin', Laurinburg 221

Howard's Barbecue, Lillington 223

Fuller's BBQ, Lumberton 224

Village Inn Barbecue, Lumberton 225

A&M Grill, Mebane 226

Eddie's Barbecue, Newton Grove 228

Smithfield's Chicken 'n Bar-B-Q, Newton Grove 230

Clyde Cooper's Barbeque, Raleigh 232

Don Murray's Barbecue and Seafood, Raleigh 234

Short Sugar's Drive-In, Reidsville 236

Gardner's Barbecue, Rocky Mount 239

Bob Melton's Barbecue, Rocky Mount 241

Ron's Barn BBQ and Seafood, Sanford 243

Holt Lake Bar-B-Que and Seafood, Smithfield 244

White Swan Restaurant, Smithfield 246

John's Barbecue and Seafood, Southern Pines 247

Annette's Bar-B-Q, Troy 249

Bland's Barbecue, Wallace 250

Cavenaughs Family Supper House, Wallace 251

Pink Supper House, Wallace 253

Bland's Barbecue, Warsaw 255

Ralph's Barbecue, Weldon 256

Jordan's Barbecue, West End 258

Joe's Barbecue Kitchen, Whiteville 259

Sutton's Barbecue, Willow Springs 260

Stephenson's Barbecue, Willow Springs 262

Flip's Bar-B-Que, Wilmington 264

Bill Ellis Barbecue, Wilson 265

Cherry's Barbecue, Wilson 267

Mitchell's Barbecue, Wilson 269

Parker's Barbecue, Wilson 272

NOTES 275

Section VI: Coastal: (See Bottom Quarter Tab)

A Map of the Coast 281

Skylight Inn, Ayden 283
Piggybacks BBQ, Creswell 286
Lane's Family Barbecue and Seafood, Edenton 287
Tuck's Restaurant, Elizabeth City 288
Bubba's Bar-B-Que, Frisco 290
B's Barbecue, Greenville 292
Captain Bob's BBQ and Seafood Restaurant, Hertford 295
Fisherman's Wharf, Jacksonville 297
King's Restaurant, Kinston 299
F.B. Duncan's Bar-B-Que, Manteo 301
Whitley's Barbecue, Murfreesboro 302
Moore's Bar-B-Que, New Bern 304
Simp's Barbecue, Roper 306
Joe's Barbecue Kitchen, Shallotte 308
Abram's Barbecue, Tarboro 310
Boss Hog Backyard Bar-B-Que, Washington 312
Hog Heaven, Washington 314
Shaw's Barbecue House, Williamston 315
Bunn's BBQ, Windsor 317

NOTES 319

Barbecue Routes 321

Recipes 327

Tips From the Pit Masters 345

Pig Parties 348

Postcard 351

Foreword

Jim Early is a native North Carolinian and a long-time resident of Winston-Salem. A graduate of law from Wake Forest University, he continues a limited civil practice and is certified as a superior court mediator. He speaks nationally and internationally on quality of life issues, stress management and achieving balance, motivating his audiences with his philosophy of life – that less is often more.

Born in Henderson, a small eastern North Carolina town close to the Virginia border, Jim inherited his love of cooking from his mother Nettie Hicks Early and her family. They all regarded eating as a form of celebration. He was exposed to good barbecue all of his life, Jim says. In fact, the Hicks family ate everything about a pig but the squeal.

Steeped in this atmosphere of great country cooking and family recipes handed down over generations, Jim took the basics of cooking and perfected those skills, developing a flair for gourmet cooking and creating new recipes.

In addition to instilling in him a love of fine cooking, Jim's early upbringing taught him principles that have stayed with him and indeed shaped his life. Jim is passionate about fair play, caring and reaching out to those who for whatever reason need a hand. Jim also has a large streak of his father's adventuresome/entrepreneurial spirit and thirst for knowledge. "I try to be a student wherever I go." Jim says, "If you're building a boat I want to watch. If you're making an afghan or carving an ice sculpture, I want to watch." This love of learning and pursuit of knowledge has led Jim in exciting and varied directions. In addition to being an avid and accomplished hunter, fisherman and gourmet cook, Jim's interests include riding and brokering Tennessee walking horses, breeding and training English Setters and Pointers and restoring British cars and classic Chris Craft mahogany speed boats. As hobbies Jim offers gourmet cooking classes at Salem College and throughout North Carolina, paints, writes, plays in bands and loves to dance.

Author

Though his interests are varied and sundry, Jim always returns to his love of hunting and cooking. Several times during the year, Jim, an experienced hunting guide, leads hunting and fishing parties to venues such as Alaska, Montana, South Dakota, the Bahamas, Scotland and Africa. These

trips are part of Jim's new company, *Business Adventure Seminars in the Bush* and include gourmet cooking classes as part of the experience. Jim shows his clients hands on preparation of the game they've taken, offering them the opportunity to experience delightful and delectable dishes and learn new recipes and cooking techniques.

Jim's hunting experiences and the recipes he has developed are the subjects of a cookbook to be published in 2004 – *Shining Times – The Adventures and Recipes of a Sportsman*. In addition to illustrations from some of the world's top wildlife artists and photographers, *Shining Times* takes the reader from the pursuit to the preparation of a variety of recipes from "campfire to the White House" in range and complexity.

In *Shining Times,* Jim transports the reader on an armchair experience through the whole hunting and cooking experience, inviting the reader to vicariously live the adventure through Jim's eyes. It is this desire to enrich a reader's life that is also the focus of this book – *The Best TAR HEEL BARBECUE Manteo to Murphy*. Jim hopes that his readers will experience his journey through the mountains, the piedmont, the flatlands and the coast and come to know the warmth and fellowship of those throughout the state who welcomed Jim and shared not only their cooking techniques but their family histories and stories as well.

"I hope each reader of this book can vicariously experience my journey...new friends and old clasped my hand...but beyond the good food and beauty of rural North Carolina, the thing that made this adventure shine for me was the people. The outpouring of friendship that I experienced, the warmth, the fellowship and the laughter will be with me all my days," he writes.

And what shall be the legacy that Jim leaves the reader? It's not only the recounting of his 18,000 mile, year-long journey, or his tales of those who spend 14 to 16 hours a day producing the best barbecue the world has to offer. Jim's critique as a chef of 140 barbecue places from the Outer Banks to the border of Tennessee provides the reader a treasure map to some of the best barbecue to be found in the Old North State. But for Jim, who has eaten barbecued sea turtle and alligator tail in the Keys and spit-roasted Kudu with the Zulu, his work exemplifies the true meaning of "service." As was his intention from the beginning of his trek to the crafting of this book, all of the proceeds from the *The Best TAR HEEL BARBECUE Manteo to Murphy* will be donated to Special Olympics, North Carolina.

Kitty Bowman, a long time member of Knollwood Baptist Church in Winston-Salem and a dear friend of Jim's once told Jim that "service" was his witness. That pretty much describes the man.

Eileen Kerr,
Freelance Writer and Marketing Consultant

14

Introduction

What is it about barbecue that invokes so much passion among its followers – those who cook, chase and consume the slow-roasting method of cooking "the other white meat"? People like Chinese, Mexican and Italian food. People like pizza, pasta and steak. But those who like barbecue are passionate about their food. For many, barbecue is an item often included in their daily living. For others, a new or favorite barbecue place is a destination. The pursuit of good barbecue is a quest that stirs them to drive hundreds of miles to a distant community or hamlet in search of a "pretty pig."

Barbecue is the "All-American" casual food. True, our ancestors cooked meat on spits over flame. But the custom of slowly roasting meat on a grid of wooden sticks at low heat over live coals was developed by Native Americans and passed on to our forefathers. Cooking barbecue – be it pork, beef, mutton, chicken or game – is as American as apple pie. Barbecue is enjoyed in all 50 states and this form of cooking is the one most often associated with celebration, be it the Fourth of July or a gathering of family and friends.

In preparation to write this book I traveled in all 100 counties of this great state, drove more than 18,000 miles, talked to more than 1,500 people and critiqued more than 200 barbecue places in six months. This journey took me from the Outer Banks to the border of Tennessee. I tried to learn as much as I could about raising hogs, methods of cooking barbecue, various kinds of sauces and dips, and the history and people who raise the hogs, cook the barbecue and those privileged to enjoy it.

After completing my journey, I concluded that:

- **BARBECUE IS COLOR BLIND**
  Native Americans shared their method of cooking meat with white settlers who later shared these skills with African Americans who developed and refined these skills in their roles as cooks and barbecue journeymen. Some of their cooking skills and secret recipes were shared with whites. Today, whites and blacks share their wonderful slow roasted product with every nationality that makes up this wonderful melting pot we call America. African Americans shared with me that long before repeal of the Jim Crow Laws, when the crops were in and it was time to celebrate, it was generally done with a pig pickin'. All who participated in the harvest and their children gathered for the feast. At this time in history the after harvest pig pickin' was perhaps the only time that blacks and whites ate, socialized and celebrated together. At that time and in that moment all differences were set aside as they celebrated and shared the meal.

15

• BARBECUE IS TRADITION

Those dedicated souls who spend 14-16 hours a day producing good barbecue take pride in the fact that their place has been in business 40, 50 or 60 years and that it was founded by their grandparents or parents and is now carried on by the third or fourth generation. Patrons of such places seem equally pleased to share that they have just found such a place or that they have eaten at such a place for 40, 50 or 60 years. People in their 70s and 80s will patiently wait at their place for their table even though other tables are open. Some people eat two or three times a day at their places because the owners, staff and ambiance affords them a "comfort zone." Such places with their retro '50s décor seem to take us back to a kinder, gentler time.

• BARBECUE IS A BONDING AGENT

Perhaps more than any other casual dining food, barbecue brings together people of different races, creeds, religions and socio-economic levels. Pull into the parking area of any good barbecue place and you will see luxury motor cars, SUVs, pickup trucks, motorcycles and junkers that barely made it to the lot. Professionals, educators, athletes, skilled and unskilled workers, unemployed and winos come together to share what may be their only common interest – good barbecue.

• BARBECUE IS UNIVERSAL

Barbecue is found in some form in each of our United States. And it is generally found in some form in every country on the planet. People like the taste of slow roasted meat. The animal or critter (or the parts thereof) that produced this treat may not have made our A list but for a certain group of people in a particular place it was – good barbecue.

I have been exposed to good barbecue all my life. I was born in Eastern North Carolina and my family later moved to the Piedmont where I have spent my adult years. My mother's maiden name was "Hicks." A hundred plus years ago the Hicks family settled in an area now known as Hicksboro outside the town of Henderson. My mother's father, Joseph Carter Hicks or "Papa," was a connoisseur of good pork. In fact, this was a calling shared by the entire Hicks family. They ate everything about a pig but the squeal. I drew the line at chitlins. Being reared in such a family where the smallest celebration was reason enough to do a pig-pickin', I came to appreciate the taste and art of cooking the "other white meat."

I have eaten good barbecue in most of our 50 states and a number of foreign countries. I have enjoyed mouth-watering ribs and good blues in Chicago. I have "kicked back" with friends in Texas to barbecue beef brisket, hotter than hell peppers, long necks and the two-step. Kansas City barbecue beef ribs have long been among my favorites. When fly fishing in the Keys I have been treated to

barbecue sea turtle, alligator tail and rattlesnake filets. They're mighty fine with a pitcher of margaritas. My hunting experiences in the wilds of the Rockies, Canada and Alaska have enabled me to share the table, stump or rock with a number of interesting characters where we dined on barbecue elk, venison, bear and even beaver. In Africa I have shared succulent roast mutton with large ranch owners and spit roasted Kudu with the Zulu. Both were equally good.

I have yet to eat barbecue that I enjoy as much as I do the good barbecue of North Carolina. It is my favorite casual-dining meal. It was my passion for this pursuit of a "pretty pig" and the encouragement of friends that prompted me to write this book.

A number of books have been written about national or regional barbecue and a couple have been written about some of the better-known barbecue places in North Carolina. But to my knowledge no book has been written that provided the reader with the location, history, cooking style, sauce style and a gourmet cook's critique of the product of some of the best barbecue places to be found in all 100 counties of the Tar Heel State. This was my goal.

I am a trial lawyer who speaks nationally on quality of life, stress management, balance and the tenets of less is often more. Therefore, I had to find a window that would permit me to do the field research for this project without stringing it out so long and to continue to serve my clients and keep my speaking engagements. Careful review indicated this was most doable May through October. In May 2001 I commenced a regime of practicing law 40 hours in four days. This usually entails 14-15 hours per day at the office. On Thursday night I would bail out and drive to the area I intended to work Friday and Saturday. A number of barbecue places are closed on Sundays, and some on Mondays.

I would arrive at some small town and find a room around midnight. At 5 a.m. on Friday I was up talking to anyone I could find at businesses, truck stops, restaurants, etc. about barbecue. The question I posed was: "If your best friend were celebrating a birthday today and wanted to eat barbecue, where in this county would you take them as a treat?" When I had a list of names I commenced my daily search. As soon as kitchen staff was in the closest restaurant so was I. When they were cutting out the lights at the last place I could find that day I trundled off to yet another small town motel and repeated this scenario on Saturday. Sunday morning I slept in and returned home to do about five hours dictation of my notes Sunday afternoon. Sunday night I crashed.

The reason I framed the barbecue question as I did for the locals was because I may have gotten a different response if I asked, "Where do you usually eat barbecue?" The person's job may not have allowed for much travel time for lunch. Thus they may eat at the closest barbecue place rather than the place they thought was the best in the county. Also if they had other constraints such as a DWI and limited privileges they probably were not going to travel 15-20 miles one way on a Moped. Others simply may be unwilling to make the effort for themselves but might go the extra mile for a friend on their birthday.

I also found that a lot of people did not venture far from their home base. There may be a good barbecue place 25 miles away on the other side of the county but for many it might as well have been on the other side of the world. People tend to stay in their "comfort zone." I have had a number of people tell me there was no good barbecue in their county, or no good barbecue in that part of the county, only to find a place that was a treasure and not known to them 15 miles down the road. To find such a place requires a lot of driving back roads and stopping at filling stations, country stores and volunteer fire departments. I spoke with truck drivers, highway patrol officers, deputy sheriffs, wrecker drivers, people on tractors in the field, and people eating at barbecue places as well as the owners.

I found that people who like barbecue and those who prepare and serve it are decidedly the friendliest people I have ever encountered. Everyone with whom I spoke – patron, owner or wait staff – could not have been more helpful with my project. Not once did I encounter an owner who was not willing to show me their place, discuss cooking methods, recipes (not the sauce) and assist in any way possible. Not once did I encounter a waitperson who acted as if he or she were doing a favor to wait on me or had an "attitude." Every waitperson that served my food did it with a smile and made me feel at home. Like the locals, I was called "honey," "sugar," "darling" and "lord child."

In an effort to be ethical and fair about critiquing each place I decided not to eat any meals, snacks or beverages while on the road. This enabled me to remain constantly hungry and wanting to eat at every place I stopped. I generally could critique five or six places a day. I would order a sample of the barbecue in all the ways that it was served – chopped, coarse chopped and sliced – along with a tablespoon of slaw (red, white or both), one hushpuppy and a milkshake cup with water and slices of lemon. I would cleanse my palate with the lemon water before attempting to taste the barbecue. I would take a bite, taste it like a wine and write what I had experienced. This was followed by more lemon water and repeated with the other styles of offerings. I tasted the sauces individually with a spoon in the same fashion. I then added sauces as I deemed necessary to the way the barbecue was served from the kitchen. I tasted the slaw and ate half a hushpuppy. I did not eat the side dishes. However, if fried chicken or brunswick stew was considered a specialty, I would try those items only. I tasted the desserts (at their insistence) at only three or four places out of more than 200 places visited. I ate Altoids between each barbecue place to again freshen my palate.

I was able to stay perpetually hungry all day since I never ate more than several spoonfuls of food and a half a hushpuppy at any one place. I did not feel it was fair to the next place I would visit if I had curbed my hunger by eating at the previous place. I also tried to prevent saturating my palate with the barbecue or sauce flavors of the previous place that would impede me from having a fresh taste for the next offering.

I actually lost 15 pounds during the six months I did field work on this book. I'm not advocating eating barbecue five or six times a day, two or three days a week for six months as a weight-loss program. I guess between eating healthy and heartwise four days a week I inadvertently backed into

a "mini" Atkins Diet on the weekends. Of more interest to me, because today's hogs have been bred to be leaner and the people operating barbecue places respect that their patrons are more fat gram conscious, we are eating a leaner more fat-free product than we have ever known. My blood pressure (generally 150) dropped to 132 from the time I had it checked before starting this project until completion six months later.

Oftentimes after I had finished an area, a traveling salesman or a barbecue aficionado would say, "Did you go to 'so-in-so's' in 'such-in-such?'" Toward the end of my fieldwork I was making long treks to the furthest reaches of the state to pick up loose ends or check out newly discovered places. After a couple of wild goose chases, I learned to do as much checking by car phone as possible. Some of the names given me were incorrect, or I discovered that the place had burned or closed several years before I arrived at the crossroads in rural Eastern North Carolina or some small mountain town. One of the places included in this book does not have a telephone, another is closed on Saturdays, many are closed on Sundays and some are closed on Sundays and Mondays. In addition to regular closings, the owners of barbecue places are pretty independent folk, and there is always the risk that the place will be closed for vacations, weddings, funerals or they simply sold out of barbecue for the day and locked the doors. I suggest you call ahead.

Inevitably when people find out that I have done this book they ask the question, "Which is the best in the state?" There is no correct (politically or otherwise) answer to this question. There are a number of good barbecue places across this great state. There are barbecue places in some areas that are equally good as barbecue places in other areas of the state but the style of cooking and sauces are different, good nonetheless. To be included in this book a barbecue place had to meet three criteria: (1) they had to cook their own pork; (2) they had to make their own sauce or dip; and (3) the barbecue, the sauces, the slaw and hushpuppies (to my taste) had to be GOOD! I made the assumption that if they could cook good barbecue, come up with their own sauce or dip and fix good slaw and hushpuppies, they could probably come up with good side dishes and desserts as well. People come to barbecue places to eat barbecue, they do not come because of banana pudding. If a place has good sides and desserts that's a plus but that is not what brings 'em in and brings 'em back.

To me, barbecue generally falls in two categories, good and not so good. The good on a scale of 1-10 can range from 5-10. A number of places I critiqued (to my taste) would fall in the 5, 6 range, meaning GOOD. Some of the places I critiqued (to my taste) would fall in the 7, 8 range, meaning BETTER. A few (to my taste) would fall in the 9, 10 range, meaning BEST. Every barbecue place included in this book is not as good as every other barbecue place included in this book. Every barbecue place included in this book is however the best (to my taste) I was able to find in that particular area.

With few exceptions the barbecue places at which I stopped that are not included in this book were not included because they did not cook their own barbecue but instead bought it from a barbe-

19

cue wholesale distributor. The 'cue was good but they didn't cook it and they generally used only commercial sauces.

For the readers' convenience, I have divided the state into four sections: Section 1 – The Mountains, Section 2 – The Piedmont, Section 3 – The Flatlands, Section 4 – Coastal. The section names were chosen because they more typically define the area. There is however an overlap of topography in every section. The barbecue in Section 1 is a hodgepodge of Florida style, Texas style, Lexington style and a few representatives of Eastern North Carolina style. The barbecue in Section 2 is primarily Lexington style and Salisbury, Gastonia, Shelby and other area variations on a theme. There are a few places offering Eastern North Carolina style and South Carolina style in this area. Section 3 is comprised of Lexington style barbecue from the Piedmont-Triad area (Winston-Salem, High Point and Greensboro) to the Research Triangle (Raleigh, Durham and Chapel Hill). From Raleigh east almost all of the barbecue places serve Eastern North Carolina-style 'cue. Section 4 barbecue places serve Eastern North Carolina-style barbecue almost exclusively except for one place that serves barbecue more attuned to the Florida style. Though the book has been divided into four sections there are in reality only two main types of barbecue being served in North Carolina (Eastern North Carolina style and Lexington style) with variations thereof occurring about every 50 miles in any direction.

I hope each reader of this book can vicariously experience my journey as I attempted to ferret out the best barbecue places in the Tar Heel State. Did I find them all? No! And if I failed to find a "treasure" that you know about, please share that information by removing the post card in the back of this book and providing this information to me. But more than that, tell the people that operate your favorite place that I somehow missed, how much you appreciate their efforts, hard work and good food and that my missing them was my loss. I can assure you that if you will share your information with me I will certainly try to visit your special place when I revise this book.

The journey that produced this book carried all of my senses to new heights and fed my soul as well. Wonderful aromas wafted from pits and chimneys. Uncommonly good food crossed my palate. New friends and old clasped my hand. My eyes beheld the shafts of first morning light on the dunes and the purple haze of sinking sun in the high country. My ears heard the sigh of the waves, the whisper of the pines and the call of quail. Beyond the good food and the beauty of rural North Carolina, the thing that made this adventure shine for me was the people. The outpouring of friendship that I experienced, the warmth, the fellowship and the laughter will be with me all my days.

Bon Appetit,

Jim Early

A Brief History Of
Tar Heel Barbecue

The earliest recorded pig pickin' in the Tar Heel State occurred on or about June 20, 1584. Recently discovered entries from the ship's log of the Elizabeth, captained by Thomas Cavendish, revealed that upon tying up at the Manteo Marina and Yacht Club, he and his men were met by a small group of bronze skinned individuals wearing Speedos, loin cloths and flip flops. Historians differ as to whether this group was Native Americans or college boys spending their summer at the beach as lifeguards. In any event this tanned contingent invited the sailors to a keg party.

When Capt'n Tommy and his merry men arrived at their hosts' encampment, they were amazed to see several whole hogs roasted to perfection on a wooden grid over hickory coals spread in an earthen pit. One crew member was heard to remark, "Now that's a pretty pig." Their hosts were most apologetic that the homebrew was a bit warm, a fact that went largely unnoticed by the Brits. Capt'n Tommy made special note that the pulled pork was the most succulent dish that he had ever encountered and the banana pudding was "killer." By some accounts the malted beverage served that night later became known as "Bud Light." There is little to support this theory, however Capt'n Tommy did mention in his log that the leader of this congenial group rode a "bitchin" Clydesdale. Except for the addition of ice and extending the guest list to include girl-type settlers, little has been done in the last 400 plus years to improve upon the tradition that was started that night.

Shortly after the momentous event described above, settlers began to make their way westward across the Old North State. This is the most plausible explanation of what happened to the Lost Colony. The opening of Interstate 40 from Wrightsville Beach to Tennessee provided easier passage for the settlers on the coast to hang out with friends in the mountains and vice versa. Soon this well-known trail became a virtual gridlock of covered wagons and pony carts especially around the settlements of Greensboro and Raleigh-Durham. Still that did not deter those hearty souls in pursuit of the casual food holy grail. They spread across the state faster than Kudzu, bringing with them thongs, shag music, Pepsi and barbecue recipes.

In Lexington, a small number of these barbecue gypsies set up shop on street corners and in front of the courthouse. In order to stay mobile and move fast (they had no vender's license), they cooked on Webber Cooking Kettles. These early barbecue journeymen, unlike their eastern cousins, cooked pork shoulders because they were easier to pick up and run with than a whole hog. These pork-roasting troubadours also monkeyed a bit with the Eastern North Carolina vinegar-base sauce. They had the audacity to put ketchup, brown sugar and God knows what else in a perfectly good barbecue sauce and call it dip. Ever looking for a marketing edge, settlers in Salisbury "tweaked" the Lexington-style dip. In desperation, settlers further south, in an effort to retain market share, adopt-

21

ed the strange habits of their southern neighbors and infused their barbecue dip with mustard. If that were not enough, settlers from Florida would visit the mountains in the summer. Some stayed. They brought with them funny clothes and strange barbecue taste. They smoked their meat like Plains Indians and slathered it in a thick molasses, brown sugar rib sauce. Is it any wonder settlers in the east shook their heads, rung their hands and muttered, "Is nothing sacred?" The results were inevitable. War!

For years now, war has raged across the Tar Heel State between barbecue aficionados and purists as to which is better – vinegar-base barbecue or tomato-base barbecue. This battle is renewed annually and makes the Civil War pale in comparison. As nearly as I can tell, the North-South line that divides these two factions appears to run through the center of the old capital building in Raleigh, the capital city. You will find a few tiny pockets of Eastern style sauce west of the line of demarcation, but no Western style dip east of this line. The passion of this cause has divided families, set brother against brother, father against son and mother against daughter. My family is no exception.

North Carolina is the source of the best barbecue in the world. I was born in Eastern North Carolina. Having lived west of the line all of my adult life, I have acquired a taste for the Lexington-style barbecue and dip and find it absolutely delicious. But my roots, my heart and my barbecue preference are (and always will be) slightly EAST of the old Capitol building.

Because most of the towns in Eastern North Carolina are so small (some not even having a movie theatre), eating becomes a social event. Four couples will get together in two cars and drive 50 to 75 miles one way to eat at a new barbecue place they heard about through the grapevine. They switch off for the ride home so that all have a chance to visit. Thus, like the local saloons out West, the barbecue places of Eastern North Carolina become the hubs of social life for many small towns. If you go out to eat barbecue, you do not go to a "barbecue café" or "barbecue restaurant." There is no such thing. You go to a "barbecue joint" or "barbecue place." I have never heard of a place that serves good barbecue described in any other fashion. Most of these places derived their origin as small Mom and Pop places, acquired a reputation and grew in size. In Eastern North Carolina when you order barbecue you will hear it pronounced "bobby-q."

Barbecue places of note in Eastern North Carolina have generally cooked whole hogs over open pits, fired with hickory and oak wood reduced to coals for cooking. Their Lexington style counterparts cook shoulders using the same methods. This process is slow and takes many, many hours of hard work and constant attention to the pits. The heat from the coals waxes and wanes. The coals have to be freshened about every 15 to 30 minutes.

Many factors have to be addressed by the pit master. Pigs raised on peanuts and pigs raised on corn have a different moisture content. There is a different moisture content in wood. Hickory burns faster and hotter than oak. You clean your pits on Sunday when you are closed. You start Monday with clean pit floors. By Friday you have five inches of ash and the coals are five inches closer to the meat. A 10-degree change in temperature affects the cooking. A change in humidity affects the cooking. These factors and the loss by death or retirement of pit masters who have carefully tended the fires for 30 or 40 years have caused most of the barbecue places, large and small, east of Raleigh to resort to gas or electricity.

There are approximately five barbecue places east of Raleigh still cooking solely with wood or charcoal. Some who claim to cook with wood actually do most of their cooking with electrical cookers and finish the product on open or enclosed pits. Thus they can put the meat on at night, set the temperature, flip the switch and go home. In the morning they fire the pits and smoke the meat for flavor for several hours before serving that day. Some, I'm advised, do not even put the meat on the pits. They simply fire the pits and throw some fat and skin on to get a good aroma in the parking lot and cook the meat entirely by electricity or gas.

There are more restaurants in the Lexington style area cooking with wood than any other area of the state. This cooking method, and the fact that most all barbecue places west of Raleigh cook only pork shoulders, in no small part accounts for the exceptionally fine barbecue produced in this area. Pork shoulders are more tender than ham, which is grainier and drier. The difference between pork shoulders and hams is about the same as the difference between chicken breasts and thighs. The darker meat of the pork shoulder has more flavor, is more moist and is certainly more tender.

In addition to the major differences between Eastern-style barbecue and Lexington-style barbecue, there are subtle differences that occur about every 50 miles within the state. These subtle changes are sometimes produced by cooking methods but more often are produced by tweaking a particular kind of sauce or dip. Though my preference is slightly tilted toward Eastern-style barbecue in which the whole hog is cooked over wood-fired pits, chopped and mixed and sauced with the classic Eastern style-sauce, I readily admit that I have eaten excellent barbecue that was cooked with gas and electricity. I also am of the opinion that if the barbecue is fresh, prepared well (not overcooked) and sauced in the kitchen, most people cannot tell the difference in cooking methods. For most it is not a matter of great importance.

Another change that has taken place in barbecue places across the state is the method by which the barbecue is chopped after it is cooked. Historically, most places, whether east or west, have hand chopped their barbecue on wooden butchers blocks with cleavers. You know it's fresh when you can hear the staccato of cleavers in the back as you eat. However a number of places east and west have turned to mechanical processes to shred their barbecue. I find most mechanically chopped barbecue to be too fine and too dry for my taste. I prefer my barbecue coarse chopped by hand.

Barbecue is generally served by itself or in combination with fried chicken and/or brunswick stew. The sides are white barbecue slaw (east), red barbecue slaw (west), boiled potatoes, french fries or potato salad, and corn bread, hushpuppies or cornsticks. The drink is always sweet iced tea or soft drinks. The dessert is traditionally pecan pie or banana pudding, pronounced "pudden."

The history of barbecue places and tobacco are interwoven. Many of the good barbecue places in Eastern North Carolina gained their regional recognition from the influx of tobacco farmers and tobacco company buyers that converged on small towns for the tobacco market in the fall each year. As these buyers moved on to other markets, they spread the word about the best barbecue places they had encountered in their travels. Barbecue also played a large role in the parties that were given in Eastern North Carolina to celebrate the end of the tobacco market when the community all had "new money." The good folk of Eastern North Carolina love a party!

Rocky Mount is not only part of the hub of Eastern North Carolina barbecue country, but also the home of what is thought to be the longest-running party in the South. As has been the custom since 1880, the *June German* is held each spring in a tobacco warehouse in Rocky Mount. It is black tie, buffet and big-name bands. Historically it began on Friday evening with music around 9 p.m. which was followed several hours later by the Grand March that preceded the midnight buffet. The orchestra played til' dawn at which time (after the advent of the automobile) the revelers departed for the beach where the party continued at various beach homes throughout the weekend. Now that's a party! As a young child, I heard about these dances from my parents and their friends. Ladies in their 80s still got dreamy eyed when they told their tales to me.

Barbecue is also intertwined with this state's politics, the church, civic organizations and higher education. All political candidates, at least all that want to win, hit the barbecue trail during their campaign. Apparently the public finds it hard to trust someone who does not like good barbecue. Barbecue pork and chicken probably account for more fundraisers than any other activity. Signs in churchyards reading *BARBECUE SATURDAY, 9 – 5* are as common in urban and rural areas as the church marquee. Civic clubs celebrate their annual get together with catered pig pickings. Barbecue is one of the favorite dishes for any tailgate party. Recently, a well-known barbecue entrepreneur left his university the largest personal gift it had ever received – more than $7 million.

Who would have thought that a barbecue and keg party 417 years ago would have such a profound effect on the development of the Tar Heel State? If those bronze lads in their flip-flops had decided to serve Capt'n Tommy and his men poached filet of sole and a fine white wine, where would we be? Would our only claim to fame be underwear and cigarettes? Would we ever have become the second largest pork-producing state in the country? Would Miss Piggy be the only "pretty pig" we had ever seen? And on a more sobering note, what if there were no "Bud Light" or barbecue?

So the next time the occasion calls for celebration, remember those men on the Outer Banks that taught us to fly long before Orville and Wilbur. Keep the fires burning; make it BARBECUE.

NC Map

THE BEST
TAR HEEL BARBECUE

Manteo to Murphy

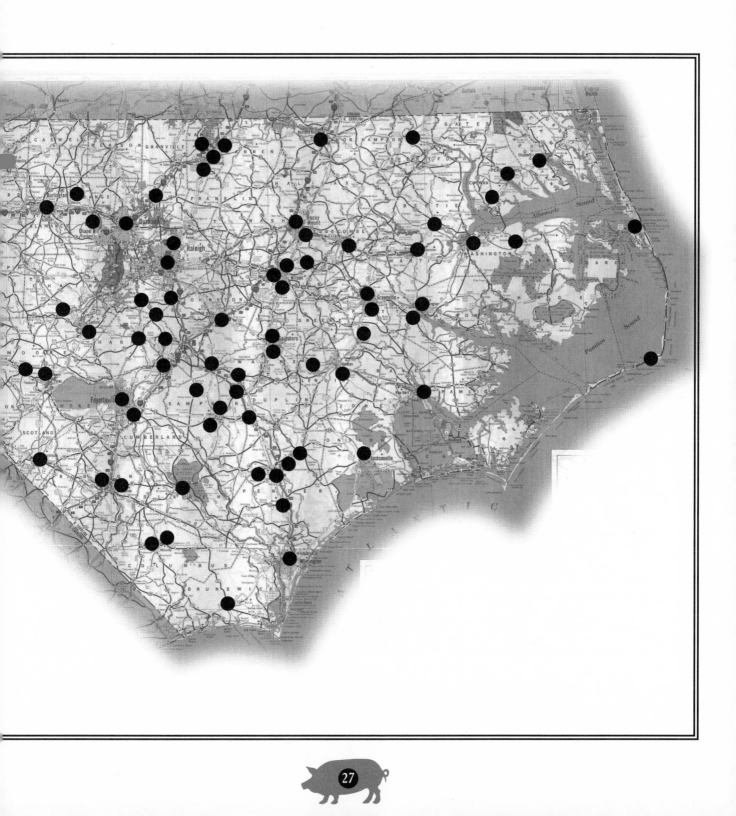

SECTION 1

The Mountains

Location

Barbecue Inn, Asheville **1**

Mountain Smoke House Barbecue, Asheville **2**

Perry's BBQ, Black Mountain **3**

Old Hickory House, Brevard **4**

The Bar-B-Q Wagon, Bryson City **5**

Skeeter's BBQ House, Canton **6**

Carolina Smokehouse, Cashiers **7**

Craig's Barbecue, Cherokee **8**

The Cajun Pig, Chimney Rock **9**

Duncan's Barbecue, Chimney Rock **10**

Dillsboro Smokehouse, Dillsboro **11**

Sam's Country Cook-Out, Edneyville **12**

The Barbecue Shack, Etowah **13**

Fat Buddies Ribs and BBQ, Franklin **14**

Rib Country, Hayesville **15**

Butts on the Creek, Maggie Valley **16**

Herb's Pit BBQ, Murphy **17**

Green River Bar-B-Que, Saluda **18**

Smoky Mountain Grill and Lee's Barbecue, Sylva **19**

Eddie's Bar-B-Que, Waynesville **20**

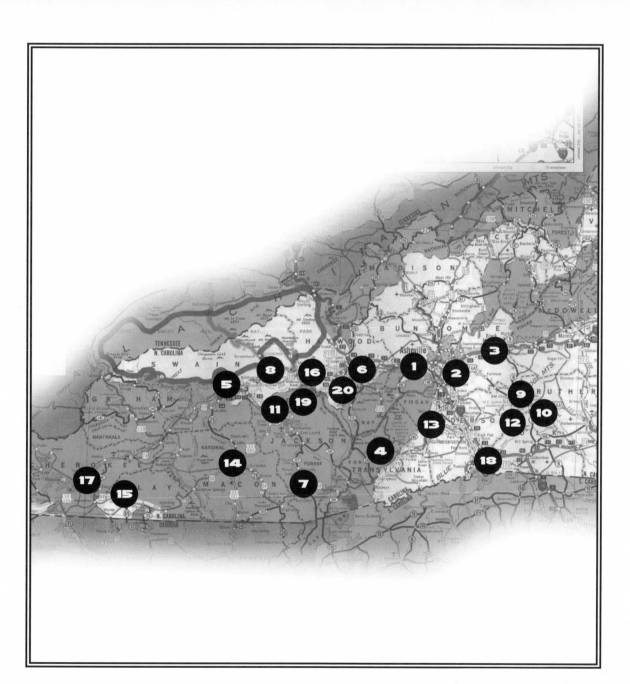

Barbecue Inn, Asheville

Built in 1961 at its present site on Patton Avenue, the Barbecue Inn is the culmination of the dream of the late Gus Kooles. Gus went to Burlington to learn how to cook barbecue pork in the Lexington style. After a six-month apprenticeship, Gus brought his newly honed skills and newly developed recipes back to his home in the mountains.

Like most barbecue places, Gus was ably assisted by his family. Gus' two sons, Woody and Chuck, and daughter-in-law Martha Kooles continued the tradition along with the assistance of Martha's two daughters, Michelle and Kimberly.

The pork shoulders are slow-cooked overnight on Nunnery Freeman electric cookers. All the meat is the freshest available. Barbecue Inn does not baste its meat while cooking. Once cooked the meat is ground and sauce is added in the kitchen. The Lexington-style dip is brought to the table hot. On the table, you will find a bottle of Eastern North Carolina vinegar and pepper hot sauce. Try both.

The chopped barbecue tastes fresh, is moderately moist, has a good pork flavor and is medium chopped. The meat is very tender with no fat or gristle. Without any sauce, the meat has a mild pork taste with no smoky flavor, since the meat is not exposed to wood smoke of any type. The chopped barbecue with the Lexington-style dip is a nice combination.

The Lexington-style dip is vinegar base with tomatoes, ketchup, honey, spices and brown sugar. It is thin, reddish brown and sweet with enough spices to give it a little zip. It is not hot at all, just pleasantly tangy. The Eastern North Carolina vinegar and hot pepper sauce at the table was the sauce of choice for me.

The slaw is moderately chopped green cabbage with carrot and no mayo taste. The hushpuppies are golden brown, have a nice crunch and are moist inside. Otherwise they are unremarkable. The brunswick stew had hunks of tomatoes and hunks of chicken, and tasted like vegetable soup with small bits of potato.

When Gus Kooles opened his Eastern North Carolina-style Barbecue Inn, as a promotion, he offered free barbecue to anyone who brought him a decorative pig like no other he had ever seen. Hundreds of people brought their pigs. There are shelves throughout the interior supporting little pigs of every shape, material and description. Children like to come and look at the pigs. The donors like to come and point out to friends their gift to Gus' dream.

Tuesday night is Senior Citizen Night

35

and those 65 or older get approximately 50 percent off menu price. There are lines out into the parking lot on Tuesday night. Martha said that various seniors have their certain table and will stand in line and let others go ahead as they wait until their table is available. The chairs they wait on are handmade and more than 100 years old.

Wednesday night is the Family Night Special. For $13.85 (normally $18.35), a family can get a full meal, all served family style in bowls and on platters.

Barbecue Inn has been written about in a number of magazines including the ones that go in airline seat pockets. The same cook has prepared this good food for the past 30 years. Try it.

The Barbecue Inn is located at 1341 Patton Ave. in Asheville, about three miles west of downtown. The Barbecue Inn is open 10:30 a.m. until 8 p.m., Monday through Thursday, and 10:30 a.m. until 9 p.m., Friday and Saturday. It's closed Sunday. Telephone number: (828) 253-9615.

HAVE BEEN INFORMED THAT RESTAURANT
HAS CLOSED SINCE FIRST PRINTING OF BOOK

Mountain Smoke House Barbecue, Asheville

Formerly located on South Spruce Street in downtown Asheville near Pack Square, Mountain Smoke House Barbecue moved in 1988 to River Ridge Marketplace shopping center.

At its new home, Mountain Smoke House (MSH) has the look of an upscale chain restaurant such as a TGI Friday's or Applebee's. Once inside, the feeling remains the same. The restaurant is large with medium-dark stained oak, vinyl and tile decor. Strategically placed are framed articles of reviews and accolades that have been written about MSH. Every good barbecue place has to have a picture of a pig doing something. MSH's answer is a white pig with sunglasses napping in a Pawley's Island hammock.

The co-owners of MSH are Marcel Proctor and his lovely wife, Catherine Mitchell Proctor, who is also the general manager. Marcel is originally from Asheville but migrated to the Big Apple to pursue a successful real estate career focusing on rehabilitating inner-city housing. Catherine, formerly a New York City attorney, is from Birmingham, Ala. Marcel learned his barbecuing skills from his daddy, Jess Proctor, who learned them from his father, John Proctor, who came to Asheville around 1900 from Laurens, S.C. Catherine learned her culinary skills from her mother as well as family and friends in Birmingham and in Charleston, S.C. Marcel attends to the cooking of the meat at MSH and Catherine conjures up upscale offerings of Old South favorites such as black-eyed peas, collard greens, crab chowder, sweet tater chips, hoppin' John and blackberry a la mode.

Marcel says he has never forgotten his father's advice, "don't feed anybody anything that you wouldn't eat yourself."

MSH is a main peg for more than 150 bus touring companies that transverse the East Coast, the Smoky Mountains and the Blue Ridge Parkway. In addition to the locals, tens of thousands of patrons from all of the country and the world have passed through the portals of MSH to experience (many for the first or the only time) North Carolina barbecue and southern cooking. Catherine and Marcel, who (in his cowboy hat, denim shirt, jeans and boots) looks to me like a Shaq-size version of Danny Glover, are truly ambassadors for Asheville and our mountains.

I tried the coarse-chopped barbecue with sauce. The meat had a good, dark smoky flavor all the way through from Marcel's slow-cooking process. Having not been exposed to too much heat, it was still moist. The meat had a slightly pink cast that comes from smoke penetrating to the bone. It comes coarsely chopped about the size of walnuts – good stuff. It tastes almost like outside brown. It is not basted when cooked and has a flavorful, nutty taste. It's a good strong start, a good finish, and a nice journey along the way.

The sauce, neither Eastern Carolina sauce nor Lexington-style dip, is reddish brown. It has a taste of vinegar, tomato, red peppers, onion, garlic, paprika and other spices blended into a tangy, tart, slightly hot liquid with just enough heat and sweetness. It leans more toward a Kansas City rib sauce, but is not as sweet or thick.

The meat is cooked in a cooker and in a manner unlike any other that I have encountered on my barbecue journeys. The cooker is a long machine about the size of a VW Bug that looks like something from Willy Wonka's Chocolate Factory. There is a front door on the cooker that opens to reveal a series of metal mesh trays about a foot or so wide and five feet long that form a rotisserie much like the seats on a Ferris Wheel. This is chain driven by an electric motor. The firebox is on the right-hand side where the hickory wood burns down to coals and is then force-air pushed by convection fans into the cooking unit. Thus, the meat is never exposed to direct heat. Trays

of Boston butts gently rotate like the blades of a Mississippi paddle wheeler while hickory smoke is pushed into the chamber. The process takes about 14 hours. The meat comes out pinkish in color all the way to the bone, which is the sign of good smoke penetration. MSH also has the distinction of being the only barbecue cooking facility in North Carolina that has been seismic tested. Get Marcel to tell you the story.

MSH has been written about in a number of magazines and newspapers in the Asheville area and the state. In one article, Marcel states that he has the best barbecue east of the Mississippi, north or south. Will Rogers was fond of saying, "if it's true it ain't bragging." Put the man to the test.

From I-40 West, take I-240 West then exit at Exit 8. When you reach the end of the exit ramp, you will be facing a McDonald's restaurant across the street. Turn right and move over to the left lane closest to the median. At the next traffic light, turn left on Fairview Road into the shopping center. You will see the Mountain Smoke House sign. Hours are 11:45 a.m. until 9 or 10 p.m., Monday through Saturday. It's open Sundays during the summer season. There are house bands on Friday and Saturday nights. Telephone number: (828) 298-8121.

Perry's BBQ, Black Mountain

Perry's BBQ opened in 1996 under the direction of Perry Cox who came to Black Mountain from Taylor, Texas, which is near Austin. He had done weekend, side-of-the-road type cooking and decided to start a place in North Carolina offering Texas-style sliced barbecue beef brisket and chopped beef. Perry soon found out that in order to be successful in the barbecue business in North Carolina you also need to offer pork. The pork went well and Perry's little place prospered.

Jack and Susan Spencer bought the place from Perry, who retired on December 31, 2000. Jack and Susan had worked with Perry since Perry's BBQ opened. Jack had been Perry's apprentice for five years. Following the age old principle, if it ain't broke, don't fix it, Jack and Susan continued cooking Texas style beef brisket and North Carolina style pork barbecue just as Perry had done with the same recipes, sauces, etc.

Jack cooks over a gas and wood-fired smoker. He cooks pork Boston butts at 200 degrees for 15 hours. The meat is all hand chopped. Jack, who does not baste while cooking, makes his own rub to put on the meat. At a certain point, the butts are encased in foil for a time for tenderness. The juices in the foil are saved as one of the ingredients in Jack's "secret sauce" that is applied in the kitchen after the meat is chopped. Jack shared that some of the ingredients in the rub are salt, pepper, garlic, pork juice and spices. This gives the meat a Southwest flavor. The beef brisket is also smoked for 14 hours and sliced as ordered.

The chopped barbecue pork had a very rich, smoky pork flavor. It is moderately chopped and has a hint of peppers. The sauce, rich with tomatoes, is Texas style in taste, not Eastern Carolina or Lexington. The meat is sauced in the kitchen and you do not need more at the table, although Texas Pete and a commercial barbecue sauce are provided.

The chopped beef was moderately chopped and has a taste much akin to the chopped pork due to the cooking methods except this one, of course, has a beef flavor.

The sliced beef is a very slow-roasted beef with a good smoky flavor and a nice brown outside edge. The meat is very tender; you can flake it with a plastic fork. It is good with the brisket sauce at the table. With the flavor of this meat, I would prefer a horseradish sauce.

The slaw is white, coarse-chopped coleslaw with the additions of celery seed, mayo and carrot chips.

To reach Perry's, take the Black Mountain/Hwy 70 exit and follow Highway 70 into Black Mountain. Perry's is on your left, just before you reach the downtown intersection. It is a gray building and is easy to spot. Hours are 11 a.m. until 7 p.m., Tuesday through Thursday, and 11 a.m. until 8 p.m., Friday and Saturday. It's closed Sunday. Telephone number: (828) 664-1446.

Old Hickory House, Brevard

The Old Hickory House in Brevard looks like an overgrown Boy Scout house or a fishing or hunting lodge. It is large, made of brown logs with white chinking and nestled in a grove of balsam trees beside the road. The Old Hickory House looks like it belongs in the mountains. The owners of this rustic old barbecue emporium are David and Carrie Guice.

Old Hickory House serves hand-chopped barbecue pork, beef and chicken, barbecue-basted chicken, hickory-smoked baked chicken, barbecue baby-back ribs, pork country spareribs (available in combinations), steaks, rainbow trout and seafood.

The moderately chopped barbecue pork comes sauced from the kitchen with a tomato-base sauce and is very tender and moist. It is tasty with a tomato prominence but needs some zip. Pork with the brown sauce at the table has more flavor but still needs some heat.

The barbecue chicken is chopped finely, sauced in the kitchen, tender, moist and has the same smoky, tomato overtones as the barbecue pork. Chicken with sauce at the table (brown) takes on a smoky flavor from the sauce. To my taste it's a good, middle-of-the-road 'cue, not too spicy not too bland.

The barbecue beef is finely chopped, tender, moist and sauced in the kitchen with what seems to be the same sauce. The only difference I could tell in the pork, beef and chicken was the flavor of the meat and texture. The brown sauce at the table is mild and slightly sweet. With the beef, it slow dances instead of doing a Highland Fling.

The slaw is moderately coarse chopped white cabbage with bits of carrot and generous mayo. It makes a good side.

Old Hickory House is located at 842 Country Club Rd. in Brevard. Hours are 5 p.m. until 8:30 p.m., Tuesday through Saturday and 11 a.m. until 2:30 p.m. on Sunday. Telephone number: (828) 884-7270.

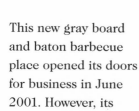

The Bar-B-Q Wagon, Bryson City

This new gray board and baton barbecue place opened its doors for business in June 2001. However, its owner, Pat Monteith, is not new to the barbecue game. For a number of years, Pat had a place a quarter of a mile up the road. Her new place is bright, fresh and rustic, as are many of the barbecue places in the mountains. Pat said all the wonderful wood in her new place is due in no small part to the fact that her husband is in the lumber business. One can eat inside or on picnic tables overlooking the river outside Pat's establishment.

Pat cooks her delicious pork offerings on a Southern Pride cooker at 200 degrees for up to 10 hours. She serves barbecue pork, barbecue beef and barbecue chicken.

The chopped barbecue pork is a fine chop (minced) and has a good deep smoky flavor with lots of outside brown. It's sauced in the kitchen with brown rib-type sauce worked into the tasty 'cue.

The sliced beef barbecue is moist and tender with good smoke penetration, a very tasty presentation.

The juicy white cabbage slaw is a moderate coarse chop with flecks of carrot and mayo. The hushpuppies are a bit greasy and heavy for my taste. The brown, crunchy shell has a cornmeal center with bell pepper flecks and onion.

The Bar-B-Q Wagon is on Highway 19 West overlooking the river in Bryson City. Hours are 11 a.m. until 8 p.m., Monday through Saturday. It's closed Sunday. Telephone number: (828) 488-9521.

Skeeter's BBQ House, Canton

Skeeter's opened April 1994 at its present site. Under the management of owners Skeeter Curtis and wife Myra, it has been called Skeeter's BBQ House from day one. Skeeter said that he mostly feeds the locals, but pulls a lot of tourists from Maggie Valley and Asheville.

Skeeter cooks electrically with a Nunnery-Freeman cooker. He cooks Boston butts (bone in) and ribs. When he caters, he adds lemon-pepper chicken and barbecue chicken. Skeeter's also offers a daily blue plate special.

The hand-chopped barbecue is moderately coarse chopped. This delectable offering is moist, rich, really good roasted pork with lots of pieces of outside brown throughout giving the 'cue a really nice flavor. While the meat comes without sauce from the kitchen, one can choose a fiery Eastern North Carolina vinegar-base sauce with red peppers or a sweeter brownish-red sauce that is thicker (about ketchup consistency). The latter has a smoky-sweet spicy flavor and some heat. This one is more of a rib sauce but many in the mountains put it on their chopped 'cue. I like the vinegar base sauce for the chopped pork and the smoky brown sauce for the ribs.

The pork ribs are TENDER with just enough brown glaze to give them a wonderful flavor and make them slightly chewy. They taste smoky, woodsy and delicious despite not being cooked over wood. Neat trick.

The hushpuppies are nice. They have a light brown, crunchy shell along with a good moist center and a wonderful cornbread taste. Isn't that what you want in a good pup? Yes.

The slaw is white cabbage with a little purple onion, carrot flecks, light mayo and seasoning. It's really good slaw for any section of the state.

Normally I don't indulge in dessert as I am about writing a barbecue book not a dessert book. However, Skeeter insisted that I try the banana pudding. Damn good. Myra makes it.

From I-40 West, take Exit 37. At the end of the ramp, turn left, go 100 yards to the stoplight, and turn right into Canton. This is a several-mile trek. When you reach downtown Canton you will be at a little junction. You will realize when you are there. Follow Highway 19/23 south. Skeeter's is a quarter mile from the junction on the left.

Skeeter's hours change with daylight savings time. The summer hours, Eastern Daylight Saving time, are 10:30 a.m. until 9 p.m., Monday through Saturday. The winter hours, Eastern Standard Time, are 10:30

a.m. until 8 p.m., Monday through Saturday.
Skeeter's is closed Sunday year round.
Telephone number: (828) 648-8595.

Carolina Smokehouse, Cashiers

Carolina Smokehouse is housed in a red wooden building nestled in evergreen trees on the north side of Highway 64 West in Cashiers. The exterior is rustic and inviting. The interior is unfinished wooden walls covered in license plates. The seating is ladder-backed chairs with wooden tables. In 1986 owners Rob and Tammy Williams bought what was then a restaurant and changed it to Carolina Smokehouse. Tammy is from this area and Rob, like many of the owners of mountain barbecue places today has roots in Florida.

Carolina Smokehouse cooks with hickory and oak on open pits. They cook Boston butts, beef briskets, St. Louis ribs and chicken.

Carolina Smokehouse serves chopped pork barbecue without sauce. While the chopped 'cue was a tiny bit dry for my taste, it did have good smoky flavor. I like it.

The chopped barbecue beef, without sauce, was also a tiny bit dry for my taste. To my palate the chopped barbecue beef had a flavor that was slightly akin to corned beef. It was different, I liked it as well.

The barbecue chicken I was served was good but not as moist as the other offerings.

The barbecue pork ribs were moist, fall-off-the-bone tender and cooked to perfection. It was the best of all the offerings I sampled.

There are two tomato base sauces: a brown hot sauce and a mild sweet sauce. The brown hot sauce is so hot eaten by itself, it will peel your tongue and blow out your eyes. There's no lasting aftertaste but your mouth is numb. The mild sweet sauce works nicely with the 'cue but for my taste was not quite enough. I suggest you add two parts sweet and one part hot to the chopped 'cue for a nice marriage.

Carolina Smokehouse in addition to making its own sauces, makes its own desserts. I am advised by the locals that the desserts are killer (this means very, very good).

Rob shared that Carolina Smokehouse provides live music for its customers on Friday and Saturday nights. Good music and good barbecue, now that's a combination that's hard to beat.

Hours are 10 a.m. until 10 p.m., Friday and Saturday, and 10 a.m. until 9 p.m., Sunday through Thursday. Telephone number: (828) 743-3200.

Craig's Barbecue, Cherokee

Craig's Barbecue is located next to Craig's Motel (not same owner) in Cherokee. I only report this barbecue place because several people said that Craig's has good barbecue. However, I am further advised that Craig's is only open for dinner and only sells barbecue on Friday and Saturday nights. I was there on Thursday at about 1 p.m. Craig's is open for breakfast from 6:30 a.m. until noon. I did not have an opportunity to taste Craig's barbecue. I am advised that it is good but could not wait a day and a half to find out.

The Cajun Pig, Chimney Rock

Tim Turner had a vision of Cajun Pig for years. He had been in Charlotte with ESP, one of the largest surveying businesses in North Carolina. Tim and his wife Deb often came to Chimney Rock on vacation and fell in love with the place. Tim did his research, decided to build his restaurant in Chimney Rock and set about to acquire land. Tim and Debbie were building a house up on the mountain and Tim was in town one day and saw a For Sale sign on some property where the restaurant now sits. Within hours, Tim had made an offer written on the back of a matchbook and the deal was done.

When Tim decided to build the restaurant as large as it is, he realized he needed more land. He went to the people on the right and they agreed to sell, but did not want Tim to tear down the house to which they were so attached. Tim agreed to redo the house and live in it and the deal was struck. Having the land he needed, Tim got logs out of British Columbia to build the Cajun Pig. These huge, blonde-skinned, treated logs make the Cajun Pig look like the home of your dreams in Montana. Tim said the building brings 'em in and the food brings 'em back.

The food is cooked slow and served fast. The Cajun Pig opened March 15, 2001.

The first day they served more than 400 people. Tim said that on Saturdays they serve more than 900 people. People drive 60 miles one way to come and eat here each week. From inside the restaurant one can look up through the plate glass windows at the top of the cathedral arch and see both Chimney Rock and Hickory Nut Falls (the falls in *Last of the Mohicans* movie).

The meat is cooked on a Southern Pride cooker. They cook Boston butts with hickory, and Texas beef brisket and chicken with mesquite. Tim pulls the skin off the ribs, applies a rub and leaves it over night. The rub contains 15 different ingredients. The ribs are then lightly smoked with mesquite wood.

All barbecue that is not consumed the day after it is cooked goes into Cajun dishes. It is not cooled, warmed over and served the next day.

Tim said they developed the sauces on their own. The sauces are cooked on Wednesdays. The five sauces are an Eastern North Carolina vinegar-base sauce, a Western North Carolina tomato-base that is smoky, a red hot sauce, a mustard sauce for the South Carolina crowd and a sweet homemade brisket dipping sauce that was developed by David Sanders who is the kitchen manager. David is from Texas. Tim and David said tourists could come here and experience their wonderful meat product and taste all of the North Carolina sauces as well as one from the Southwest.

The red hot sauce, "fire in a bottle" is pretty hot stuff. There's lots of cayenne here. Watch this one, it will blow your doors off. The smoky rib sauce is brown, sweet, spicy and is just the right trick for the ribs. The yellow mustard sauce is tart and spicy. It is a delicious version of a South Carolina favorite. The Texas brisket sauce has a smoky, molasses taste, very good – a brisket bride.

Tim and his partner David sometimes get a plate and come out and sit among the customers and listen to what the customers' comments are about their food and sauces to see how they might improve them.

The brisket has a good, rich smoky flavor with good penetration throughout. It's very tender and surprisingly moist for brisket.

The hand-chopped barbecue pork comes in large pieces and is very tender and moist. It has a good wood-smoked flavor. The hickory really comes through here. It comes from the kitchen unsauced but with the Eastern North Carolina sauce you are carried to the best of the Sandhills. The chopped barbecue with the "fire-in-a-bottle" sauce is HOT. A mustard sauce, a South

Carolina favorite, is also available.

The pork ribs are pink to the bone with good smoke penetration. They have a nice crusty outer surface. The rub is excellent and carries the ribs to new heights.

The barbecue chicken looks like the centerfold in a *Southern Living* Thanksgiving or Christmas magazine. The crisp, golden-brown skin has no burn spots or black edges. The smoky mesquite flavor shines through. The meat is very moist; even the breast had tiny droplets of juices throughout. If this is not the best chicken you have ever had you will have trouble remembering better.

The red Lexington slaw is dark, spicy and as good as you will find.

The white Eastern North Carolina slaw has a good fresh cabbage taste complete with spices and light mayo.

The Cajun Pig is located in downtown Chimney Rock. You can't miss it; it's huge. It is a piece of Montana sitting on Main Street.

The Cajun Pig is open Thursday through Sunday only. They are open 11 a.m. until 8 p.m., Thursday and Sunday, and from 11 a.m. until 11 p.m., Friday and Saturday. They stop serving dinner at 8:30 p.m. but do continue to serve sandwiches and such until closing. Telephone number: (828) 625-0701.

Duncan's Barbecue, Chimney Rock

Owner Dave Duncan and wife Janet opened this tiny mom and pop barbecue in 1967. The meat is cooked on a Barbecue King rotisserie smoker with hickory wood. Dave cooks ribs, three-and-down spareribs, chicken, pork shoulders and Boston butts. In the off season, he barbecues bear, venison and even rattlesnakes for his friends.

Dave used to cook outside. He would put up a sign; "chicken will be off at 4:30, 5:00." You could smell the good barbecue chicken smell all over town. I remember this from more than 20 years ago when I was involved with sports cars and the Chimney Rock hill climb. People would line up, plate in hand, for Dave's barbecue chicken. Dave can't do that now due to rules and regulations. Pity.

The chopped barbecue is minced, moist and sauced in the kitchen with a tomato-base sauce that is mild. There is also a hot sauce and fine pepper chow-chow to light it up at the table.

The sliced barbecue is much smokier than the chopped barbecue. It has a deep, wood-smoked taste with brown pieces that give it the flavor. It's tender.

The ribs are tender and moist with a good roast pork taste. There's a dark, nutty flavor but it's a little fatty. The sauce adds a brighter, mild, sweet and sour taste. It's very good.

Hours are 11 a.m. until 6 or 8 p.m., Wednesday through Sunday. It's closed Monday and Tuesday. Telephone number: (828) 625-1578.

Dillsboro Smokehouse, Dillsboro

The walls of Dillsboro Smokehouse are covered with college pennants, license plates, business cards and pig stuff. Dillsboro Smokehouse cooks pork shoulders and butts, beef briskets and Danish babyback ribs.

The chopped pork barbecue comes from the kitchen without sauce. The meat is a moderate chop, very moist and has a good roast pork flavor. There are four sauces at the table: a homemade pepper vinegar; a red liquid hot sauce with lots of heat; a hick-ory smoke and a mild sauce that is slightly spicy, slightly sweet.

From Highway 23/74, take Exit 81 onto Haywood Street. Dillsboro Smokehouse is on the right. It is a brown, weathered board and baton building. It's open all year. Hours are 11 a.m. until 9 p.m., Monday through Thursday, 11 a.m. until 10 p.m., Friday and Saturday and 11 p.m. until 8 p.m., Sunday. Telephone number: (828) 586-9556.

Sam's Country Cook-Out, Edneyville

Owner Sam Fowler, a fine-looking, redheaded lady from Texas, took over what was formerly a burger joint in 2000. Sam's mother ran restaurants all of Sam's life. Sam teethed on a grill. Sam's cook is Jackie McMurray, who has been cooking pigs for 25 years. No stranger to cooking, Jackie's grandpa was a cook in the Marines. Jackie started his cooking at family cook-outs. His brother had a catering business. Jackie said it seemed like the family had been in the food business all of their lives.

The slogan on the front of Sam's Country Cook-Out reads, "Put some South in your mouth." This they do. Sam's cooks sliced and chopped barbecue pork, barbecue country ribs (not babyback), sliced barbecue beef and catfish.

The meat is cooked with gas and hickory wood in a Southern Pride rotisserie cooker. Jackie says he roasts his meat for 24 hours.

The moderately chopped barbecue pork has a tasty, nutty flavor and is moist and tender. The outside brown is mixed in for a very nice offering. It tastes good without sauce. But consider saucing at the table with the reddish sauce; it tastes wonderful.

The barbecue country ribs are so tender, so moist and so good you don't want to swallow. There's a little bit of fat still on and the cooking method gives the ribs a pound-the-table, country good taste. Try some.

They serve a number of side dishes including collard greens, black-eyed peas, maple-candied yams, and fried green tomatoes. The desserts are to die for. Try the fried pies.

The slaw is white cabbage with carrot chips and light mayo. It has a good fresh taste. The hushpuppies have a medium brown, nice shell covering a moist cornbread center.

The sauce is red, slightly sweet with peppers and spices, and quite different for the mountains. Sam's sauce is not as smoky as some of the mountain sauces. It's definitely not a Lexington style, and certainly not an Eastern North Carolina vinegar-base sauce. This sauce is different and it's good.

Sam's building is unfinished board and baton construction with a red tin roof and has trees for support posts out front. You can see a cookin' fire to the side of the building. It looks like a real barbecue place.

Sam's Country Cook-Out is on Highway 64 in Edneyville, which is between Hendersonville and Chimney Rock. Hours are 6 a.m. until 9 p.m., Friday and Saturday, and 6 a.m. until 3 p.m., Tuesday through Thursday. It's closed Sunday and Monday. Telephone number: (828) 685-0031.

The Barbecue Shack, Etowah

Just west of Horseshoe on Highway 64 is the community of Etowah, on the short list for the next Olympic site. Both of these communities lay between Brevard and Hendersonville, closer to Hendersonville. Etowah is the home base for the culmination of Gene Miles' business success. Gene started years ago at a Dairy Queen in Hendersonville. Later, the Miles family and the Todds formed a partnership that owns the Shack. Shawn, Gene's oldest son, and Justin, Gene's youngest son, run the place along with Mary Lee, Gene's wife. Gene passed away several years ago. The Shack draws customers from Asheville, Hendersonville and Lake Toxaway as well as mountain tourists.

The Shack is one of those few places still cooking with wood-fired pits. It has a raised brick pit with a firebox at the end. The pit holds a goodly number of Boston butts. The slowly roasted pork is then chopped with a Hobart chopper. The Shack boils and shreds its chicken. The beef brisket is sliced.

The chopped barbecue pork is rich, tender and comes sauced in the kitchen with a tomato-base sauce. The smoke from the pits comes through despite the meat being finely chopped. The tomato base sauce is one of the favorites of this area. It is not a Lexington-style dip but more of a Southwestern-type sauce.

The chicken has a nice, mild chicken taste. There is no barbecue flavor here. Remember the chicken is boiled and shredded by hand. The barbecue flavor is imparted to the chicken through the sauce.

The beef barbecue is tender, moist, fully chopped and has a good, mild pit-roasted beef flavor.

There are three sauces at the table. One is brown, labeled "mild" in a blue bottle (Cattleman's Classic). The second is red, marked "spicy" in a yellow bottle (Open Pit). The third is brown, marked "hot" in a red bottle (Cattleman's Hot and Spicy).

The Shack was built in 1983 and opened in 1984. The interior has brown-stained paneling, a stone chimney, pine floors and is very rustic. The Shack is the perfect setting for a pig pickin' in the mountains (Monday nights).

Take Highway 64 east from Brevard. The Shack is on your left the moment you enter the Etowah community. It is rustic, reddish-brown clapboard with a front and side porch with rockers. There is a sign on the roof but not at the road. As you drive east on Highway 64, trees obscure the Shack. From Hendersonville, take Highway 64 west, the Shack is on the western skirts of Etowah on the right. Hours are 11 a.m. until 9 p.m., Wednesday through Monday. It's closed Tuesday. Telephone number: (828) 891-3200.

Fat Buddies Ribs and BBQ, Franklin

Placemats that double as brown take-home bags, beer stein glasses, tin plates with a red-and-white-checkered paper liner, reddish-brown paneling, tin walls covered with antique farm implements, wooden tables and captain's chairs make up the décor at Fat Buddies.

The owners are Chuck and Judy St. John. Chuck was a big time winter vegetable farmer in Florida for 30 years. He decided he wanted to get out of the farming business and open a restaurant and almost opened one in the Keys. The Keys' loss was North Carolina's gain. Chuck came to Highlands and fell in love with the area. He and Judy moved up here in 1995 and opened the restaurant in August 1999.

Fat Buddies delicious pork is cooked in an Old Hickory cooker. He cooks Canadian pork collars, beef-eye round and Danish ribs. He said the mad cow scare stopped the importation of Danish ribs for awhile so he used St. Louis ribs. Now that the matter has cleared, he is back to Danish ribs.

Chuck cooks with pecan wood that he procures from South Carolina and Georgia. He has a friend who is a schoolteacher moonlighting as a tree man or a tree man moonlighting as a teacher, Chuck's not sure which, that keeps him in good supply.

Chuck and Judy have enticed three of their sons to the area, all of whom work with mom and dad. There's a daughter who Chuck says they have yet to capture but are working on.

When the boys were young they were all in the 4-H Club and raised their own steers. The children's fathers encouraged the youth and provided funds for the 4-H Club through an informal buy-back program. If the children's beeves did not bring the price the fathers thought they should, the fathers would buy them back through the bank and the bank would tell each father what they owed at the end of the sale. Thus, Chuck and his farmer friends became known as the "Fat Buddies." Chuck liked the role and the name so he brought it with him from Florida.

The sliced barbecue pork at Fat Buddies is pink throughout with good smoke penetration. It has a wonderful smoky taste and is ever so tender. It is very, very moist without sauce, cooked to absolute perfection. The sliced pork with the sweet brown sauce is wonderfully rich. With the caramel-colored mustard sauce, it is tangy, not hot and very tasty. With the hot sauce, your taste buds really perk up. It's just hot enough. With the Franklin Firehouse Sauce, get the hose. This wolf in sheep's clothing will light your fire and is only for the very brave.

The sliced beef is pink with good smoky overtones. It has a nutty flavor, is tender to fork, has a nice brown edge and imparts a wonderful woodsy, brown, rich outdoors flavor.

The babyback ribs are the most tender and succulent ribs you have ever tasted. If your fork is not on a rib bone, it will fall through these ribs. There is just enough searing and glaze to lightly crisp the outside. When you bite into these four-inch morsels of maddening goodness, you will say, "I'm ready, heaven is at hand."

The barbecue chicken is pink throughout and done to the bone. It has a wonderful smoked flavor and is exceptionally moist all the way through. With the brown sugar-smoky sauce, this is too good to swallow.

The baked beans have a sweet smoky flavor that is enhanced with just the right spices... a good offering.

The sides also include black-eyed pea soup in a rich broth with chunks of potatoes, smoked meat and spices – damn good. The brunswick stew is delicious and has some fire. The slaw is a moderate coarse chopped white cabbage with nice carrot flakes, celery seed and moderately light mayo. It is so crisp, so fresh with just enough tartness to offset the sweet smoky sauce and the rich smoky meat.

Hours are Monday through Saturday from 11 a.m. until 2:30 p.m.; Monday through Thursday from 5 p.m. until 8 p.m.; and Friday and Saturday from 5 p.m. until 9 p.m. Telephone number: (828) 349-4743. Also visit Buddies at www.fatbuddiesribsandbbq.com.

Rib Country, Hayesville

Owner Danny Craig was selling food for SYSCO when his current business partner moved to the mountains from Florida. Danny's partner opened a place in Highlands. Danny liked his food and worked for him for awhile. Danny wanted to live in Hayesville, so he opened Rib Country in June 2000. His partner continued to run the one in Highlands. Plus, they jointly own one in Georgia.

Everything is cooked on site with an Old Hickory gas cooker using pecan wood from Georgia. Rib Country uses only Danish babyback ribs. Danny makes his own sauces (four) served at the table. Rib Country serves barbecue pork (sliced), barbecue beef, smoked turkey, barbecue chicken and all kinds of combinations along with lots of sides. Drinks are served in mug-style pint

mason jars.

The inside of the restaurant has gold-toned pine paneling, ladder-back chairs and walls decorated with horse collars and farm implements. There are checkerboards for your entertainment and pigs made from different materials everywhere. As you walk in the front door, there are antique gas and wood stoves. It's clean as a pin and staffed by nice people. Danny Craig is a nice looking, neat, affable young man who looks like he may have been a wide receiver.

The sliced beef has a rich wood-smoked flavor. It's tender, moist and exceptional.

The babyback ribs are succulent, so tender it falls off the bone. This delicacy has a smoky flavor and a rich, slightly sweet taste. The combination of smokiness and sweetness makes for an absolute taste symphony – just enough outside crunch to go with the moist melt in your mouth meat.

The slaw is a moderate coarse chopped white cabbage with chips of carrot, celery seed and light mayonnaise. It's very crisp, fresh and tasty – an excellent counter balance to the richness of the 'cue.

The mustard sauce (in the yellow bottle) has a spicy taste. The brown mustard has a sweetness that coupled with the yellow mustard is very tasty. The regular sweet sauce (in the brown bottle) has a nice brown sugar and spice taste for the sweet tooth. The hot sauce (red bottle) is the brown sauce ratcheted up to a fiery, smoky liquid with a KICK. The XXX hot sauce (red bottle with XXX Hot on it) carries the same warning that XXX carries with a skin flick, it is HOT, HOT, HOT. Check your homeowners insurance before imbibing; this one will burn your house down.

From Highway 64, take Highway 69 to the junction of Highway 64 business. Follow Highway 64 business to Rib Country, which is about 100 yards on your left. Summer hours are 12 p.m. until 2 p.m. and 5 until close, Monday through Friday; noon until 3 p.m. and 5 p.m. until close on Saturday; and 12 p.m. until 3 p.m. on Sunday. Call for winter hours. Telephone number: (828) 389-9597.

57

Butts on the Creek, Maggie Valley

Butts on the Creek is the inspiration of owner Joe Kilgore. Picture three round pink pig bottoms sitting on a bench having a meal. This is Butts on the Creek. Though only 6 years old, Butts on the Creek has become one of the places to eat in Maggie Valley. It was built as is on the present site. It has a rustic exterior and a bright varnished wood interior, Butts

would be an attractive place situated anywhere, but when you nestle it back in the trees on a beautiful creek, you have a very picturesque mountain setting.

Joe said he had no family barbecue history; he just built this lovely place and started cooking. He said trial and error produced the cooking style and the sauces that are spicy, mustard and molasses.

Joe cooks his pork for 14 hours and his beef for 10 hours with hickory wood. The chicken, ribs and pork tenderloin are cooked over apple wood. The cooker is a Southern Pride smoker that does an excellent job for this type of cooking.

The sliced beef is good roast beef with a smoky overtone and is as moist as roast beef gets. It is not dry, but not juicy either. I found it best with the molasses sauce or the mustard sauce.

The pulled pork is smoky, tender, juicy and delicious with good smoke penetration. It's a delightful offering and needs nothing. But, if one is to sauce, I like the hot vinegar base sauce or the brown mustard sauce best.

The sliced pork is tasty but a bit dry, as most sliced pork offerings are likely to be. It has a nutty flavor with slight smoky nuances. It's best with hot vinegar base sauce or brown mustard sauce.

The pulled beef is pink, moist, chewy (not tough) and tender with good smoke penetration. While it's a flavorful offering without sauce, it's best with brown molasses or brown mustard sauce.

The hand-pulled chicken is a moderately fine chop, moist, tender, hint of smoke, good bird.

The very fresh slaw is crunchy white cabbage with nips of carrot, celery seed and light mayo. The hushpuppies are fairly large with a brown crust and a moist center. There's a hint of bell pepper (not hot, just tasty). The pups are homemade, not a pre-mix; they use Three Rivers Cornmeal Mix.

Butts on the Creek is on your right proceeding south on Highway 19 in downtown Maggie Valley. You should look carefully as it sits back from the road in the trees and below road level. Plus, the sign is obscured by their neighbor's sign. If you

miss it, turn around. It's well worth it. Imbibe at their fine bar and enjoy watching Joe's sister blow glass (her studio is in Butts).

Hours are 11:30 a.m. until 9 p.m., Tuesday through Saturday, and 11:30 a.m. until 8 p.m., Sunday. It's closed Monday and is open from May until December. Telephone number: (828) 926-7885.

Herb's Pit BBQ, Murphy

Herb's Pit BBQ in Murphy opened in 1982. Like so many good barbecues it is the typical family run restaurant. Hoover and Helen Gibson started this Western North Carolina barbecue mecca. Their son is the kitchen cook and their daughter-in-law is the manager of the wait staff. Helen comes in every day to oversee and lend a hand. Herb still does all the cooking on the pits.

The restaurant interior is warm pine paneling. Double doors open to buffet and kitchen. There is a screened porch on the back for bug-free outdoor dining.

The meat is cooked on open pits with hickory wood. They cook pork loins for the sliced barbecue and chopped. They barbecue St. Louis-style ribs and whole chickens.

Herb's pulls a lot of business from the Ocoee River area. The Ocoee was the river used for sculling in the 1996 Summer Olympics held in Atlanta. There are lots of rafters and kayakers in this area. Eagle Ranch often brings its resident water rats here to eat. Eagle, located five or six miles west of the Tennessee line, is a ranch for rafters, hikers, horseback riding, etc. People come from Murphy, Andrews, Hayesville and Copperhill, Tenn. to eat Herb's wonderful food.

The staff has been together for more than five years and they're very friendly, truly Southern hospitality at its best.

Herb serves chopped barbecue pork and beef, sliced barbecue pork and beef, barbecue ribs and chicken. Herb also serves steaks, prime rib, shrimp, grilled chicken and mountain rainbow trout. Herb's desserts are famous four-layer pies.

The chopped barbecue is hand chopped medium with nice meaty pieces. It comes sauced from the kitchen. It has moderately sweet rib-type sauce and you don't need to add anything at the table. The pork has a rich brown flavor; it is hard to taste the smokiness fully because of the sweet sauce, however the cooking method and sauce work.

The sliced barbecue pork has a deeper smoky flavor than the chopped. It's very moist and very tender. You can cut it with a fork. It goes really well with the sauce used in the kitchen, the same sauce as the chopped.

The barbecue chicken has a slightly crisp skin and good smoky flavor all the way to the bone. It's very moist with juicy droplets inside. The house barbecue sauce on the bird is something to crow about.

The barbecue pork ribs are tender with just enough outside crust and glaze to

60

make these ribs sing. They are meaty, chewy and good to the point of being sinful.

The slaw is a moderate coarse chop of white and red cabbage with carrots and light mayo. This very fresh coleslaw has a refreshing taste to balance the sweet sauce of the 'cue. It's just good.

The hushpuppies, although a bit greasy, have a light brown shell and a good crunch with a moist center and a good cornbread taste.

The sliced beef barbecue is slow roasted to perfection with a Kansas City-style house sauce that elevates this dish to the sublime. Soooooooooo tender, soooooooooo good. Look out Texas, here comes Herb's.

The sauce is a brown, thick Kansas City-style sauce with a sweet and sour taste.

It coats well on chicken, ribs and sliced barbecue beef. This is exceptionally good food.

There are specials Wednesday through Sunday. Wednesday is country dinner day; Thursday is prime rib day; Friday is all-you-can-eat popcorn shrimp and fish day; Saturday is all-you-can-eat crab legs day and Sunday is the "church special."

Take Highway 64 West out of Murphy for 16 miles. Herb's is on your left. It is a small white building with turquoise trim surrounded by trees. You will have to go past Herb's and cut across and come back east on Highway 64 East for 200 yards. Hours are 11 a.m. until 9 p.m., Sunday through Thursday, and 11 a.m. until 10 p.m., Friday and Saturday. Telephone number: (828) 494-5367.

Green River Bar-B-Que, Saluda

Owner Daryl "Kim" Talbot and wife Melanie opened the Green River Bar-B-Que in 1984. This tiny barbecue establishment is just up the street and over the bridge from the historic depot in downtown Saluda. Across the street from the depot is a sign that tells you that the Saluda grade is the steepest standard gauge mainline railroad grade in the U.S. Opened in 1878, the grade is three miles long and crests at the point of the sign. Past this point, you cross over the bridge and you are facing Green River Bar-B-Que.

Kim, the mayor of Saluda, said that he used to cook with wood over pits. After many years, he grew tired of the 160-degree temperature in the pit room and switched to electric cooking. He now cooks with a Cook Shack and hickory wood. Kim cooks pork shoulders and beef top round. In addition to serving the locals and summer tourists, Kim caters to Asheville, Spartanburg and Greenville, S.C.

Green River serves chopped pork barbecue, sliced barbecue beef, barbecue chicken and barbecue pork ribs. One of its offerings, the Saluda Stuffer, is a half loaf of their homemade Italian bread hollowed out and stuffed with chopped barbecue. The Hog Trough is the whole loaf version.

The moderately chopped barbecue pork is moist, brown-and-white mixed, slightly dry, chewy and not sauced in the kitchen. With the mustard sauce, it is a good South Carolina-style 'cue. With the mild sauce, it was kinda bland. With the hot sauce, it was best.

The sliced barbecue beef without sauce was very tender, moist and had a good roast beef flavor. It's best with the mustard sauce. My second choice would be the hot sauce.

The sliced barbecue pork was also tender, moist and had a good roast pork flavor. Again, try it with the mustard sauce.

The barbecue pork ribs were sauced in the kitchen with a house chicken and rib sauce. This is a kind of sweet mustard sauce, not hot and mildly spicy. The ribs were slightly tough and a bit too chewy for my taste. The ribs had a good pork flavor but seemed to have been cooked a bit too fast.

The barbecue chicken was sauced in the kitchen with the chicken and rib sauce. It was fairly moist and the breast was tender. Add a few drops of the hot sauce and it really turns this bird up a click. The chicken is also good with the mustard sauce. Try both.

The slaw is a moderately coarse chopped white cabbage with celery seed. It's fresh and crunchy.

The sauces are mild, hot, volcano, mustard, chicken and rib, and down East. There are 22 side offerings and six desserts.

When you come into Saluda, exit at I-26, and follow the signs into downtown Saluda. When you reach the historic depot area, on the right you will see an old restored depot building painted yellow with green trim and reddish brown doors. The sign across the street tells about the Saluda grade. Proceed up the hill and over the bridge and Green River Bar-B-Que will be on your immediate left. Hours are 11 a.m. until 9 p.m., Friday and Saturday, and 11 a.m. until 8 p.m. after Labor Day and on Tuesday, Wednesday and Thursday. It's closed Sunday and Monday. Telephone number: (828) 749-9892.

Smoky Mountain Grill and Lee's Barbecue, Sylva

Owner Lee Ewart has been cooking good pork barbecue at this establishment for more than 15 years. Lee's Barbecue cooks fresh, never-frozen Boston butts every night for about 14 hours. They sell out every day and the 'cue never goes into the cooler. What you eat was cooked the night before, no leftovers.

Lee's cooks with a Southern Pride cooker, gas/wood smoker.

The finely chopped barbecue pork is moist with good roast pork flavor. The pork has a good nutty flavor from the outside brown without any sauce. With sauce added this becomes a good Lexington-style 'cue. You would think you were in the Piedmont instead of the mountains. The sauce is a vinegar base, Lexington-style sauce served hot at the table. It is a reddish-brown, peppery dip with tomato prominence, but enough peppers and spices to make it a good Lexington-style dip without a tomatoey taste.

The moderately chopped slaw is a red Lexington style also. It is very tart, tangy and a nice combo with the 'cue.

Sides include baked beans, coleslaw, Lexington-style slaw and sauce.

Hours are 6 a.m. until 9 p.m., Monday through Saturday, and 11 a.m. until 9 p.m., Sunday. Telephone number: (828) 586-3490.

Eddie's Bar-B-Que, Waynesville

Owner Eddie Gibbs retired to Jonathan Valley from Jacksonville, Florida in 1996. Eddie, who had a catering business in Florida, decided to open a restaurant in Jonathan because it is such a pretty area. He bought the present site in 1996 and built his restaurant. Eddie's opened May 1997. The infamous I-40 rock-slide occurred six weeks after they opened. Interstate 40 was closed and Eddie's had just opened. This hiatus continued for five months. Eddie said that once I-40 reopened and traffic passed through the area, business has been good ever since. He said locals account for about 80 percent of his business. Tourists are missing a good bet here.

Eddie cooks with a Southern Pride rotary cooker. He cooks pork collars (they are pre-trimmed shoulders) that he gets from Canada. He said this is the leanest cut of pork you can buy. The meat is boneless and you can slice it or chop it.

The ribs are St. Louis-style pork ribs.

When he decided to open his barbe-cue place, Eddie traveled about the state trying to decide whether to cook Lexington style or Eastern North Carolina style. He discussed it with his wife and they decided they would do what they knew how to do best and let the chips fall where they may. The chips have been falling favorably ever since.

The chopped bar-becue pork is ever so smoky with a very rich, wonderful pork taste. It is tender, moist, delicious 'cue with any of Eddie's choice of sauces. Eddie marinates this wonderful offering in salt and pepper, but does not baste during cooking.

The sliced pork has deep smoke penetration. It is pink at the edge, big-time tender and absolutely delicious. This 'cue is wonderful with any of Eddie's sauces.

The pork ribs are the best smoky ribs you will ever eat. Eddie said a customer, whom he had never met, told him after a plate of Eddie's delicious ribs that he was a barbecue judge and had judged cook-offs all over the state and knew ribs. He said Eddie's ribs were the best he'd ever eaten. I agree.

The slaw is white cabbage with flecks of carrot, light mayo and a hint of sweetness. It's very good. The baked beans are killer. The hushpuppies are crisp with a golden-brown shell, a nice center, good cornbread taste and are not heavy or greasy.

Eddie has several sauces. One is a brown sauce which is a good, mild, slightly tangy, medium-thick sauce. Another is a mustard sauce which is slightly sweet, hot, tangy, and a good change of pace. Eddie's meat has such a wonderful flavor without sauce it is almost criminal to put sauce on it.

Eddie's ribs are so tender that Eddie said a man comes to eat ribs every week that does not have a tooth in his head. This pleases Eddie and he is justifiably proud of his wonderful food. Tuesday is all-you-can-eat rib night. Wednesday is catfish, just to change the pace. Thursday is chicken and Saturday night is barbecue prime rib smoked five to six hours. Eddie said it's to die for.

Driving into Maggie Valley on Highway 19 south, you will see Eddie's sign. From Highway 19 South, turn right at the stoplight on Highway 276 north and go three miles. Eddie's BBQ is on the right. Hours are 11 a.m. until 9 p.m., Tuesday through Saturday, and 11 a.m. until 8 p.m., Sunday. It's closed Monday and open only May through October. Telephone number: (828) 926-5353.

Notes

Notes

SECTION II

The Piedmont

Location

Log Cabin Barbecue, Albemarle **1**

Whispering Pines Cafe, Albemarle **2**

Speedy Lohr's BBQ of Arcadia, Arcadia **3**

Pappy's Barbeque, Banner Elk **4**

Bubba's Barbecue, Charlotte **5**

Gary's Bar-B-Que, China Grove **6**

Little Richard's Lexington Bar-B-Que, Clemmons **7**

Troutman's Bar-B-Q, Concord **8**

Bennett's Smokehouse and Saloon, Conover **9**

The Hickory Log, Barbecue, Forest City **10**

R.O.'s Barbecue, Gastonia **11**

M&K Barbecue and Country Cooking, Granite Quarry **12**

Kepley's Bar-B-Q, High Point **13**

Wallace Brother's BBQ, Lambsburg, VA **14**

Hannah's Bar-B-Que, Lenoir **15**

The Barbecue Center, Inc., Lexington **16**

Jimmy's Barbecue, Lexington **17**

Lexington Barbecue, Lexington **18**

Bar-B-Que King, Lincolnton **19**

Spear's BBQ & Grill, Linville Falls **20**

Location

Fuzzy's, Madison **21**

Deano's Barbecue, Mocksville **22**

Lancaster's BBQ, Mooresville **23**

Timberwood's Family Restaurant, Morganton **24**

Snappy Lunch, Mount Airy **25**

Doc's Deli, North Wilkesboro **26**

Arey's Barbecue, Rockwell **27**

The Barbecue Place, Rutherfordton **28**

Hendrix Barbeque, Salisbury **29**

Richard's Bar-B-Q, Salisbury **30**

Wink's Bar-B-Que, Salisbury **31**

Alston Bridges Barbecue, Inc., Shelby **32**

Bridges Barbecue Lodge, Shelby **33**

Carolina Bar-B-Q, Statesville **34**

Little Pigs Barbecue, Statesville **35**

Scotz BBQ and Diner, Taylorsville **36**

Stamey's Barbecue, Tyro **37**

Smoky Mountain Barbecue, West Jefferson **38**

Hill's Lexington Barbecue, Winston-Salem **39**

Little Richard's Bar-B-Que, Winston-Salem **40**

Hall's BBQ Restaurant, Yadkinville **41**

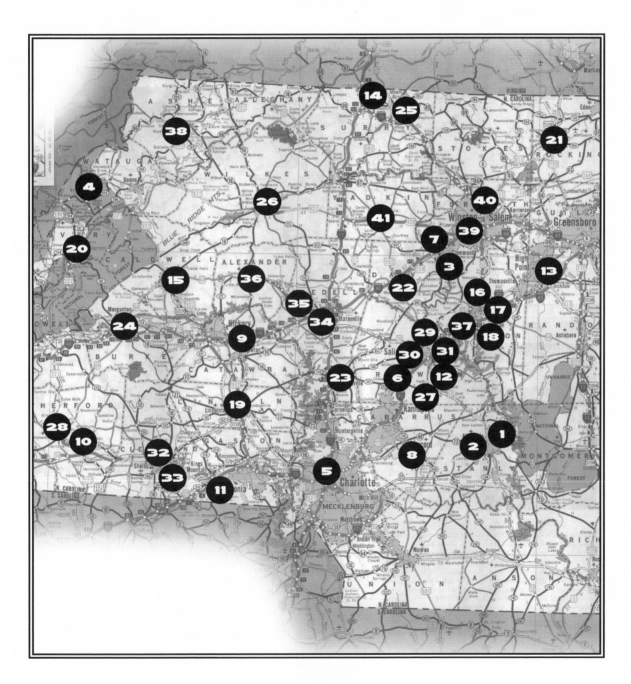

Log Cabin Barbecue, Albemarle

As you enter the town of Albemarle on Highway 52 South, on the left you will spot a rustic red log restaurant with green doors. Close your eyes (after you've parked) and you will think you are in Montana. The Log Cabin Barbecue (LCB) looks like it should be surrounded with pinion trees and have snow-capped mountains in the background.

In such a setting one would expect to be served steak or barbecue beef ribs with a Texas or Kansas City sauce instead of pork barbecue as is the fare here.

Edie Almond, who formerly owned the restaurant with her son Glen, now has sole ownership having purchased Glen's interest several years ago. This place remains pretty much the same as it has for the past dozen years. LCB continues to cook its mouth watering pork shoulders on pits over hickory coals in a red log smokehouse located on the rear of the property. You don't have to ask if they use hickory or oak. As you approach the smokehouse, you are immediately confronted with the pungent smell of split hickory wood. Split hickory wood (on its best day) smells like a horse barn. If it's wet, it smells even worse. But, oh, does it add flavor when reduced to coals and shoveled into a barbecue pit.

After LCB's wonderful barbecue is cooked to a state of perfection, it is allowed to cool and then broken down. The heart of the shoulder (the larger muscle) is pulled for slicing. The rest of the shoulder is hand chopped into a moderately chopped offering and a coarse-chopped offering. When you order the chopped, the coarse chopped or the sliced barbecue, you are in for a treat.

The chopped barbecue is rather finely chopped yet still moist. It is not sauced in the kitchen. You can taste a hint of the basting sauce from the cooking pit. The 'cue has a rich, deep, smoky, woodsy flavor. The outside brown and inside white mix well together. It is served so each person can sauce at the table to their liking. The sauce at the table is fiery. Be careful here. It doesn't take much, so try a few a drops at a time. The sliced barbecue has brown edges and a pinkness running toward the center, which is evidence of good smoke penetration. The sliced barbecue is very tender and takes on the taste and texture of a pig pickin'. It is ever so moist, ever so good and definitely my favorite. Take me home country road. Tell your waitperson you want your sliced barbecue thick sliced like pulled pork. Edie or one of her helpers will fix it just to your liking.

The slaw is a white, fresh, crisp cabbage with flakes of carrot. It was a teeny bit heavy on the mayo for my taste but overall it's very good. The red slaw is not like your usual Lexington-style slaw. It is red with chips of pimento and is made up of moderately coarse white cabbage with vinegar, tomatoes and spices.

The hushpuppies have a brown, crisp outer shell with a good moist center and nice cornbread flavor.

The vinegar-base sauce for the 'cue is reddish in color with lots of fiery peppers and spices. There is a reason the sauce is red and it is not tomato paste or ketchup. It is a hot one.

Edie shared that for a number of years before purchasing an interest in LCB, she worked with her sister, Lavada Doby, at Whispering Pines several miles down the road. Naturally Edie knew how to make all the products offered by Whispering Pines. When Edie bought her interest in LCB, she promised her sister that she would not pirate her recipes and would come up with her own sauce. Edie said she had experimented with a number of different ingredients before settling on the recipe that she now uses to sauce her delicious 'cue. The lady knows her barbecue.

In my treks across the state looking for good barbecue places, I had only encountered one incident of a woman working on the barbecue pits. This was Leola, a black lady who worked with the men on the pits at Hursey's Barbecue in Burlington. Well we've come a long way baby. LCB has a female pit master (or would it be pit mistress?). Edie recently hired Rhonda Smith to run her barbecue pits. Rhonda is a tall young woman in her 30s who is more than capable of doing what has been thought of historically as a "man's job." Edie said Rhonda could swing a case of 60-pound meat with the best of them as well as push a dolly loaded five feet high with split hickory wood. When showing me her smokehouse, Edie invited me to lift one of the cast iron doors that must be raised every 45 minutes in order to freshen the coals. Well I figured if a woman could do it, I could do it without bending my knees. Oops, Rhonda's stock went up another 10 points. My visit to Rhonda's smokehouse left me with three indelible impressions: (1) Rhonda keeps an immaculate work place; (2) Rhonda cooks scrumptious barbecue; and (3) if I ever get backed into a corner at a bar, I would surely like to have Rhonda on my side.

Wednesday night is barbecue chicken night. You must try the barbecue chicken cooked on open pits over live hickory coals. It's worth the trip.

Hours are 10 a.m. until 9 p.m., Monday through Saturday. It's closed Sunday. Telephone number: (704) 982-5257.

Whispering Pines Cafe, Albemarle

Lonnie L. Doby built Whispering Pines in 1945 outside the city limits of Albemarle. Before going into the food business, Lonnie was in dry cleaning for a number of years. Lonnie ran this place by himself for eight years before he and Lavada married in 1954. Lonnie retired in 1966 due to poor health and Lavada has run Whispering Pines ever since.

Lavada said that she was a workhorse when she married Lonnie. She did what six short-order girls now do. She said she did it all from memory with no pencil or pads. Lavada added to her skills until she could perform every facet of the barbecue business. This came in handy when Lonnie became ill and she had to take over the whole operation.

Whispering Pines still does everything the old-fashioned way. The curb service is not done with speakers but instead looks like something from the movie American Graffiti. Pretty young schoolgirls come out and take your order at your car. Curb service represents 50 percent of Whispering Pines business. Locals and beach travelers on Highway 52 stop for some good 'cue to eat along the way or take home for lunch or supper.

Not a lot has changed at Whispering Pines in nearly 60 years of operation, including Lavada. When you go, take note of the 1948 National cash register. The meat is still cooked all night, three times a week and served all day. Jason Morton runs the two big brick barbecue pits on either side of a large firebox. The floor is broken tile and the place is clean as a whistle.

Lavada said that years ago the business was about 35 percent transit and 65 percent Cannon Mills. She says now the business is still about 65 percent locals and 35 percent transit. She said, "things change but the business has always been consistent."

The chopped barbecue was a good, rich, brown barbecue with full flavor and outside brown mixed for that wonderful woodsy taste. It's very moist but not greasy at all.

The sliced barbecue had some outside brown that had a deep, powerful smoky, campfire flavor. It's extremely tender and moist with a deep pink color indicative of good smoke penetration.

The vinegar-base sauce has no tomatoes and is dark brown in color. It has lots of spices. Yee Haw! Cayenne, the peppers ride again. This sauce is not for ice cream. A little sauce at the table goes a long way. To my taste, the sauce is better on the sliced than

77

the chopped barbecue.

The barbecue chicken had a spicy, soft, not crispy skin. The breast that I tried was moist and had beads of juice and a dusting of pepper on the skin that gave a wonderful taste to the really fresh, moist meat inside.

The slaw is red and very coarsely chopped. A pronounced cabbage taste balanced well with green bell peppers, red bell peppers, vinegar and spices, which really kick it up.

The hushpuppies were brown, crunchy, moist, not greasy and had a good taste.

In addition to its barbecue treats, Whispering Pines serves 22 different sandwiches along with the usual sides.

As you enter Albemarle on Highway 52 South, Whispering Pines Cafe is located on the right side of the road. The lot is fairly large but the building is not. Look for a 1950s-style pine tree in front of a rather diminutive diner with a drive-in and pits on the rear. Whispering Pines has four four-top tables, two two-top tables and a counter with seven seats.

Hours are 9 a.m. to 9:30 p.m., Tuesday through Saturday. It's closed Monday and Sunday. Telephone number: (704) 982-6184.

Speedy Lohr's BBQ of Arcadia

Roger Lohr ran Speedy Lohr's BBQ for a number of years under the name of Arcadia Barbecue. Several years ago, Roger placed the business under the umbrella of his father's corporation and changed the name to Speedy Lohr's. Roger's father, Paul "Speedy" Lohr, is an old hand in the barbecue business, having trained under the watchful eye of Warner Stamey at Stamey's Drive-In in Lexington and Old Hickory Barbecue, also in Lexington. Speedy also trained under Paul and Joe Cope at Stamey's.

Speedy purchased Tussy's Drive-In from Holland Tussy and continued running that restaurant under that name. Speedy ultimately opened several other restaurants bearing the name Speedy Lohr's BBQ. All of these restaurants incorporated the barbecue experience and recipes that Speedy learned from Warner Stamey.

Speedy retired within the last couple of years and recently lamented to Roger that he missed serving people barbecue.

A certain amount of mystery shrouds the origin of Eldridge Overby's nickname "Short Sugar." There is no mystery to Paul Lohr's nickname "Speedy." Paul played football in high school. The first time he touched the ball in a game, he ran 80 yards for a touchdown. He's been called "Speedy" ever since.

Paul has interests outside the barbecue arena. He runs coon dogs, has 25 beagles and bass fishes with a passion.

Roger Lohr trained under his dad and now operates the Speedy Lohr's in Arcadia. Roger says that people come from Lexington, the barbecue mecca eight miles away to eat at Speedy Lohr's in Arcadia. Davidson County probably has more barbecue places per capita than any county in the country. Roger said there were approximately 38 barbecue places in Davidson County. Of which, about 20 are located in and around the town of Lexington.

John, Roger's brother, went to college. Roger on the other hand, said he tried college for awhile, missed the barbecue business and went back to work with his dad. Roger's dad was of the old barbecue school which says, "If it's not cooked over coals, it's not barbecue." Roger said his dad could not accept a microwave oven for a long time and balked when Roger wanted to install an electrical warmer to keep meat warm after cooking during rush periods. Roger finally persuaded his dad to allow the microwave and the electric warmer in the kitchen. Roger said he still looks at it and shakes his head.

Roger not only feeds the locals but

ships his barbecue as far away as Michigan, Florida, Alaska and most other states. Roger said that it takes a minimum of a year to train a barbecue cook to the point that you can leave him by himself while cooking. Roger's meat is cooked fresh daily. He said if you try to make it in large quantities and carry it over, it loses its freshness. He said that he can taste barbecue and know immediately if it was cooked that day or the day before.

The sauce at Speedy Lohr's BBQ is a Lexington-style dip. It is brown, thicker than some, slightly tomatoey and peppery with spices that fit in very nicely. It has overall good balance and clings to the meat well. It is not too hot and has a good finish.

The chopped barbecue comes sauced from the kitchen. The chopped 'cue is slightly drier than the coarse-chopped or sliced barbecue. The chopped pieces are large enough to retain the flavor of the meat with the sauce. It has plenty of taste – good, bright vinegar-peppery taste with a good finish. The chopped barbecue is not heavy and you know you just had some good stuff.

The coarse-chopped barbecue is tender as can be. It's moist and comes sauced from the kitchen fairly generously. I would not want more sauce at the table. The dip and the meat are a good combo. The coarse-chopped 'cue comes in much larger pieces. It has a good, light, smoky flavor that is enhanced by the dip.

The sliced barbecue is the white part of the shoulder. It is very moist and sauced in the kitchen. It is very flavorful and tangy. The pepper comes through but does not overwhelm the meat. It can be eaten as dessert or entrée.

All the meat is cooked on a pit over hickory slabs. Roger cooks the old simple way. He cooks just shoulders, about 10 pounds each. He said this cooks down to eight or nine pounds when done. He said his pork shoulders used to come with a big slab of fat. Now shoulders are filleted, trimmed and do not have as much fat. Roger purchases his pork shoulders from Orrell's. They are Lundy's, Smithfield and Hatfield brands. Roger said the timing on the cooking is very critical. If the meat is too done, it is dry and if not done enough, it won't mix right. Roger mixes white lean and brown outside together to create good blend.

The red slaw is vinegary but not too hot, and is a nice compliment to the barbecue. The slaw and the coarse-chopped barbecue are a marriage made in heaven.

Speedy Lohr's BBQ is located on Highway 150 South in Arcadia, approximately 15 miles south of Winston-Salem. Hours are 8 a.m. to 6 p.m., Monday through Saturday. It's closed Sunday. Catering service is available. Telephone number: (336) 764-5509.

Pappy's Barbeque, Banner Elk

Pappy's Barbeque, which opened in 1987, is owned by Robert C. Schwebke. In the mid-1990s, Rick Ballou was hired as general manager. Rick, who has been a chef for 35 years, says cooking pigs has been part of his life since his early years in Florida. He remembers having friends over when he lived in the Keys and cooking pigs in the sand.

A graduate of the Culinary Institute of America, Rick was on the short list to be sec-

ond in command as chef to one of our former presidents. He has cooked barbecue at a number of places in Florida. He recalls doing parties for Jimmy Buffett and other celebrities such as NFL Hall of Fame player Terry Bradshaw, former NFL coach Don Shula and NASCAR driver Harry Gant.

Rick has the build of an NFL pulling guard. His neck, shoulders, arms and hands convey a strength born of many hours of hard work. Rick is not a tall man, but when he steps into his kitchen and does his thing with the 'cue, he is 7-foot-4 and can slam dunk from the top of the key. His pleasant smile immediately lets you know that you are welcome and he will do all that he can to serve you a good meal and contribute to your having a pleasant time in the mountains.

Rick says that he likes to let his food speak for his skills. His food has certainly done that. When Rick took over the restaurant, it sat 45 people. In 1999, they added two new rooms and a deck. It now seats 160 people. A year later they redid and paved the parking lot and added attractive landscaping to the already welcoming look of the log building which houses Pappy's.

In 1994, Rick started serving three meals a day. The breakfast crowd enjoys Rick's smoked pork loin, which is sliced like a ham. The breakfast menu includes all the usual things one might expect, but the smoked pork loin is Rick's specialty. Rick says that the restaurant serves between 140,000 and 150,000 people a year. It has been written up in *America* by Charles Kuralt and *Southern Living* magazine.

Pappy's cooks a variety of meats. Rick says that in season, they cook about 500 pounds of pork butts per night. He said he tried shoulders but there was too much waste and too much fat. He prefers the Boston Butt cut. They also smoke about 50 pounds of turkey and 60-95 pounds of ribs per day.

In addition, they smoke chicken breast. Rick prefers the breast to the dark meat. The chicken is sold in quarters. If one wants a half chicken, they get two breasts. Rick used to smoke babyback ribs; now he uses St. Louis ribs. All the meat is cooked in two smokers. One is an Old Hickory smoker that will hold 850 pounds of meat. It is fired by propane and cooks at a steady, regulated heat. The smoke is generated from inserting pieces of hickory into the firebox that burns and imparts the hickory smoke flavor to the meat. The smaller cooker is a Southern Pride, which holds 350 pounds of meat. It is fired by propane and also uses wood inserts.

Rick said that he uses local hickory wood almost exclusively. He said that when the apple orchard farmers prune and clear their orchards, he gets apple wood from them and adds it to the hickory to produce a little sweeter flavored smoke. Rick said the hickory from different areas produces a different flavor of smoke. He prefers the hickory from his local area to that found anywhere else he has cooked. He said that another chef from Canada who stopped at his restaurant was so taken with the flavor that the local hickory produced that he took wood home with him in hopes of duplicating the flavor.

Rick says he uses approximately two hickory logs every 24 hours. He believes the secret to his success is using the right amount of smoke. Rick believes that wood,

like grapes, takes on the qualities of the surrounding environment. He equated the difference in wood flavor to the difference in placing beehives in different areas and getting different flavors of honey.

The pork loin served by Pappy's originally started out as a breakfast item. It has caught on with the patrons and Rick now makes pork loin sandwiches and sells about 35 pounds per day.

Rick also cooks about 50 pounds of beef sirloin butts per day. This is sold as a plate or in sandwiches. Another item of particular interest is smoked prime rib. This is a smoked boneless rib eye done to perfection.

Pappy's barbecue pork is hand chopped the old-fashioned way. Rick does not put any sauce on his meat while it is cooking. He said that the sauce they use would caramelize and blacken. He does not find this attractive and feels his customers would not either. He also believes this would change the delicate smoked flavor of his meat. The sauce is served at the table in an original form and a hot form. To make the sauce, Rick starts with Cattleman's Barbecue Sauce as a base and adds his own special touches including cinnamon sticks, apple juice and molasses. The hot sauce is simply the original sauce with cayenne pepper added.

I tried a generous sample of the chopped barbecue pork, smoked pork loin, smoked turkey and smoked beef sirloin butt sliced. To my taste the chopped barbecue had a very mild smoked flavor and was a bit on the dry side. I'm aware that a large number of people prefer their barbecue dry in both the eastern and western part of the state. However, I like mine moist and this generally entails a little fat. Pappy's barbecue has little or no fat. I found the smoked pork loin had a very delicate, almost veal-like flavor with hints of smoke. It also was a bit dry for my taste but, again, it had no fat at all. The smoked turkey was moist, aromatic and had a delightful light smoked taste. The smoked beef was not as moist as the turkey but more so than the pork. It too had a light smoked flavor. All were good.

The sauce was neither an Eastern North Carolina vinegar-base sauce nor a Lexington-style dip. The original sauce was brown in color, slightly sweet, slightly tangy and thicker than either Eastern North Carolina sauce or Lexington-style dip. It does not fit the mold of either. To my taste, it was more akin to a Kansas City kind of barbecue sauce. On my palate, I found the sauce went best with the beef, turkey, chopped barbecue and pork loin in that order. The hotter sauce was just that, hotter because of the cayenne pepper, but not a particularly different flavor. Since Pappy's serves a host of people from all over the country traveling along the Blue Ridge Parkway and into our mountains,

Rick's hybrid sauce may please more people than either the pure Eastern North Carolina vinegar-base sauce or the tomato-added Lexington-style dip. I found Rick's sauce more like Bubba's sauce on Hatteras Island than any other sauce I have encountered across the state. Bottom line: it's good meat, good sauce and good eatin'.

His sides include baked beans, coleslaw, corn on the cob and Texas toast. All of Rick's sandwiches are served on Texas toast unless a customer requests a bun. Rick says the Texas toast holds up better than a bun and does not come apart in a customer's hand.

Cooking barbecue is a job that requires a passion. One has to want to feed and please others. Otherwise, people would not put in the long hours and hard work that it takes to produce a good barbecue product. Rick has this passion. You can see it in his eyes when he talks about his cooking, the products he prepares and the service he provides his customers. The Boone/Grandfather Mountain area is lucky to have Pappy's as one of its neighbors.

Pappy's is located 13 miles west of Boone on Highway 105 toward Grandfather Mountain, near the Banner Elk exit. Pappy's is open seven days a week. Hours are 7 a.m. to 9 p.m., Monday through Saturday, and 8 a.m. to 9 p.m., Sunday. Telephone number: (704) 898-6777.

Bubba's Barbecue, Charlotte

Owned by Ralph "Bubba" Miller, Bubba's Barbecue Restaurant was the barbecue place mentioned most by all of the inquiries I made in or around the Charlotte area.

Bubba himself pit cooks the pork shoulders over wood on site. In fact, Robin Hanes, the charming manager of Bubba's, said that Bubba is the only one who cooks the 'cue. He comes in, tends the fires and cooks the meat all night. The barbecue is chopped by hand. Staff takes over the daytime duties while Bubba gets some well-earned rest.

The chopped barbecue was a fine to moderate chop and a little dry, but moist enough to have a pleasant, good pork taste without sauce. It is sauced in the kitchen with an Eastern North Carolina sauce. The sauce and the meat form a good mix and are nice to each other. I suggest you taste before you sauce at the table. Pretty flakes of red pepper and seeds wink at you from behind meaty pieces of delicious slow-roasted, smoky pork. This is truly Eastern North Carolina barbecue.

The pork ribs had a good smoky flavor. The meaty ribs had a rich, brown taste and were very tender and lean with no fat. The ribs are sauced in the kitchen with Bubba's chicken and rib sauce. This thicker rib sauce makes a really good combo with the ribs.

The barbecue chicken had a crisp skin and a rich, smoky flavor. The breast was a little dry, but it was still tasty. I had let the breast sit while I talked to Robin too long with the food on the table, so it might have been more moist when served. Even so, a bite touched lightly in Bubba's wonderful chicken and rib sauce made for mighty fine eating.

The brunswick stew has tomatoes, potatoes, corn, lima beans, green beans and lots of chicken. It is thick and has a strong corn flavor, not corn kernel but cornmeal. It was my least favorite of all the offerings.

The slaw is slightly yellow by design and has a good fresh cabbage taste. It is moderately chopped with celery seeds and mustard. It's a nice change of pace from traditional white or red slaw of the area.

The hushpuppies were dark golden brown with a good outside crunch and a very moist inside. It had a nice cornbread taste and was not greasy.

The vinegar-base barbecue sauce is an Eastern North Carolina style with crushed red pepper and spices. It is delicious on the chopped barbecue.

The chicken and rib barbecue sauce is a dark reddish-brown, Kansas City-style sauce. It is smoky, rich, slightly sweet, spicy and very, very good!

From I-77 North, take Exit 16B and turn right. Cross over I-77 and Bubba's is a quarter of a mile on the left. From I-77

South, take the exit for Sunset Road, turn right at top of the ramp and Bubba's is a quarter of a mile on the left. Hours are 11 a.m. to 10 p.m., 7 days a week. Telephone number: (704) 393-2000.

Gary's Bar-B-Que, China Grove

Gary's is a long-established big name in barbecue in this area and across the state. Pictures just inside the door show the original Gary's Drive-In Diner. When you enter, what you immediately see in front of your eyes is about the size of the old Gary's. This landmark restaurant has expanded many, many times.

Gary's emits a bright and cheerful ambiance and it has to be one of the cleanest barbecue or any other kind of restaurants around. If Gary has not cornered the market on every antique tin soft drink advertisement in Christendom, few have escaped his grasp. The panel walls of Gary's are chock-a-block full of antique soft drink signs and wall clocks that Gary has collected over more than 25 years of collecting. Also, part of the restaurant encompasses a climate-controlled mirrored room that houses three of Gary's vintage show-cars, a Corvette and two T-Birds. Drool but don't touch.

Gary looks as if he may have just retired from a career in pro football. He is tall, big with closely cropped gray hair, twinkling blue eyes and a ready smile that makes you immediately feel at home. While I interviewed Gary, it seemed that every one of the hundreds of people that came in the door wanted to shake his hand or touch his shoulder and let him know they were there. I am sure his warm, outgoing personality and friendly manner, along with his excellent pork product, have had no small bearing on the success that Gary has enjoyed over the years.

Gary opened his first establishment in 1971 and has added on three times. Gary worked at a barbecue place in Rowan County and then went to college. He said college did not hold a fascination for him and he wanted to do something else. He decided the quickest way to put 50 cents in his pocket was to cook and sell barbecue, which at that time sold for 50 cents per sandwich. Gary originally cooked with wood but later switched to electric. He now has 14 Nunnery-Freeman cookers out back which produce his wonderful pork product.

The chopped barbecue comes from the kitchen moderately chopped but not fine. It has a good Eastern North Carolina taste but is not hot with peppers.

The sliced barbecue is as tender as a mother's love and has a good, rich, roasted-pork flavor. The sliced barbecue pork with Gary's sauce makes you just want to squeal.

The sauce is a reddish-brown vinegar-base sauce with black pepper, red pepper, and spices. With no tomatoes, this sauce walks in lockstep with its eastern cousins. It is not a Lexington-style dip as it's much thinner and vinegary. It has a strong start, a strong finish and no lingering aftertaste.

The slaw is a red Lexington-style variety: moderately chopped, crunchy, very tart, and not too sweet as Lexington-style slaw sometimes can be.

The hushpuppies are large and have a crunchy brown outside. They weren't greasy but were a little dry on the inside for my taste.

The brunswick stew was thick with tomatoes, corn, baby lima beans, carrots and lots of chicken. Gary says there are potatoes in there but I did not run across them. It had a good flavor, but it had an unusual taste for brunswick stew. It is not sweet like many Eastern North Carolina offerings. The spices used create a taste almost like low-country clam chowder broth.

It is different.

While I was there, Gary went back to the kitchen and brought me a pulled piece of outside brown that, with some of his sauce added, was as good as I have ever eaten. Barbecue is the ticket here.

Owner Gary Ritchie did well when he picked Roger Hinson as his manager. He has also selected some of the nicest, most attentive servers one could ever hope to find.

From I-85 South, take Exit 68 (Highway 29 South) and go 1.5 miles. Gary's is on the left. You will have to do a U-turn at the light just beyond Gary's and come back on Highway 29 North for about 100 yards.

Hours are 10 a.m. to 9:30 p.m., Monday through Saturday. It's closed Sunday. Telephone number: (704) 857-8314.

Little Richard's Lexington Bar-B-Que, Clemmons

I am blessed to have a number of good friends in the Greek community in Winston-Salem. Nick Karagiorgis, owner of Little Richard's Lexington Bar-B-Que in Clemmons, is one of those friends.

Little Richard's Lexington Bar-B-Que in Clemmons bears the same name but is not a part of Little Richard's Bar-B-Que in Winston-Salem. Nick has been in the restaurant business for a number of years and each of his restaurants has been among the best of its type wherever it was located. Nick's venture into barbecue in Clemmons is no exception.

Little Richard's in Clemmons cooks with a Southern Pride smoker and hardwood. The long slow roasting with indirect heat and wood smoke blown into the cooking chamber produces a rich, woodsy, campfire like product that is slightly pink in color due to deep smoke penetration. Most people in this area are not accustomed to pink pork or pink chicken. The staff said they have to do a lot of explaining.

The chopped barbecue pork is a nice coarse chopped offering with a good roast pork flavor. It is a mix of pink, white and outside brown meat producing a good roast pork flavor that really shines through. It has just a teeny bit of seasoning at the kitchen producing a mouth watering treat for the barbecue aficionado or novice pretty pig chaser alike.

For my palate it needs a dash of Little Richard's house sauce to raise it a click or two.

The coarse chopped barbecue pork is walnut sized bites of absolute perfection. Slightly pink in color indicates good smoke penetration here. This offering is very, very tasty with a scrumptious, smoky, roast pork flavor seldom found in this area. The coarse chopped barbecue pork satisfied my barbecue desires without adding sauce at the table. However if one wishes more zip or spiciness I suggest a tiny dash of Little Richard's homemade dip or the smoky, brown rib sauce. Either is a good choice. A very light dip of one of these rich smoky morsels into each type of sauce produces hog heaven.

The sliced barbecue pork is so tender, it literally melts in your mouth. This offering presents slightly pink from good smoke penetration with a lovely border of brown, creating outstanding barbecue by anyone's yardstick. This is gooooood 'cue.

Little Richard's red Lexington style barbecue slaw is fresh, tart, tangy and just the ticket for Little Richard's chopped roast pork offering.

Hours are 10 a.m. until 9 p.m., Monday through Saturday. It's closed Sunday. Telephone number: (336) 766-0401.

88

Troutman's Bar-B-Q, Concord

Get your hot dogs, hamburgers, barbecue, Mercedes, Ford, Chevrolet, BMW and building lots right here. Raiford Troutman has it all. Raiford, ever the entrepreneur, wanted to be a businessman. And that he has become.

Raiford's dad was a farmer. Though admiring his dad along with the energy and effort he expended into running a farm, Raiford decided at a very young age that farming was not the life for him. That's good news for barbecue lovers.

At age 17, Raiford was working for Concord Bakery running a bread route. He observed the different restaurants where he delivered his bread and decided that cooking and selling barbecue appealed to him. A building that had housed a barbecue restaurant was on the market and Raiford bought it. There was no barbecue history in his family. Being an only child, he was not following in the footsteps of a sibling or parent, nor did he have cousins, uncles or aunts to pass along barbecue cooking secrets and family recipes.

Young Raiford grabbed his bootstraps, hitched himself up and became his own man. Today Raiford owns three Troutman Bar-B-Q's in Concord, a five-acre car and truck sales operation (Troutman Motors) and a real estate business. Raiford said that

he had been in the car business for 57 years, the real estate business for 43 years and the barbecue business for 40 years. Not shabby for a young man who started out peddling bread at age 17.

Troutman's Bar-B-Q has cooked barbecue on pits with wood in the traditional manner since it opened. Today, the restaurants cook with electricity and pits and wood. Most day-to-day cooking is done on a Nunnery Freeman Kook Rite Kooker with hickory inserts. However, during Christmas week, Troutman's will cook more than 1,200 shoulders all with pits and hickory wood. Raiford said that most all large catering is done on wood-fired pits. Raiford attributes his success in the barbecue business to four things: (1) careful selection of quality meats; (2) time-honored cooking methods; (3) making his own special sauce; and (4) the slaw. Raiford's attention to detail is carried out in all three of his restaurants by more than 100 employees.

Rightfully proud of his restaurant's good barbecue, Raiford said that 15 years ago there was a debate between a group of barbecue restaurants in Texas and North Carolina as to which had the better barbecue. It was decided (by whom I know not) that Texas would pick its 10 top Texas-style barbecue restaurants to cook a meal and

North Carolina would do the same. Troutman's was one of the 10 chosen to represent North Carolina. **The Charlotte Observer** covered this friendly feud and the copy made for interesting reading.

I have had the pleasure of eating at Troutman's Bar-B-Q a number of times on my travels to and from the Charlotte area. A recent visit swayed any fears that I may have harbored that Troutman's wonderful barbecue may have changed. It has not. The same

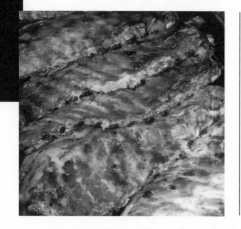

sauces and the same good 'cue that has brought them in for 40 years still brings them back.

I found the chopped barbecue to be very tender, mouth-water-

ing 'cue. It's moderately chopped and very lean with no fat or gristle. The rich, roasted-pork taste has slight nutty nuances. The barbecue contained a good mix of brown and white and produced a very fresh taste. It is not sauced in the kitchen. There is a mild sauce (Cattleman's) on the table along with the homemade vinegar-base sauce. The vinegar-base sauce is far and away my favorite. It has fire and the more you shake

it, the hotter it gets.

The sliced barbecue was just plain scrumptious roast pork in big pig pickin'-sized hunks. It was so tender you could cut it with a fork. It will be some of the best pork you ever tasted. It was so good without the sauce that I was reluctant to put sauce on it. However, with just a tiny bit of the homemade hot sauce, it won my heart.

Troutman's slaw is a Salisbury-style red-and-white slaw. It is coarse chopped with white cabbage, chips of tomato and pimento, water, salt and vinegar. This offering has a good fresh taste and is a typically good representation of the Salisbury area barbecue slaw.

The hushpuppies were light, yet crispy with a golden outer shell and a moist cornbread center that had hints of sweetness. Plainly put – nice pup.

Troutman's homemade sauce is a vinegar-base Eastern North Carolina-type sauce with lots of Cayenne. If you try it by itself, it will pucker your lips, cauterize your tongue, put beads on your brow and blow off doors.

If you are in the Concord area heading south on Highway 601, take the left fork onto Church Street at the hospital. Troutman's is about a quarter of a mile up the road on the left. If you don't have time to sit down and enjoy one of Troutman's delicious barbecue plates, get a couple of barbecue sandwiches and a Pepsi to go.

Better yet, call ahead to the car lot and pick up a Mercedes. I wouldn't be surprised if Raiford threw in a couple of barbecue sandwiches and a drink.

Troutman's is open at all three locations from 5:30 a.m. until 10 p.m., seven days a week. The Highway 601 location's telephone number: (704) 786-9714. The 362 Church St. telephone number: (704) 786-5213. The 128 West Franklin St. in Mt. Pleasant's telephone number: (704) 436-9806.

Bennett's Smokehouse and Saloon, Conover

Bennett's was started as a chain in Denver, Colo. Bennett Shotwell, a petroleum executive who loved to barbecue in his backyard, decided to turn his week-end passion into an avocation. Bennett grew up around barbecue in Texas where he learned the fine art of preparing great-tasting barbecued meats. Good friends and family enjoyed the results of the long hours of preparation.

In June 1985, Bennett opened the doors to his first restaurant in Denver and it was an immediate success. Bennett's Pit Bar-B-Que won the Denver Post's Reader's Choice Award for the best barbecue in Denver for six consecutive years beginning in 1988.

Bennett decided to franchise his dream and WSMP (Western Sizzlin' and Mom and Pop's) bought franchise rights to the concept. WSMP opened a Bennett's in Conover and four other places. WSMP sold the other franchises but kept the Bennett's in Conover. Ken Moser and Michael Hodges are the owners.

Having opened in 1988, Bennett's was slow to convince the locals that slow-smoked Texas beef brisket was barbecue. Ken Moser said that the first year they thought they would have to close the doors. But with any change, good or bad, it takes

people a while to adjust. The locals have surely adjusted. The place was packed when I was there. The good food is not only enjoyed by the locals but by a host of I-40 travelers, traveling east and west.

The place is upscale with the chain look of a Lone Star or Sagebrush steakhouse. It has Western décor with saddles, hides, mounted deer and NASCAR memorabilia. It is the perfect place to kick back and listen to Garth Brooks sing "Wild Horses."

The meat is cooked on a rotisserie with natural gas and hickory-wood inserts.

The sliced pork was tender, smoked through and had good flavor with hints of sweetness and nuttiness – a nice grain to the meat. Using the house sauce, the pork took on a Western taste with some tomatoey flavor and dark smoky overtones. Spices danced in the shadows. The sliced beef was just yummy and had a steak-like flavor. This bodacious bovine was tender and the outside brown edge roped in the smoky flavor. When partnered with the house sauce, the beef was slightly sweet, pungent and had spicy flavors that rode point.

The sauce was a reddish-brown, thick Kansas City-type sauce. It is a perfect mate for beef and sliced pork but I couldn't imagine it would be a good partner for chopped pork. The spiciness steps up and holds its

own but does not fight with the mellow, dark, smoky flavors – good balance.

The slaw was white, medium-coarse chopped with a good crisp flavor. It sparkles with carrots and red cabbage and light mayo.

The barbecue chicken is smoked to the bone. The skin is golden brown, country good and rich with a brown nutty flavor. The chicken breast had a slightly pink cast from the smoke, not from being undercooked. It was not dry at all. The sauce and the chicken together are very tasty. The tartness of the sauce cuts the slightly greasy taste of

the chicken skin that all good chicken has. They make good sidekicks.

From I-40 West, take Exit 128. At the top of the ramp, turn left and travel two-tenths of a mile. Bennett's is located on the left. From I-40 East, take Exit 128. At the top of the ramp, turn right and travel two-tenths of a mile and Bennett's is on your left.

Bennett's is open 11 a.m. until 10 p.m. Sunday through Thursday, and 11 a.m. until 11 p.m., Friday and Saturday. Telephone number: (828) 464-6967.

The Hickory Log Barbecue, Forest City

Owner Bill Gold opened The Hickory Log Barbecue in September 1968 at its current site. Originally the barbecue place was the present counter stool area and the tables you see as you enter the door. Eric, Bill Gold's son, now manages The Log, which doubled in size in 1980.

The Hickory Log cooks electrically with a Nunnery-Freeman Kook Rite Kooker. The Log cooks pork shoulders and beef brisket. They slice the big shoulder muscle of the pork and chop the rest.

They serve chopped, sliced and coarse-chopped barbecue pork, also sliced and chopped barbecue beef.

The chopped barbecue beef (minced) is chopped fine; it has a good beef flavor and is sauced in the kitchen. The beef has a rich woodsy, smoky taste.

The chopped barbecue pork (minced) is also chopped fine, it has a good pork flavor, and some brown outside gives it a woodsy, smoky flavor. It is sauced in the kitchen.

The coarse-chopped pork is large pieces pulled from the hog. This is like a pig pickin'. It is tender to fork, has a good rich pork taste and does not hold the sauce like the minced; therefore, it is not as mushy. This is the one!

The sliced beef has a good roast beef flavor.

The sauce is a vinegar base Lexington-style dip.

The sides are onion rings, french fries, barbecue beans and hushpuppies. The slaw is red Lexington style. It's a bit runny, tart and twangy but it has a good taste.

The coarse pulled pork is my 'cue of choice here. The chopped barbecue beef and the chopped barbecue pork were both over sauced for my taste. Both of these offerings came to the table soupy. I suggest you ask the waitperson to have the kitchen not sauce and serve the sauce on the side.

Hours are 11 a.m. until 8 p.m., Tuesday through Thursday, and 11 a.m. until 9 p.m., Friday and Saturday. It's closed Sunday and Monday. Telephone number: (828) 245-6241.

94

R.O.'s Barbecue, Gastonia

Great food, friendly environment and special employees are the secret to R.O.'s success, which dates back to the mid-1950s. James McDonnell says the other attributes of R.O.'s success are the 11 ingredients he puts in his "heavenly slaw." Ruth Black Hoffman prepares the top-secret slaw each week. R.O.'s barbecue sandwich is a North Carolina classic.

The barbecue pork is cooked electrically, sliced thinly (like shaved) and served on a warm hamburger bun with the heavenly slaw.

The slaw is a pinkish color, kinda like 1000 Island dressing with about the same consistency.

My sandwich was a sliced barbecue sandwich that was served warm with a generous amount of sliced (shaved) 'cue and a light spread of the heavenly slaw. It makes for a really good barbecue sandwich. I did not eat the minced barbecue sandwich.

This is a popular take-out place. It has a large parking lot and about 10 young men who hop curb. The orders are filled quickly and the service is prompt. There are booths inside for those who would like to come in and eat at a table.

From I-85, exit onto Highway 321 South, come up to Airline Road, take a right on Airline Road and go 1.5 miles. R.O.'s is on the right.

Hours are 9:30 a.m. until 10 p.m., Monday through Saturday. It's closed Sunday. Telephone number: (704) 866-8143.

M&K Barbecue and Country Cooking, Granite Quarry

M&K Barbecue and Country Cooking, opened in 1990 by Myran and Kathy Thomas, is just what the name implies – good barbecue and country cooking. Myran is not a stranger to either. His father spent quite a few years cooking barbecue at the old Wink's Barbecue in Salisbury. Then he went to Concord and worked at Troutman's Barbecue. Myran learned his cooking skills from his dad and learned them well. Until Myran and Kathy opened M&K, Myran was a long-distance truck driver, which provided him with more than a nodding acquaintance with country cooking, good and otherwise.

M&K Barbecue and Country Cooking is a white cinder-block building with gray trim and looks like an old filling station/auto garage combination. The reason it looks this way is because in a former life it was. Whoever performed this transformation had large barbecuing ideas. In the rear of the building, M&K has six large table-height concrete pits with steel doors the size of flatbed trailers. At one cooking, M&K has the capacity to cook 360 pork shoulders, a small heard of buffalo, Tyson Foods chicken production for the year or several large elephants and a rabbit.

The firebox that feeds the pits is called "The Train." This contraption looks like the engine from the "The Little Engine That Could" and sits beside the railroad tracks behind M&K's building. It is a large rusty cylinder affair that looks as if someone took a gasoline tanker, cut it in half, and put three chimneys on top. The wood is burned in The Train and the coals are dropped into a wheelbarrow underneath to fire the pits. M&K rarely uses all of this cooking capacity at one time. Most of its day-to-day cooking is done with pits on the north side of the building.

In late 2001, during a visit to M&K, Myran took great pride, and rightly so, in showing me the blueprints for the next transformation phase of M&K's barbecue operation. Myran and Kathy are building new stand-alone pits on the north side of the building that will have a daily cooking capacity of about 70-80 shoulders. Myran said this is about all he and his staff can handle in a day for sit-down service. The new pits will be connected to the building by a walkway. Parking facilities will be enlarged and there are plans for an expansion of dining room facilities that will double the seating capacity. New kitchen, new coolers, new air conditioning – the works.

Fortunately the time-honored traditions of slowly roasting pork over live hickory coals and hand chopping it when it is done are not among the changes taking place at M&K Barbecue and Country Cooking. Myran said he will continue to produce the same products in the same manner and that all he is seeking is more space for his customers and better logistical configuration for his business.

On my latest visit to M&K, I found the barbecue was still excellent. The chopped barbecue was moderately coarse chopped and sauced in the kitchen with hot basting sauce. The 'cue had a good mix of outside brown and inside white. I could not see or taste any fat or skin. The chopped barbecue was very lean, moist and very, very tasty. This little piggy had a rich roasted pork flavor and a smoky, woodsy, almost sweet taste. It's wonderful 'cue.

The coarse-chopped barbecue was an offering of nice and tender hunky pieces that melt in your mouth. The outside brown and inside white gave this 'cue a scrumptious flavor and a nice texture. The flavor of the coarse-chopped 'cue is rich, robust, smoky, nutty, slightly sweet and so fresh.

The sliced barbecue is Myran's good 'cue at its best. These thick, tender slices of yummy roast pork are almost like a pig pickin'. It is lean with no fat and so tender you can cut it with a fork. This is pound-the-table good pork barbecue. Alternating bites of outside brown and inside white kept my

taste buds dancing.

The homemade red basting sauce is bright reddish-brown and rather fiery. It's used in the kitchen for saucing purposes. There are commercial sauces available on the table. I much prefer the homemade sauce to the commercial offerings.

The slaw is white cabbage with a strong vinegar taste and specks of celery seed. This slaw is tart and good but kind of soupy for my taste.

The hushpuppies are walnut-sized with a crisp, brown outer shell. The moist center and rich cornbread taste with an ever so slight greasy taste makes them just right.

In addition to his wonderful barbecue, Myran also serves a host of country meat entrees and 26 vegetables. If your journey on Highway 52 finds you in Granite Quarry early in the morning, be sure and stop for breakfast. This is the place. Myran said that on Saturday he sells about three cases of eggs along with his wonderful pork products and other breakfast goodies.

Following Highway 52 South from Salisbury, M&K Barbecue and Country Cooking will be on your right when you reach the little village of Granite Quarry. Hours are 6 a.m. until 9 p.m., Monday through Friday, and 6 a.m. until 3 p.m., Saturday. It's closed Sunday. Telephone number: (704) 279-8976.

Kepley's Bar-B-Q, High Point

Kepley's is a barbecue place in the tradition of most barbecue places that are more than 50 years old. Barbecue is their game. But for those that have not acquired a taste for this wonderful stuff, they have hamburgers, cheeseburgers and hot dogs.

The barbecue used to be pit cooked over hard wood. Some years ago, they switched to cooking their pork on electric

cookers. They still chop the meat by hand. Kepley's claims it's the only place in High Point that still chops by hand.

If you want to work at Kepley's, have a backup plan. The employees at Kepley's are not only friendly and willing to serve, but many have worked there since Noah docked the Ark. The four Austin sisters – Molly, Kay, Cathy and Sandy – have worked at Kepley's for more than 75 years collectively. Other longtime employees of Kepley's include Peggy Hayden (more than 30 years), Dennis Carroll (more than 30 years) and Gary Wooten (almost 25 years). Gary

oversees the cooking; Molly and Kay make the red slaw.

Hayden Kepley, known to most as H.O., founded the business in 1948. Later, Charles Johnson, H.O.'s son-in-law, and Bob Burleson ran the business. Charles is retired now. Bob Burleson and his daughter Susan own and operate the establishment.

Little has changed at Kepley's since 1948 and the good folk of High Point seem to like it that way. They did switch from wood to electric, but most people seem to find the barbecue just as good as ever. In 1960, Bill Smith came to work there. He didn't particularly care for the hushpuppies; so, he added granulated onion to the recipe. Other than that, the good food and the service with a smile have remained the same.

Before H.O. Kepley came to High Point, he had a barbecue place in Salisbury named the Red Hog. You will note that the hog on the sign out front is red, not black and white like most. H.O. Kepley also did catering for private parties, wedding receptions and the like at the Kepley Barn on Highway 68. The Kepley Barn, built in 1970, burned Jan. 4, 2001. It was not rebuilt.

The chopped barbecue comes medium-coarse chopped (not fine or mushy). It has a vinegary taste much like Eastern North Carolina-style sauce. The outside brown is mixed with the rest of the meat and that gives the chopped product texture and more flavor. It is a little dry without dip. Once dip is added at the table, the meat is plenty moist. You don't need much.

The coarse chopped is very tender, almost like veal. One can hardly detect any sauce. It's very moist yet has no fat. It has a good cooked-pork taste. When you add sauce at the table, the flavor of the barbecue really kicks in. The vinegar and pepper taste is predominant.

The sliced barbecue is very tender, moist and has a nice offering without sauce. It has almost a sweet taste and has a very light pork taste. When you add hot sauce, the meat becomes more alive with flavor.

They only serve red slaw. It is finely chopped and has a vinegary taste. It's a good traveling companion for the 'cue.

The dip used at Kepley's is the brainchild of the founder's brother-in-law. Mrs. Kepley's brother worked on the railroad in Salisbury. He concocted the original sauce and gave the recipe to Mrs. Kepley, who shared it with H.O. It has not changed in more than 53 years. It is a vinegar-base dip that is applied after cooking when they chop

the meat. They coat the meat lightly. One employee said that it is vinegar with ground black pepper and pinch of salt. It is boiled and cooked down and applied to the meat just before serving. The house hot sauce served at the table also contains colored vinegar, ground red pepper and is boiled off (reduced). The hot sauce at the table has more zip and one would probably want just a dash on the meat to make it sparkle.

The hushpuppies are crunchy outside and moist inside with a hint of onion flavor that produces a nice touch.

Like most good barbecue places, Kepley's has served movie stars. Tommy Lee Jones ate there when on location in High Point. Kepley's regulars include Kyle Petty and his wife Patty. One older gentleman said he was sorry about hearing that Kepley's Barn burned down, but it really didn't bother him much as long as nothing changed at Kepley's Bar-B-Q. Nothing has.

Kepley's is located in downtown High Point at 1304 North Main St. Kepley's is open 8 a.m. until 8:30 p.m., Monday through Saturday. It's closed Sunday. Telephone number: (336) 884-1021.

Wallace Brother's BBQ, Lambsburg, VA

Wallace Brother's BBQ, located just off I-77 north in Lambsburg, VA, is a few hundred yards over the North Carolina border. Joe Wallace, the owner of Wallace Brother's, said that if you step off the back side of his property, you are back in North Carolina and that's close enough for me.

Joe Wallace was born in Midway, just outside of Lexington. At age 15, he went to work for Country Kitchen in Lexington and has been in the barbecue business for 25 years. Joe cooked at Country Kitchen for 15 years. In 1995, he bought the present site of Wallace Brother's BBQ. He said the building had been allowed to get run down. It was covered in vines, the lot was grown up and the windows were broken out. Joe rolled up his sleeves and made this place into a first-class barbecue stop. He put in pits and cooks barbecue on open pits with hickory wood in the old-fashioned style.

Joe says he only cooks Lundy pork shoulders. This first-class product is slowly cooked over live hickory coals for eight to 12 hours. The time depends upon moisture in the pork, change in temperature, humidity, moisture in the wood and a number of other variables that go with cooking meat over live coals.

Joe's pork products are cut-with-a-fork tender and have a rich nutty flavor from the hickory and good smoke penetration.

The chopped barbecue is heavily chopped. There are lots of good bites here. It's a cut above moderate chopped. It comes sauced from the kitchen and is very moist and tasty.

The coarse chopped barbecue consists of large meaty chunks cooked just right. It's tender, moist and cut the right way so as not to be tough by grain. This offering comes sauced from the kitchen in a good Lexington-style dip with a bright peppery flavor that goes well with the delicious pork smoky overtones that carry throughout.

The sliced barbecue consists of large, thick, melt-in-your-mouth pieces of tender pork like it was pulled from the pig. It has a good, rich and fresh pork flavor with delicate, smoky nuances and tangy peppers.

I really enjoyed all three cuts of barbecue but the coarse chopped and the sliced were my favorites as they were most akin to a pig pickin'.

Joe's hushpuppies are made with Sweet Betsy Meal, which had its origin in 1757. The pups have a light, golden-brown, crispy shell and are moist inside. It's not greasy at all.

They make a red Lexington-style slaw. It's coarse chopped and tangy as the vinegar

100

shines through but does not overwhelm the fresh cabbage and peppery spices. It has a lot of crunch and is a nice side with the pork.

The dip is reddish-brown Lexington style. It's a vinegar-dip sauce with spices and peppers. IT HAS PEPPERS. By itself, the dip is hot on the palate but perfectly wonderful served on the pork. The dip at the table was served warm. This dip stands tall. It is hot, tangy and sweet as Joe uses Hunt's Ketchup and Saurer Spices. Joe said he got his recipe years ago from Leroy McCarn in Lexington.

Wallace Brother's BBQ is your last opportunity to get really good North Carolina Barbecue before entering Virginia on I-77 north. And, it's your first opportunity to get good North Carolina barbecue upon entering the state from Virginia on I-77 south. In either event, it is well worth your while to make the very short detour off the interstate for this good 'cue.

From I-77 north, take Virginia Exit 1. At the stop sign at the end of the exit ramp, turn right. Immediately take another right and come back south on the rural road for less than half a mile. Wallace Brother's is on the right. When you are at the stop sign at the end of the ramp, you will see the Wallace Brother's red sign across the road with the arrow pointing back toward the restaurant. From I-77 south take the last exit for Virginia, go under I-77 and take the first road to your right. The Wallace Brother's sign is less than half a mile on your right. Summer hours are 11 a.m. until 9 p.m., Tuesday through Sunday. It's closed on Monday. Winter hours are 11 a.m. until 8 p.m. Telephone number: (276) 755-3291.

Hannah's Bar-B-Que, Lenoir

Owned by James Hannah, Hannah's Bar-B-Que in Lenoir has that weathered patina of a retro 1950s drive-in restaurant. The reason for this is that Hannah's has been aging at this spot quite nicely for the past 19 years. It has drive-in diagonal parking under a canopy out front and a sit-down diner restaurant inside. You expect to see pretty high school girls on roller skates come up to your car to take your order but, alas, they don't. The décor is clean, slightly worn and has that warm feeling that this is where the locals eat (and they do).

Hannah's finely chopped barbecue pork is moderately moist and comes sauced from the kitchen. It has flecks of red and black pepper and a mild pork flavor which starts light and finishes light without the addition of sauce. With the addition of Hannah's Eastern North Carolina sauce you have Fred and Ginger. They dance well together.

The sliced barbecue pork is ever so tender and tastes like baked ham with a hint of smoky flavor. It was a tiny bit dry, as is the tendency with most slow-cooked hams.

Hannah's homemade Eastern North Carolina-style barbecue sauce is an amber, peach-colored sauce with a predominate vinegar taste accompanied by crushed red pepper. The sauce has some sugar in it, which is unusual for an Eastern North Carolina-style sauce, and has a slightly sweet taste. It is particularly good on the chopped 'cue more so than the sliced.

Hannah's Texas-style sauce is a red peppery sauce with a pronounced taste of ketchup, vinegar, peppers and spices in that order. This sauce is mildly hot and to my taste was best on the sliced barbecue.

The barbecue chicken is baked in a pan topped with the Texas sauce while it cooks. Additional sauce is ladled over the chicken when served. The chicken was very tender but a bit overwhelmed with the sauce as served. Since the chicken is baked, it does not have a smoky or barbecue flavor without the addition of sauce. To my taste it was more like chicken creole substituting barbecue sauce. It was tender, tasty and good, but did not have a slow-roasted flavor.

The pork ribs are also baked with Hannah's Texas sauce. Like the chicken, the baking produced a very tender product that was a welcomed treat but lacked any smoky or barbecue flavor without the sauce. The ribs had additional Texas sauce ladled over them before serving. Again, I found the sauce a bit overwhelming for the taste of the meat.

When ordering the chicken or ribs at

Hannah's I would suggest having the kitchen hold the sauce and bring it heated as a side dish. Sometimes less is more.

The hushpuppies were golden with a crisp, crunchy outer shell. The center was moist and it had a good cornbread flavor.

They make white slaw that has a good cabbage flavor with flecks of carrot, celery seed, light mayo and vinegar. This slaw has a nice fresh crisp taste that makes it a terrific companion for Hannah's 'cue, especially with the Texas sauce.

Hannah's serves chopped pork, sliced pork, Texas-style barbecue beef, barbecue chicken and barbecue pork ribs. All are served as sandwiches, trays, combos and an all-you-can-eat special for $7.99. Extras are the usual barbecue fare: slaw, fries, onion rings, barbecue beans, hushpuppies and chili cheese fries.

For those who have yet to acquire a taste for that wonderful casual food known as barbecue, Hannah's also has hot dogs and hamburgers.

Hannah's serves soft drinks, tea and lemonade. Desserts are barbecue standards apple pie and pecan pie but no banana pudding.

Hannah's has two other locations in Claremont and Hickory. Hannah's Bar-B-Que in Lenoir is located on Highway 321 on the left on the north side of Lenoir just after the light for Highway 15 and Highway 90. Look for a big red pig with the name Hannah's Bar-B-Que. Hours are 11 a.m. until 9:30 p.m., Monday through Saturday. It's closed Sunday. Telephone number: (828) 754-7032.

The Barbecue Center, Inc., Lexington

The Barbecue Center, Inc. is the oldest barbecue establishment in downtown Lexington that still cooks on pits. It has been featured in *Southern Living* magazine, on the TV show "Good Morning America" and in any number of newspapers. This bastion of Lexington-style barbecue started years ago across the street from its current site as a dairy center serving ice cream. They built a small barbecue pit to have something to sell in the winter when the ice cream business slowed. They moved in the late 1950s but they still sell a lot of ice cream.

When the Barbecue Festival started, The Barbecue Center, Inc.'s name skyrocketed. Now they are fortunate enough to have their product shipped to 30 states including Hawaii. They also ship to Puerto Rico.

The business is family owned by Sonny and Nancy Conrad and their two sons Cecil and Michael. The business still has that same drive-in dairy bar feel today. The ambiance is warm, family friendly and inviting. Cecil was my host and shared information, food and fellowship while his mom, Nancy, was busy greeting customers, making humongous banana splits, and showing an 8x10 picture of her newest grandchild to friends. You immediately felt like you're in the right place.

The Barbecue Center, Inc. has played a large part in the lives of many of the residents of Lexington. It was the northern turnaround for cruising teenagers during the '50s. Old Hickory at the other end of town was the southern turnaround. Thus, The Barbecue Center, Inc. was the hub of social life for a large number of Lexington citizens during their youth. They still faithfully return for good food and fellowship. With its excellent product and generous servings, the young people of Lexington today are regulars as well.

Tim Queen, Pitmaster at his chopping block.

Tim Queen, who has been on the job with The Center since the late '80s, mans the pits. The pit master before him was there for 22 years. Cecil said they cook the barbecue to 170 degrees internal temperature at the center. The health department requires 140 to 160 degrees minimum. He said that 180 degrees is too done. They have found 170 degrees produces the best possible product.

The pork, shoulders only, is cooked on open pit with 85 percent hickory and 15 percent oak hardwoods. It is slow cooked for 8-12 hours. After it is cooked, the meat is taken apart by hand and chopped. The methods used are direct descendents of Stamey and Swicegood, who used to cook in front of the courthouse in Lexington.

The Center separates its light and dark meat for slicing. Some people want outside brown, some want white, some want extra fat, and some want no fat. The barbecue is served custom-made to the customers' order.

The chopped barbecue is moist, tender, medium chopped, tomatoey and peppery. It's generously sauced in the kitchen with a hint of vinegar and a hint of sugar. It's tasty – slightly tangy, not too tart. It has a good finish with no heavy aftertaste.

The coarse chopped barbecue is very, very tender with a good, smoky flavor. It holds hands nicely with the dip.

The sliced barbecue is very tender with a great smoky flavor and outside brown. This is the ticket.

The chopped barbecue with the red slaw, which is slightly tart (ketchup, vinegar, pepper, salt, sugar and crisp cabbage) works well together. The slaw does not fight or overwhelm the flavor of the meat.

The light brown, vinegar-base sauce is comprised of ketchup, pepper, salt, water and hot peppers. It's very tangy alone but calms down on the meat.

The Center has the usual sides: slaw, potatoes, salad, fries, onion rings and hushpuppies. They're all good. They also have country ham, fried chicken and barbecue chicken.

The desserts are homemade pies, banana pudding and ice cream. I observed the construction of one their famous banana splits. This concoction looked like something that would be shared by an entire table from a segment of *Happy Days*. Bring friends.

The Barbecue Center, Inc. is located at 900 North Main St. in downtown Lexington. From the I-85 Business loop, also known as U.S. 29/70, follow the signs into downtown Lexington. You'll go directly onto Main Street and The Center is at the north end of the street. The Center is open 6 a.m. until 9 p.m., Monday through Wednesday, and 6 a.m. until 10 p.m., Thursday through Saturday. It's closed Sunday. Telephone number: (336) 248-4633

Jimmy's Barbecue, Lexington

Located just off Business I-85 in Lexington, Jimmy's has been at its present location since 1970. The building was originally built by J.B. Carlton and used as Carlton's Barbecue until the 1970s. When Carlton decided to hang up his cooking apron in 1977, Jimmy Harvey, who had been an employee of Carlton's for many years, bought the business and renamed it Jimmy's Barbecue.

Jimmy had other mentors whose names were household words in the Lexington barbecue world, Warner Stamey and Sid Weaver to name a couple. Jimmy had worked with some of barbecue's most noted figures for 28 years before opening his own barbecue place. Having celebrated his 60th year in the barbecue business, Jimmy has pretty much got this pig cookin' thing figured out.

While maintaining the elder statesman role in Jimmy's Barbecue, Jimmy Harvey and his wife, Betty, have turned over the day-to-day management of the business to their sons, Terry (General Manager) and Kemp. Jimmy's two daughters, Karin and Kirksey, also work in the business full time along with part-time assistance from six grandchildren. Terry has worked with his dad since he was a child. He has been in the business since 1985. Described by one employee as a non-stop worker and a smart business man, Terry, with the assistance of his brother and two sisters, seems to keep Jimmy's heading down the right track with a secure future.

Jimmy's barbecue is pit cooked and kept warm in electric cookers. The electric cookers are used primarily for backup during the Barbecue Festival. The meat is cooked over oak and hickory for heat and flavor. Hickory breaks down to coals quicker. The meat is not basted while cooking. They cook pork shoulders through the week and chicken Thursday through Sunday.

Steve Presley said that the hallmark of Jimmy's Barbecue is that it is consistently good in quality and they are persistent about perfection at every level of their business. He said that Jimmy's Barbecue gets compliments even before people taste it.

The chopped barbecue comes in generous pieces sauced from the kitchen. It has a mild tomatoey taste with a hint of vinegar. It's light on pepper and very moist – one of the most moist chopped barbecues in the Lexington area.

The coarse chopped barbecue is very, very tender with large chunks that taste like pork filet. The outside brown has a woodsy flavor. It's not heavily smoked but does have a good rich brown taste. It's lightly sauced in the kitchen.

The sliced barbecue is fall-off-the-bone tender. It's a little drier than the chopped but still good and moist. With the outside skin, the flavor really comes through.

The red slaw is tart and tangy with a vinegar taste that does not overwhelm the cabbage taste. It has a slight peppery finish. The white slaw is creamy, crisp cabbage with carrot and light mayo blended well.

The brown sauce is slightly hot with peppers up front. It's thin, tomatoey and spicy. It's a nice blend and definitely a Lexington-style dip. When eaten alone it has a good zing and a nice finish with no hot aftertaste. On chopped barbecue, it has just the right amount of zip to compliment any fat taste that one needs to savor the meat. On coarse-chopped barbecue, the sauce jacks it up a bit. It's a little over the top on the sliced barbecue. The dip, chopped bar-becue and red slaw form a delectable family of flavors that would please the harshest critics. The chopped barbecue and white slaw is like kissing your sister, not very exciting.

Barbecue chicken is a favorite on Thursday through Sunday. The chicken has a wonderful, light, smoky flavor and is moist and tender with a crisp skin. It's a treat.

The desserts consist mainly of cakes (homemade coconut and chocolate) plus pies and a dessert named pig pickin's.

Jimmy's is located at 1703 Cotts Grove Rd., just off Business I-85 in Lexington. Take Exit 91 (the Southmont exit), turn south on N.C. 8 and Jimmy's is on the right. Hours are 6 a.m. to 10:30 p.m., Wednesday through Monday. It's closed Tuesday. Telephone number: (336) 357-2311.

Lexington Barbecue, Lexington

Owned by barbecue icon Wayne Monk, Lexington Barbecue (formerly Lexington #1), has been producing fine products since the early 1960s at its location on I-85 bypass on the outskirts of Lexington.

Cooking barbecue for sale in Lexington originated around 1920 mainly through the efforts of Sid Weaver, George Ridenhour and Jess Swicegood. They decided to cook at the courthouse while court was in session. Lexington is the county seat for Davidson County. The circuit judge came through every so

Wayne Monk

often and tried cases. From these humble beginnings of canvas tents and quasi portable pits, this cottage industry arose. It seems these early entrepreneurs knew how to market their product. There was no air conditioning and when the aroma of good barbecue cooked over open pits wafted into the courthouse, the judge was never reluctant to call an early recess for lunch. These barbecue troubadours also produced barbecue for the tobacco market.

I am told that in the beginning the men cooking barbecue in Lexington tried whole hogs, as was the custom in Eastern North Carolina. Out of necessity, they went to shoulders because they were easier to handle and cooked quicker on the small portable pits.

In the late 1930s, Warner Stamey returned to Lexington from Shelby and bought the old Jess Swicegood place. In the mid 1950s, Stamey's apprentice was a young man named Wayne Monk. Wayne learned the craft well, opened his own place in 1962. Today Wayne Monk is one of the godfathers of barbecue in North Carolina and is held in high esteem anywhere barbecuers gather. He oversees one of the most streamlined, efficient and impeccably clean barbecue operations I have ever seen.

Wayne, in addition to overseeing the entire operation, is generally out front meeting and serving customers. Everybody wants to speak to Wayne. As with most good barbecue businesses, Wayne is ably assisted by family. His able assistants include his son Rick, daughters Kelly and Julie, son-in-law

Keith "Bubba" Wright and a host of nieces and nephews.

Bubba has worked for Wayne for 25 years. This is amazing since Bubba, an athletically built, nice-looking young man does not appear to be much over 25 years old.

Bubba said that they cook over five pits with hickory wood and some oak. He said all hickory cooks twice as hot and twice as fast. As long as they can get it Bubba said they would continue to use all hickory. They cook pork shoulders and smoked turkey breasts. Bubba said they average around 8,000 pounds of pork per week. He said their pork shoulders are about 18 pounds green from a hog dressing out, approximately 250 pounds. Lexington Barbecue buys from Lundy Packing in Clinton. Even though Lundy was bought out by a company in St. Louis, Bubba said they are still able to get the premium meat they have always used. Bubba said hogs fed on peanuts have a different moisture content than hogs fed on corn.

Every pig they cook, though uniformly consistent with industry standards when purchased, will come out a tiny bit different from the others, Bubba said. Some come out smoky, some come out piggy, and some come out sweet. None of this is bad, just different. Bubba said the quality of the wood, the humidity and temperature all effect cooking over coals. The variables change

one firing to another. If the fire is too hot, the meat sweats and sticks. If the fire is not hot enough, the meat does not cook done.

Ashes are removed from the pit on Sundays so the pits are clean Mondays. By the end of the week, there is a bed of ash that is 2, 3 and even 4 inches deep that must be taken into account. For instance, the coals will be closer to the meat on Fridays than it is earlier in the week.

Bubba said they salt their meat before cooking but do not baste during cooking. The dip is applied after cooking. He said their product was consistently good and they don't mix it. The different parts of the shoulder – outside brown, regular, white lean, etc. – are separated so customers can order the type of barbecue they prefer.

Lexington Barbecue does not ship and does not cater.

The sauce is a Lexington-style dip. It is thin more like a marinade. It's not a basting sauce. The milder sauce is applied to the meat in the kitchen. There is a hotter sauce at the table.

The medium-coarse, chopped barbecue was good with lots of brown skin in tiny bits intermingled. The slight taste of fat added to the excellent flavor. The meat had smoky overtones and was not crunchy but was slightly chewy (because of the brown). It was oh so good.

The coarse chopped barbecue was in

big hunks and came sauced in the kitchen generously enough for me. It was ever so tender with some brown and a slightly smoky flavor.

The sliced barbecue is so tender, so smoky and so good.

The red slaw is not so red as other barbecue houses; it is a wonderful blend of red and white with no mayonnaise. It has a sweet-and-sour taste. It's very good.

The dip applied in the kitchen is thin, brown, spicy, peppery and hot but not too hot. It is 75 percent water with salt, sugar and black and red peppers. It is much, much milder when applied to the meat. It's great combined with the chopped barbecue. Bubba said that they sell three times more chopped barbecue than the sliced.

The sliced barbecue with the dip applied in the kitchen is a union of smoky meat and tangy sauce. It's to die for.

Lexington Barbecue is located on the I-85 business loop, also known as U.S. 29/70, which runs through High Point, Thomasville and Lexington. Approaching Lexington from the north, follow the signs

for Charlotte rather than bearing left to enter downtown Lexington. You will see the restaurant on the right. It has easy access via service drive-offs. From the south, follow

the I-85 Business signs. You will spot the large white restaurant building on your left. You will exit right onto a service drive and then cloverleaf under the main highway right into the parking lot.

Lexington Barbecue is open 10 a.m. to 9:30 p.m., Monday through Saturday. It's closed Sunday. The telephone number: (336) 249-9814.

Bar-B-Que King, Lincolnton

After having been told by a number of people in surrounding counties that they did not know of any good barbecue places in Lincoln County, I was more than a little surprised to find Bar-B-Que King. It is not only a large barbecue place in the county but a very good barbecue place as well.

Owner Steve Abernathy opened the Bar-B-Que King in 1971. Steve apparently followed the adage "Build a better mouse trap and they will come." For come, they do. When I was there at 6 p.m. on a Thursday night, the big parking lot was chock-a-block full and there were lines of people out the door as people happily waited their turn for some of Steve's delicious 'cue.

The chopped barbecue has a good, hearty roasted pork flavor. The outside brown mixed with the inside white produces a nutty, rich brown taste without any sauce. The 'cue is moderately moist without sauce and has hints of smokiness.

The sliced barbecue pork was cut-with-a-fork tender and moist, especially for sliced pork. It had a good, rich, pork flavor. I found the sliced barbecue delicious without any sauce. It tasted like roast pork and apricots.

The slaw is white with flecks of celery seed and no mayonnaise. It has a good, crisp, tart, fresh cabbage taste.

The hushpuppies had a golden outer shell with a light crunch, a very moist center and a good cornbread flavor. These are really good pups.

Bar-B-Que King's Eastern North Carolina sauce is a reddish-amber sauce with a mild twang that has a hint of an apricot taste. I know it is not apricots but it tastes like that to me. I found this slightly sweet sauce was very good on the chopped 'cue and the sliced 'cue as well.

Bar-B-Que King's jalapeno sauce is a reddish sauce with jalapeno slices floating about. This one is an attention getter. By itself, it will light your fire. On the chopped 'cue, it behaves very well. I like it. It also goes well with the sliced 'cue. Use sparingly to avoid overwhelming the taste of Steve's delicious pork products. Try mixing one-third jalapeno sauce and two-thirds Eastern North Carolina sauce. Experiment.

To reach Bar-B-Que King traveling south on Highway 321, take Exit 24 and follow 150 East. Go through six traffic lights. Bar-B-Que King is on your left, across from the Winn-Dixie store. It is a large red brick building with a fairly large parking lot.

Hours are 10 a.m. until 8 p.m., Monday through Saturday. It's closed Sunday. Telephone number: (704) 735-1112.

111

Spear's BBQ & Grill, Linville Falls

Spear's owner David Huskins says the tiny (and the operative word here is tiny) village of Linville Falls was the little Las Vegas of the mountain when the government was building the Blue Ridge Parkway.

It seems the original restaurant was started in Linville Falls in the 1930s by David's uncle and aunt, Guy and Phyllis Huskins. David's Uncle Guy and Aunt Phyl ran the Rock House Restaurant in Linville Falls. They had legal beer and liquor downstairs and illegal liquor and slots upstairs, David said. The federal government would bus the CCC workers (working on the parkway) to Linville Falls on Friday nights and pick them up on Monday mornings.

The little crossroads of Linville Falls had five taverns. David said that his aunt also ran a pleasure palace known as Phyl's Cabins. Phyl's "ladies of the evening" gave a whole new meaning to the term "full menu." With the advent of prohibition, the taverns in Linville Falls, including the Rock House, met an early demise. Ever the entrepreneurs, Uncle Guy and Aunt Phyl built more rooms to go with Phyl's Cabins and the place was called Huskins Tourist Court. The name was later changed to Linville Falls Motel.

Uncle Guy and Aunt Phyl never had any children. They ran the Rock House Restaurant and the Linville Falls Motel in the spring, summer and fall and spent the winter in Florida. Eventually they gave up running the Rock House Restaurant. Then they opened a Dairy Bar on the site of the present Spears Barbecue Grill. Uncle Guy died and Aunt Phyl had major health problems. David Huskins' dad lived down the road and had his own restaurant in Marion. David's dad leased the business from Aunt Phyl and ran it for a while.

When David got out of college in 1974, he wanted to move back to the mountains. David had a degree in community college administration. David's dad sold the business to David. At that time, David was a bachelor, worked full time at the community college and ran the restaurant seasonally. He would close in October and would reopen in April. David met Betty and they married and decided to give the businesses all of their time and energies. They opened the lodge year round. The restaurant grew from a sandwich and soft ice cream place to a sit down restaurant by 1985. They added the dining room and started serving full service for three meals a day. The restaurant was called Linville Falls Restaurant and was next door to the Linville Falls Lodge, formerly the Linville Falls Motel. David decided to reconfigure and find his niche. David decided his niche was barbecue. The story goes like this.

William Cable of Elk Park raised trout commercially. One day William couldn't make delivery so David and Betty rode up to get trout for the restaurant. David noticed William had a big homemade smoker. David's uncle, Joe, was a barbecue connoisseur and also happened to be a skilled welder. William invited David to take the cooker back to the restaurant and see how he liked it. David was taken with William's rig and made some modifications. He had Uncle Joe make one for him.

After deciding to make barbecue the focal point of his restaurant he changed the name of the restaurant from Linville Falls Restaurant to Spear's BBQ & Grill. Spear is the middle name of David's son Jonathan and also the name of David's grandfather, who was named for nearby Spear Tops Mountain.

Eric Queen, David's stepson manages the restaurant for David. Eric has a degree in hospitality management. He said he cooks his pork on Uncle Joe's version of William Cable's cooker for 10 and a half to 14 hours, depending upon the weather. Eric uses a blend of apple wood and hickory slabs. Eric cooks boneless Boston butts. He said he could get two cases on the smoker at

one time. I had the opportunity to observe the smoker fully loaded and several hours away from done. It was eye candy and the aroma was heavenly.

The meat comes off the smoker and Eric lets it cool for about a half-hour. It is then sealed and put in the cooler to bring the temperature down to a point where it can be sliced without mushing. The meat is then sliced, placed on a flat grill, sauced, turned, sauced and plated by chef Andy Hinshaw, who has been at Spear's for 12 years.

Spear's BBQ & Grill uses Cattleman's Choice Smoky Barbecue Sauce as a base and then tweaks it with their own additional ingredients. David said they tried other brands, but they didn't go as well, and they couldn't make their own sauce as good as Cattleman's.

The ribs and chicken are cooked on a commercial Cook Shack Cooker. The ribs are steamed for a few minutes after smoking. They are grilled and sauced as ordered. Spear's BBQ & Grill cooks the pork on the outside smoker at 150 degrees for about 10 hours and then raises the temperature to 185 degrees to finish.

The sliced barbecue pork is thinly sliced (a quarter of an inch or less). It has a dark, smoky edge that adds good flavor to the inside white. The pork is sauced in the kitchen with a Southwestern style tomato-base house sauce. It's not Lexington style even though it has ketchup. It doesn't have the vinegar base of a Lexington-style sauce.

The chopped barbecue pork is very tender, very moist and has a rich smoky flavor from slow smoking. I would prefer sauce on the side in order to experience the flavor of the hickory and apple wood smoke more.

The ribs are sweet, smoky flavored from both the cooking method (Cook Shack) and the smoky sauce. The ribs are juicy and fall-off-the-bone tender. Again sauce on the side would be my preference.

Spear's barbecue beans are spicy but not too much so. The beans are served in a rich, sweet, smoky broth with onions and meat. The beans are tender with just enough fire.

The coleslaw is coarse-chopped white cabbage and chopped red cabbage with carrot strips and mayo. The good crisp flavor goes well with the dark smoky taste of the meat.

Sadly, Aunt Phyl and Phyl's Cabins are no longer a part of the tiny village of Linville Falls. On a happier note, Spear's is serving the best barbecue ever. To enjoy Spear's fine food look for Spear's BBQ & Grill on the corner of Hwy 221 and Hwy 183 in Linville Falls, just a stones throw from the Blue Ridge Parkway off milepost 317.

Hours are 11:30 a.m. until 9 p.m. daily, April-October. November-March Spear's operates weekends only, 5 p.m. until 9 p.m., Friday and 11:30 a.m. until 9 p.m., Saturday and Sunday. Telephone number is (828) 765-2658.

Fuzzy's, Madison

Fuzzy's restaurant in Madison has been synonymous with good barbecue since T.H. "Fuzzy" Nelson established it in 1954. Fuzzy's has always enjoyed a good name among barbecue aficionados in the north/northwestern area of North Carolina. Unless one had family or business in the area or were traveling highway 311 or 220, Fuzzy's would not be in most peoples' everyday path. It certainly has not received the exposure that some of the eastern barbecue restaurants have received by virtue of being on highways leading to the coast.

Jennifer Cardwell, neither rain, snow...or broken arm...

In any event, despite being slightly out of the way, Fuzzy's has gained a following that certainly puts it in the forefront of good barbecue places in our state.

Most barbecue buffs are familiar with the two attempts to market North Carolina barbecue in New York City. Fuzzy's barbecue was the barbecue of choice for both ventures. Neither of these ventures proved to be successful despite offering some of the state's best barbecue. From good sources, it appears that the attempts to sell North Carolina barbecue in New York City failed because of the local proprietor in New York failing to understand how to market and serve barbecue.

With minor refurbishment, the restaurant basically remains unchanged since its origin.

Fuzzy's chopped barbecue is prepared from New Lean Generation pork butts, which are at least 90 percent lean. It's one percent fat or less per serving. This is less fat content than skinless chicken, which is 1.2 percent fat. Fuzzy uses only the finest hams for his sliced barbecue. All meat is cooked fresh daily over hickory-fired pits in the kitchen that opens directly to the chopping boards. There are no food additives or preservatives in Fuzzy's barbecue.

In addition to barbecue, Fuzzy's serves a variety of soups, salads, sandwiches, dinner plates, hushpuppies, fries, potato salad, baked beans, baked potatoes, onion rings, corn dogs, cheese fries and fried cheese sticks.

In addition to sweet or unsweetened tea, the beverages are soft drinks, milk, juice, coffee and homemade lemonade.

Desserts are homemade banana pudding, hand-dipped ice cream, pie and cobbler, with or without the ice cream.

Fuzzy's chopped barbecue is very lean with a good smoky flavor. It is really ground rather than chopped, the way many prepare their barbecue today. The barbecue comes from the kitchen generously sauced. Fuzzy's dip, which has always been one of his claims to fame, is a Lexington-style blend of vinegar, ketchup and other ingredients. It has a slightly vinegary, tomatoey taste with peppers that shine through but do not overwhelm. I found the barbecue to be moist and zesty with good aroma and great taste. Note of caution: Do not add dip at the table until tasting the meat as served.

Fuzzy serves a red Lexington-style slaw that is tangy, finely chopped, slightly vinegary and mildly hot. Eastern white slaw is also served. It has a good cabbage taste and is a little more coarsely chopped than the red slaw. The potato salad had a slight mustard taste but it does not compete with the mayo, pickles and onions.

The sliced ham barbecue was moist, tender and had a great flavor. It had good grain. One does not need to add anything to this dish as it comes nicely sauced from the kitchen. It's to kill for. The brunswick stew was good. It's medium thick, tomatoey with lima beans, diced potatoes and plenty of meat that includes chicken, beef and pork.

The baked beans, while slightly sweet, were above average.

The meat is prepared by Chris Barton and the restaurant runs smoothly under the careful eye of veteran manager Ricky Bullins.

Freddy Nelson, son of the founder, operates the Fuzzy's wholesale business and sells barbecue to stores. This operation is carried on at a separate unit behind Fuzzy's restaurant. The barbecue is cooked in the same way with the same dip but in greater volume. Fuzzy's also has an extensive catering business. Fuzzy's is open 5 a.m. until 10 p.m. on weekdays and until 11 p.m. on the weekend. Telephone number: (336) 427-4130.

Traveling south on U.S. 220 Bypass, exit onto U.S. 311 and follow it into Madison. Turn north onto Business U.S. 220 and follow it until you see Fuzzy's. From the north, exit off the bypass onto Business U.S. 220 and follow it towards Madison until you see Fuzzy's sign with the black-and-white pig.

Deano's Barbecue, Mocksville

Jovial owner Dean Allen began his barbecue experience as a curb boy for William M. "Buck" Miller at Buck's Barbecue Restaurant in the summer of 1961. Dean continued to work summers and part-time throughout his high school years at Buck's Barbecue and Hilltop Barbecue.

After completing high school, Dean ran his own barbecue catering business for a number of years until he decided to go into the restaurant and catering business in 1975. Buck Miller retired in 1975 and Dean took over his place and changed the name to Deano's. It remained Deano's from 1975 to 1981. Dean then transferred his restaurant business to the site of Odell "Boney" Hendrix's restaurant in Davie County. Deano's occupied this site until 1985.

From 1985 to date, Dean has carried

Dean Allen

on an extensive barbecue catering business. Missing the camaraderie and fellowship that had been so much a part of his restaurants, Dean took the plunge and went back into the restaurant business at the present site on July 15, 1998.

The present Deano's is a warm, golden hued log building facing Church Street in Mocksville. A stranger is immediately made welcome and to feel at home upon entering Dean's place.

Dean cooks primarily shoulders and some Boston butts. His pork is cooked over pits with hickory wood. Dean has a large double-door firebox adjoining his pits. Everything is new – brick, steel and tile. The hickory burns down and the coals are moved from the firebox by shovel under the pits. Dean cooks about 40-50 shoulders per week, sometimes many more when large catering parties are scheduled.

In addition to the usual extensive list of drive-in restaurant sandwiches, Dean has a specialty. It is his pimento cheeseburger. I would rather have one of these than dessert.

Deano's chopped barbecue comes generously sauced from the kitchen. It is very moist, vinegary, slightly sweet, hot (but not too much so) and is pound-the-table good. Deano's coarse-chopped barbecue (my favorite) is sauced while cooking but not additionally in the kitchen. It tastes like moist ham. Good outside brown meat is mixed in with the regular chopped and coarse chopped meat. These slightly brown pieces of meat keep the barbecue from having a gray appearance, as is the case with so many barbecue places. In addition, they give each bite that pungent smoky taste that makes the flavor explode in your mouth.

Deano's sliced barbecue is the white part of the shoulder. It is moist, tender and melts in your mouth. When it holds hands with the sauce, they dance!

Deano's has red slaw which is coarse chopped, vinegary and slightly tart. Also available is white slaw, which is coarse chopped and light on the mayo.

The sauce, the secret to any good barbecue, is a thin, light-brown sauce that is a vinegar base with some sugar, some Texas Pete, some barbecue sauce, some lemon, some ketchup, some water, some salt & pepper, some hot sauce and Dean's own blend of secret spices. There are also a few other ingredients that he would not share. The sauce is slightly peppery, slightly sweet with plenty of zip but not overly hot. The sauce is more like Eastern North Carolina but could be called Lexington-style dip; its leaning is more toward its eastern cousins than the Lexington side of the family.

Dean said that he thought the quality of meat today had changed some from his early days in the barbecue business. He said that the quality of meat may not be quite as high as it was when he initially went into the barbecue business, but the highest quality that he is able to get is at least uniform day in and day out. Dean said that his pork shoulders used to be wider and flatter and are now more narrow and thicker. He feels this has to do with what the pigs are being fed today and the push to put weight on them and get them to market quickly.

Having had Buck Miller and Boney Hendrix as mentors, Dean has learned the barbecue trade from two of the oldest barbecue people in this area. He said they told him the first three hours of smoke would look like steam because it is cooking the water out of the meat. When the water gets out and the meat gets hot enough, it will start dripping. That's when you get the flavor. The rest of the time the meat remains on the pit, it's just cooking down to be done enough to serve. The smoke tells the story. When it changes colors, you are getting the good stuff.

Desserts at Deano's consist of all homemade pies and cakes. If you should be lucky enough to be there when Dean has some of his mother's persimmon pudding, you will immediately ask to be adopted.

Dean was recognized in the book, *Good Food - American Specialties* by Jan and Michael Stern.

Deano's Barbecue is located just off of South Main Street in downtown Mocksville. To find it, exit I-40 at the 601 Exit and proceed south on 601 until you are in downtown Mocksville at the junction of South Main Street and U.S. 158 East. Turn left on South Main Street and follow South Main and U.S. 158 through two traffic signals. The next left is Church Street. Turn left on Church Street, proceed approximately 100 yards and Deano's is on the left. The hours are 11 a.m. to 8 p.m., Monday through Saturday. It's closed on Sunday. Telephone number: (336) 751-5820.

Lancaster's BBQ, Mooresville

Jeff Lancaster, who grew up in Goldsboro eating Eastern North Carolina-style barbecue, and his wife Terry, who grew up in Mooresville, own Lancaster's BBQ.

When Jeff got out of the service he went into the restaurant business at Curie Beach in the early 1960s. This was followed by a career with a sign company. In December 1986 Jeff's dad, Bud, had an employee named Joe that wanted to go into the barbecue business. NASCAR racing was just coming into its own so Jeff and Joe decided that racing, signage and barbecue was a good mix. Jeff poked his toe into the barbecue waters. His first venture was an old gas station down the street from his present site. It had three booths and seated 12 people. Carefully measuring his successes, Jeff moved to the current site, which now contains the front door and arcade room. He could seat 80 people. Successes mounted. With its expansion, the site can now seat 280 people comfortably. There are plans to add seating for 90 more. Jeff said that the next phase of Lancaster's BBQ will be Lancaster's Hog Trough Saloon which will cater more to the Harley crowd.

Jeff not only cooks good 'cue but seems to be a very astute business man as well with more than just a little of the Midas touch. This seems to run in Jeff's family. Jeff's grandfather, Tony Lancaster, started Big Daddy's fish emporium several miles down the road. This later passed to Tony's son Bud, Jeff's dad, and is now run by Jeff's brother, Freddy Lancaster. Cooking and serving good food and a strong association with racing seems to be in the blood of the Lancaster men. Jeff is no exception and I predict more successes for this fast-paced barbecue entrepreneur.

The barbecue is moderately chopped with a light vinegar taste. With chips of red pepper, this is classic Eastern North Carolina barbecue and as good as most any barbecue in Eastern North Carolina. I like it just the way it comes from the kitchen. It is certainly one of the best Eastern North Carolina 'cues west of Raleigh.

They have two sauces: a really good Eastern North Carolina sauce and a spicy rib/chicken sauce that is a bit sweeter. Terry said they developed this sauce for the Northern people that are more accustomed to a sweeter rib-type sauce.

The slaw is yellow with a mustard-mayo base. It has a fresh, crisp cabbage taste. It's really good and great with the 'cue.

The hushpuppies are light with a golden crust, a moist center and good cornbread taste with a hint of sweetness.

This place is a mecca for NASCAR fans. The walls are covered with parts of NASCAR automobiles and every kind of NASCAR memorabilia known to man. There is a full-size bus sitting in the middle of the floor across from the bar. For kids young and old, there is a separate room with a dozen or more driving machines where you can vicariously experience driving a racecar. This room, with various video games, was designed for children to be entertained while out with their parents. Sometimes the adults actually let the children play.

If you like NASCAR and good barbecue, this is the place.

From I-77, take the Mooresville exit (Highway 150). Go east for approximately 1.8 miles and you will see the Lancaster's BBQ sign on your right. Turn left on Rinehardt Road, go less than half a mile, and Lancaster's is on your right.

Lancaster's hours are 11 a.m. until 10 p.m., Monday through Friday, and 12 p.m. until 10 p.m., Saturday. It's closed Sunday. Telephone number: (704) 663-5807.

Timberwood's Family Restaurant, Morganton

When traveling east or west on I-40, take Exit 106 to Timberwood's Family Restaurant. The only sign you will see from the road reads, "Rainbow Inn and Restaurant." This is a motel with a restaurant. The restaurant now has a new name; Timberwood's Family Restaurant and a new owner, Phil Scarboro. The original restaurant has been here since the 1950s. Phil has been here since 2001. However, Phil is not new to the food business. He spent 12 years in the pizza business and the past 11 years at the Emporium Restaurant. Phil has left intact the same cooks, the same suppliers, the same menu and, he said with a smile, "the same prices."

Timberwood's cooks pork shoulders. Some are chopped, some are pulled and all are cooked electrically without wood.

This place has been mecca for locals for almost 50 years. Some locals eat here three times a day, six days a week, and twice on Sunday. People come here to celebrate their anniversaries, birthdays and any other event that goes hand-in-hand with good food.

In addition to the barbecue, Timberwood's has country ham, tenderloin and a host of country vegetables. The seafood consists of flounder, perch, jumbo shrimp and Calabash shrimp. You can get the seafood fried or broiled. Several steaks are available (sirloin and rib eye). There are 12 different sandwiches, wings and salads. The desserts consist of homemade peach and strawberry cobblers and hot fudge brownies with ice cream.

Timberwood's is a clean, bright, family restaurant that has good food cooked by good people and served by good people. The new owner is good people too.

The chopped barbecue is good. It's moist and has some brown specks from the outside edge – just good pork taste. It is not ground too fine, about medium chopped. With the house sauce, the chopped barbecue, to my palate, tastes like a good middle-of-the-road Lexington style. It still needs some zip.

The sauce is thin but not watery, has some spices, reddish in color, tomatoey and tangy but not hot. The sauce could use more spark in the form of peppers and spices to balance the tomato taste.

The dip was a sweet, tomatoey liquid, very mild, doesn't step up, and has a soft finish. On the meat, it was too sweet for my taste.

The white slaw is bright with carrot flakes and has good cabbage taste. It's a nice accompaniment to the 'cue. The red slaw is crisp with good zip, but not too much so. The cabbage steps up and the spices are close behind. There's just enough juice, and a good peppery finish.

The hushpuppies are absolutely delicious with a crisp brown outer layer and a moist inside.

The moist and tender fried chicken tastes like your mama made it... if she were the best country cook in the county. The chicken has a golden skin with that old-fashioned kind of taste one gets from cooking in a black iron skillet using fatback drippings. It's slightly greasy, the way good chicken should be. After all, just the right amount of that good fat taste is what we're seeking when we eat fried chicken.

If Timberwood's tweaks or reinvents its barbecue sauce and dip to the level of the fried chicken, they will have a barbecue and sauce combo that will be hard to guard.

From I-40 West near Morganton, take Exit 106 and turn left at the end of the exit way. Cross over I-40 and turn left into the Rainbow Inn parking lot. From I-40 East, take Exit 106, turn right at the end of the exit way, and turn left into the Rainbow Inn parking lot.

Hours are from 6 a.m. to 9 p.m., Monday through Saturday, and 7 a.m. to 3:30 p.m., Sunday. Telephone number: (828) 433-1767.

Snappy Lunch, Mt. Airy

One of Surry County's historical landmarks, the Snappy Lunch is Mt. Airy's oldest continuous-running eating establishment.

It opened in 1923 under the direction of George Roberson and Deuce Hod. After just a few months, Deuce sold his interest to Ben Edwards. In 1943, Charles Dowell began working there for $10 a week for then owners – George Roberson and Raymond Hemrick. In 1951, Charles Dowell bought George's half of the business. In those days, you could buy a bologna sandwich for a nickel and a hot dog for a dime at the Snappy Lunch. Students, including Andy Griffith, would come there for lunch. At that time, the schools had no cafeterias.

Charles Dowell making one of his famous pork chop sandwiches.

In 1960, Charles bought Raymond Hemrick's half of the café, making him the sole owner.

In an early episode of the *Andy Griffith Show* titled, "Andy the Matchmaker," Andy suggested to Barney that they go to the Snappy Lunch to get a bite to eat. Andy also mentions Snappy Lunch in his version of the song "Silhouettes."

More recently in a television news interview, Andy Griffith talked about getting a hot dog and a bottle of soda pop for 15 cents at Snappy Lunch when he was a young boy.

Since the 1960s, the Snappy Lunch has been the subject of numerous news articles and publications as well as TV news stories locally and nationally. Television personalities including Oprah Winfrey, Lou Ferigno and Donna Fargo, who is originally from Mt. Airy, have visited Snappy Lunch.

The house specialty is the pork chop sandwich created by Charles Dowell. This delightful pork rendition brings thousands of tourists to the Snappy Lunch each year. Charles cuts the meat himself. Each pork chop is cut from a whole boneless pork loin. Charles then takes each trimmed pork chop (about three-quarter inch thick) and slides it into the top of his vintage Tenderator (a small, white enamel countertop machine shaped vaguely like a toaster, but with a slot at the bottom as well as the top). The machine's whirring blades cut tiny parallel incisions front and back on the pork as it passes through top to bottom. This ancient contraption, discovered by Charles many years ago in an antique shop, is one of the secrets to Charles legendary sandwiches. The Tenderator's tiny incisions tenderize the meat without compressing it. The meat is much more tender than when it is processed in a "cuber" or tenderized with a mallet. The meat is then lightly battered in a special batter concocted by Charles, who then cooks it on a grill in the front window so all passers-by can see. This wonderful treat "all the way" is served on a hamburger bun and topped with condiments of mustard, chili, slaw, onions and tomato. Charles also makes the chili and the slaw.

Charles says his chili is the little thing that turned out big. When Charles first started serving pork chop sandwiches, he had a tomato-base chili sauce that he added to his offering. Charles said it was so thin that it ran straight off the chops. One day in an effort to improve his product, Charles took everything that was on the grill – pork chops, ham, sausage, hamburger, tenderloin (eight different kinds of meat all together) and ran them through the food processor with tomatoes and spices. This chili proved

to be the ticket. It was thick, good and it made all the difference. Charles' masterpiece served all the way comes to the table encased in wax paper. I suggest you open the paper to expose one part of the sandwich and keep the rest to cradle this treat as there is no way to eat this meal without making a minor mess. The pork chop itself is about 4 inches wide and can be up to 8 inches long. Thus, it sticks out of the hamburger bun several places. With all the condiments, this double-handed sandwich is a meal. There is a sink and towels for you to wash up after you have enjoyed one of Charles' treats.

Charles said that he used to slow roast the pork all night long and then chopped and sliced it for barbecue. When he created his famous pork chop sandwich, the demand became so great that he no longer has time to do the barbecue. I am well aware that pork cooked on a grill and offered up in the manner that Charles serves it is not "barbecue." However, if we are going to stretch the definition of barbecue to include pork roasted over electricity and gas, I am willing to throw in the grill if it produces a product as wonderful as the pork chop sandwich made at Snappy Lunch.

Since Snappy Lunch has a limited seating capacity, I suggest you arrive early and cue up as the lunch hour ends at 1:45 p.m. and they lock the doors. If you want a breakfast to die for, Charles starts serving that at 5:45 a.m. A visit to Snappy Lunch, meeting Charles, and enjoying one of his famous pork chop sandwiches is an experience worthy of anyone's detour from Highway 52 or just a trip to the mountains to enjoy the fall foliage and a gastronomic delight.

From Highway 52 North, turn right at the 601 junction and onto Rockford Street (sign says downtown) and continue for almost a mile. Turn left at the Andy Griffith Playhouse onto Dixie Street, cross the next street, go a half block further and turn right into the municipal parking lot. Walk up the walkway onto North Main Street, Snappy Lunch is located on your right next to Floyd's Barbershop at 125 N. Main St.

Hours are 5:45 a.m. until 1:45 p.m., Monday, Tuesday, Wednesday and Friday, and 5:45 a.m. until 1:15 p.m., Thursday and Saturday. Telephone number: (336) 786-4931.

Doc's Deli,
North Wilkesboro

Owner Ronnie "Ozzy" Osborne has owned and operated Doc's Deli for a few short years so the place is not as steeped in history and tradition as are a number of good barbecue places across the state. The separation ends there. Doc's does have three things in common with the other good barbecue places: (1) they cook their meat on premises; (2) they make their own sauce; and (3) the barbecue is good.

Ozzy is not a stranger to the food business. Having been in catering for more than 10 years he decided to open his own place in 1999 – a good decision.

Ozzy said that he starts his Smithfield Boston butts on a custom-made gas cooker and finishes the pork with hickory wood fired in a wood stove that is drafted back through the cooker. All 'cue is chopped by hand the old-fashioned way.

The chopped barbecue pork is moderately coarse and tender, tender, tender. The chopped 'cue has a full-flavored, rich, pork taste with brown smoky nuances and wonderful nutty overtones. Specks of red and black pepper peek at you and promise a hint of spiciness. This is delivered admirably. Ronnie cooks really good barbecue. The 'cue comes sauced from the kitchen and, in my estimation, does not need more.

The homemade barbecue sauce is a twangy, reddish-brown, Lexington-style dip with crushed red and black peppers and a pronounced vinegar and pepper flavor with spices. It is medium hot to hot by itself. It calms down on the 'cue quite nicely. Use sparingly here because it tastes great without any additional sauce other than that supplied by the kitchen.

In addition to Ozzy's wonderful barbecue, he provides 16 types of sandwiches and eight starters including buffalo wings and buffalo shrimp. Ozzy serves seven different plates. A barbecue plate was omitted in the printing of the menu but is available, ask your waitperson. There are two soups. Try the black bean Santa Fe.

It has the usual barbecue place drinks (no alcohol) and homemade desserts.

To reach Doc's Deli going north on Highway 421, take the Bushy Mountain exit. At the top of the exit ramp, take a right and go through two stoplights. Across from the ABC store, take a left and then take the first right. Doc's Deli is on the right on Cherry Street. Hours are 11 a.m. until 8 p.m., Monday through Friday. It's closed weekends. Telephone: (336) 838-1977.

Arey's Barbecue, Rockwell

Arey's Barbecue used to be known as Darrell's Barbecue. In the early '40s, Darrell Galloway, brother of Lavada Doby of Whispering Pines Barbecue in Albemarle, opened his barbecue restaurant in this tiny former filling station on the corner of a small side street in downtown Rockwell. With its dollhouse look and steeply pitched roof it is classic Pure Oil architecture.

This landmark barbecue place changed hands in 1995 when Dick and Pat Arey purchased it. Several years ago, Dick passed away. However, Arey's continues nicely under Pat's guiding hand and watchful eye along with a number of ladies who assist her. When Dick did the cooking, the barbecue was cooked over wood. After his death, Pat said that firing pits and cooking barbecue all night and running the front was too much for her and the other ladies. The barbecue is now cooked electrically on a Barbecue King. Pat still insists that it all be chopped by hand.

The chopped barbecue was kinda dry without sauce. It was light, airy and had some good outside brown meat that gave flavor to an otherwise roasted pork taste. With mild sauce, the chopped 'cue was tasty. With the hot sauce; you better have water nearby. I found a few drops of each on the 'cue worked well.

The sliced barbecue was lighter, pink on the outside and moderately tender. It had a good pork taste but, again, it too was kinda dry without sauce. With the mild sauce, it was moister. With the hot sauce, it was a bit much for me. A blend of both is still the way to go here.

The red Lexington-style slaw consists of cabbage, tomatoes, salt, sugar and, of course, vinegar. It's chopped moderately coarse and vinegar is definitely the predominant taste.

The hushpuppies were overcooked, too brown and too crunchy. This took away from the overall flavor.

The mild sauce is a light reddish-brown with a vinegar base plus pepper and various spices but it also has wine, which is something not usually found in barbecue sauces in this state. The hot sauce is a very dark reddish-brown. It is served with tongs, this one has lots of fire. Be sure to wear a lead apron.

The décor of Arey's will fascinate boys and girls of all ages, especially NASCAR fans. There is racing memorabilia on the ceiling and the walls that showcases every type of miniature NASCAR car for every team over the years. In addition, there are miniature biplanes and miniature tractor trailers.

Arey's Barbecue is off Highway 52 in downtown Rockwell. Hours are 5:30 a.m. until 9 p.m., Wednesday through Saturday, and 5:30 a.m. until 1 p.m., Tuesday. It's closed on Sunday and Monday. Telephone number: (704) 279-6300.

The Barbecue Place, Rutherfordton

Owners Darvin and Opal Crain had been in the commercial hog farm business in Rutherford County for many years. They used to sell more than 150 pigs a week. Around 1995 the couple decided to cook pigs instead of feed pigs. They purchased an old auto parts building and remodeled. The Barbecue Place was born.

The Hickory Log in Forest City, which is part of the Rutherfordton, Spindale and Forest City triangle, had been the main source of barbecue in the county for many years. When the Crains opened, they decided to offer a different sauce than the Hickory Log, which uses an Eastern Carolina vinegar base. This sauce has 14 ingredients. They also have a sweeter sauce for ribs and chicken. The pork barbecue is offered chopped and sliced.

Darvin cooks on a custom-made cooker that he designed and made. This cooker is gas fired but has wood inserted into a firebox at the end to give smoke flavor. The pork cooks slowly all night for 15 hours. Darvin cooks hams and shoulders. He chops the shoulders and slices the ham. He takes the meat off the grill, breaks the shoulders down and after they have cooled some, he chops the entire shoulder. Chopping too soon while the meat is hot will cause the meat to mush.

The chopped barbecue is moderately fine chopped, moist and tender. It has a good roast pork flavor and the sauce is a nice addition.

The sliced ham is very, very tender and has a good, fresh roast pork taste. The sauce tastes like a Christmas glaze.

The sauce has molasses, brown sugar, ketchup, vinegar, cloves, bay leaves, red and black pepper, Worcestershire, lemon juice and a few other goodies. It is served hot at the table. It is dark brown with hints of sweetness and a smoky, molasses & brown sugar taste. It has enough spices to make it jump. It's Darvin's own recipe and it's very good.

The red slaw is a good Lexington style with a tart vinegar taste. The white slaw is finely chopped white cabbage with flecks of carrot and light mayo. This is good coleslaw.

Hours are 11 a.m. until 8 p.m., Monday through Thursday, and 11 a.m. until 8:30 p.m., Friday and Saturday. It's closed Sunday. Telephone number: (828) 287-2020.

Hendrix Barbeque, Salisbury

Owned and operated by Billy and Timmy Garris, Hendrix Barbeque was started in 1954 by Wilbur and Homer Hendrix.

Born in Lexington, Billy is no stranger to barbecue. He lived near Old Hickory Barbecue in Lexington that was operated by Paul and Ennis Cope. Billy started working at Old Hickory in 1969 at age 13. Billy's brother Timmy followed at age 12.

After their experience at Old Hickory, the brothers started cooking for Dunn at Speedy's Barbecue. Timmy worked at Speedy's for 17 years and Billy worked there for four and a half years before moving on to Jerry Laxton's in Salisbury. At that time, Laxton was renting Hendrix Barbeque. Billy bought Hendrix Barbeque from Jerry Laxton and his wife Emily in 1989.

The pork is cooked with electricity and hickory chips. Hendrix cooks shoulders and Boston butts. All the meat is hand chopped.

The chopped barbecue is a moderate chop that comes sauced from the kitchen. It has a sweet taste, good flavor and is very moist. You can't detect the smoke here; the rich outside brown gives the 'cue its flavor, not the smoke.

The vinegar-base sauce is reddish with a hint of tomato. It is moderately mild, not fiery, with black pepper and other spices. It is a hybrid Salisbury sauce that is something of an Eastern North Carolina sauce with a Lexington touch but with less tomato taste.

The hushpuppies were good, crunchy and moist.

The slaw is a Lexington-style red barbecue slaw, but contains more sugar than most Lexington-style slaw. It is chopped moderately coarse with vinegar and black pepper. It's juicy and fairly tart.

Hendrix Barbeque was voted #1 in the "Salisbury Taste of the Town" competition in 1997.

Billy and Timmy Garris both look like football players. Billy could also double as Randy Owens, the lead singer with Alabama. Billy has dreamed about buying and rebuilding the Old Hickory Barbecue in Lexington where he and Timmy worked as teenagers. I am sure the good people of Salisbury would rather he just dream about it and continue to make and serve his good 'cue in Rowan County.

Hendrix Barbeque is located at 2488 Statesville Blvd. in Salisbury. Hours are 5 a.m. until 9:30 p.m., Monday through Saturday. Hendrix closes at 9 p.m. in the winter. It's closed Sunday. Telephone number: (704) 633-9838.

Richard's Bar-B-Q, Salisbury

When I started asking people on the street, in convenience stores and at filling stations in Spencer and Salisbury where they would go for the best barbecue in the area, three names came up repeatedly. One of these names was Richard's Bar-B-Q.

Richard's Bar-B-Q was originally T&F Barbecue and opened its doors on Council Street (just off Main Street near the courthouse) in Salisbury in 1935. This tiny side-street establishment only had seven stools at a counter. T&F's owners, Popeye Trexler and Grant Fories, served such a good product that people had to stand outside on the sidewalk and eat their sandwiches. Still they came.

It was the "biggest little place" in North Carolina says C.G. "Guy" Clodfelter when he and Tom Heffner worked there as teenagers. Guy and Tom ultimately bought the place and continued to run it for many years. Guy sold his interest to Tom due to poor health. The Heffner family moved the business down the street to its present location on North Main Street.

Tom Heffner Jr. took over the operation after his father began to pull back from daily management of the business. Tom Jr. put Richard Monroe in charge as manager in 1974. There is a picture on the wall of young Richard chopping barbecue as part of a Salisbury Post article from July 15, 1979. If he had Cher beside him, you might think he was Sonny Bono.

T&F remained small because of limited parking and Tom Heffner was content for the business to remain that way. His good product and his regular customers meant more than a bulging cash register.

From the outset, T&F's barbecue was cooked on pits with a firebox in the old traditional manner. Shoulders, 10 to 15-pounds, were slow cooked to a golden brown, brought from the pit one at a time and not chopped until ordered to keep the pork fresh and moist. To say that the sandwiches were handmade is true in more ways than one. Wearing rubber gloves, Richard would pick up a bun with one hand, grab a handful of chopped barbecue with the other, place it on a bun, grab a handful of slaw, pack it, top it, and serve it. Since Richard has rather large hands, the portions at his restaurant have always been generous.

Because of its proximity to the courthouse, Richard's regular customers consist of a large number of the courthouse crowd interspersed with a few winos. Richard said 55 percent of his regular customers eat here four times a week or more.

The barbecue is still pit cooked over

an open pit using 90 percent hickory and 10 percent oak. A man who works for a tree company keeps Richard continually supplied with split wood and monitors his wood rack. Richard cleans his firebox everyday and puts the wood for the next cooking in after it is clean. He said the heat from the firebrick would dry the next batch of wood just like a kiln. Richard said you could light the next batch with a match. As with most barbecue places, the firebox is fed from the wood rack from the outside and coals are removed from the inside and shoveled under the pits. When Richard opened the cover over the pit, it revealed about 20 golden-brown shoulders ready for chopping.

Richard hand chops the barbecue. It is chopped larger than most, but not coarse. It has a good smoky pork flavor and deep smoke penetration from the slow roasting. It is very fresh. The inside white mixed with the outside brown keeps the 'cue moist. It was surprisingly good without sauce. With the sauce, your taste buds tell you that you are somewhere east of Raleigh as it tastes like a fine offering of Eastern North Carolina-style barbecue.

The sauce is Eastern North Carolina-style vinegar base with red pepper and spices. The sauce without meat is fairly hot, not a torch but still hot. On the meat it is the perfect accompaniment for Richard's 'cue.

The barbecue chicken is just simply delicious.

The slaw is white and moist but not juicy. It has a good cabbage and pepper taste. The hushpuppies are large, brown, crunchy outside and moist inside with a good cornbread taste.

Richard's Bar-B-Q is located just off North Main Street in Salisbury. You can't miss it. The hours are 6 a.m. to 9 p.m., Monday through Saturday. It's closed Sunday. Seating is limited and the crowds are large. Telephone number: (704) 636-9561.

Wink's Bar-B-Que and Seafood, Salisbury

Billing itself "King of Barbecue," Wink's Bar-B-Que and Seafood does not have the traditional pig on its sign outside but instead has the King of the Beasts (a la Lion King) wearing a crown. This motif is carried over on the t-shirts of dozens of busy employees scurrying about inside.

Wink's Bar-B-Que and Seafood was the brainchild of "Wink" Wansler almost 50 years ago. At one time, there were several Wink's Bar-B-Que and Seafood places in and about the Rowan area. Today there is only one.

In 1973, Dwight Martin bought Wink's from Wansler. Dwight and his family continued to run the place until they were forced to move by the city this year. Since the city caused the move, the city allowed Wink's to be "grandfathered" under the pit-cooking method. Thus, Wink's was allowed to continue to pit cook on its new site. Wink's has only been at its present site since 2001. The present Wink's is about 10 times the size of the former. The tremendous amount of wood out back to fire the barbecue pits lets you know that there is a lot of good cooking going on here.

The pits are fired with hickory wood supplied by a man from Denton, which is a big lumber area.

Wink's is able to seat a small army as well as supply the needs of hundreds driving by. At lunch time when I was there, the large paved parking lot was filled and cars and trucks were sprawled all over the side streets to get the same good food Wink's has produced since the 1950s.

Dwight Martin is ably assisted in this endeavor by his sons, Kelly and Byron, and daughters, Sharon and Dinah.

The pork shoulders are roasted slowly over wood coals and hand chopped.

The chopped barbecue is moderately coarse with nice large pieces. It is moist and has a good smoky flavor with outside brown mixed in with inside white. A nice pink color shows the smoke penetration. It has a nutty flavor and is not sauced in the kitchen. With barbecue sauce, it has a nice mild, rich flavor. It's a good beginning and a good finish with no lingering aftertaste.

The sliced barbecue is thick and pink throughout (smoked to the bone). It's tender and very moist for sliced barbecue. The sauce helps bring out the nutty brown flavor from the hickory wood. It tastes like pulled pork from a pig pickin'. It's the best.

The sauce has a bright vinegar taste with spices but it's not too fiery by itself. It's orangey-red in color and tastes like a hybrid Eastern North Carolina/Lexington offering.

I found the sauce plenty spicy, but not hot with peppers.

They serve a red Lexington-style slaw and it's very good. The hushpuppies are bigger than golf balls and crunchy. They're not greasy and are moist inside. These are just nice pups.

Not only does Wink's serve delicious barbecue but also steaks, prime rib, seafood, sandwiches and a full page of breakfast items. Breakfast is served all day. Wink's has a variety of soups including oyster stew when in season. This is topped with 10 desserts, including banana pudding.

Wink's is located at 509 Faith Rd. in Salisbury. From I-85, take the exit for Highway 52 toward Albemarle. If on Highway 52 South already, you will cross under I-85. As soon as you cross under or exit I-85 onto Highway 52 South, Faith Road veers off to the right from Highway 52 (immediately east of the I-85 bridge). Continue on Faith Road for approximately three-quarters of a mile. Wink's will be on your right. The hours are 5 a.m until 9 p.m., Monday through Saturday. It's closed Sunday. Telephone number: (704) 637-2410.

Alston Bridges Barbecue, Inc., Shelby

One of the reasons good Lexington barbecue is found in Shelby is Warner Stamey, who was a barbecue guru, entrepreneur and teacher of most of the successful Piedmont barbecue notables. One of the other reasons is Alston Bridges, Warner Stamey's attentive protégé.

In 1950, Warner Stamey opened a restaurant with Alston Bridges. Alston Bridges, who is Stamey's brother-in-law, eventually bought Stamey's interest. Alston and his wife Mabel opened the place as their own in 1956.

Alston and Mabel Bridges had five boys: Kent, Bob, Milton, Don and Dennis. Of the five, Kent is the only son that remains in the business. Kent said the other brother's wives were not too pleased with the long hours of a barbecue man. Kent's wife Linda works with Kent in the business daily. Kent and Linda have four children: Michelle, Jay, Reid and Laura. Michelle, Jay and Reid work in the business along with their mother and father. Michelle runs the line with her mother while Reid and Jay both cook with their dad. Kent said there are two to three members of the Bridges family working at all times when the business is open. He said they work hard and play hard as a family.

Alston Bridges Barbecue is the only barbecue place I know of that is closed on Saturday and Sunday. Kent said they discussed it as a family and decided that his and Linda's children needed to be with their children on the weekends to participate in all the things that the grandkids were doing. Kent said people told him he would go broke if he closed on Saturdays. With twinkling eyes and a big grin, he said he loves the way they are going broke.

Kent said that he bought some lots up on the New River and built a home for him and Linda to spend the weekends. "This is my psychiatrist," he said. About every Thursday he said he gets to feeling that "I need to get to the river." Kent said that after a weekend in the mountains he's ready to come back and fight the fires for another week.

Kent, who turned 60 in 2001, said that he was blessed to have good long-term help that had been with the business for a number of years. He said some of the people that work here worked part-time in high school, weekends during college and after college until they could find the job they were seeking. Everyone pulls together at Alston Bridges, family and employees.

Alston Bridges uses a Nunnery-Freeman Kook Rite Kooker. Kent said they constantly had to adjust things despite using the same products and recipes for 50 years. He said that sometimes the vinegar was a bit different. Sometimes the cabbage tastes like horseradish. You have to stay on top of your product and recipes, and adjust because just making them the same way with the same products over and over does not always produce the same taste or product you desire.

The sliced pork barbecue comes as a large chop that's very moist and very tender. It has good roast pork taste with smoky overtones and hints of nuttiness. With the sauce, oh mama, this is good 'cue. This chopped barbecue is like a pulled pig. I really like it.

The coarse chopped is moist and as tender as a mother's love with large thumb-size pieces that melt in your mouth. It's rich, slightly nutty and delicious. It was so tender I could hardly keep it on the fork to dip in the sauce.

The coarse chopped outside brown is wonderful 'cue that puts a word craftsman to his task. The flavor is nutty brown, smoky and rich. These wonderful chewy morsels of pork are most tender with that bit of brown that gives it that delicious woodsy flavor.

The ribs have a wonderful caramelized glaze and are tender. Fall-off-the-bone meat wrapped around a pork Popsicle, what a treat! It is chewy enough. These ribs are

hard to stop eating.

The regular chopped barbecue is finely minced and, without sauce, is a bit dry for my taste. It had some good brown in it and the flavor was good but it was still a bit dry. The sauce makes all the difference as it jumps to life and has just the right amount of moisture, becoming a classic Lexington-style chopped 'cue.

The sauce is a reddish Lexington-style dip with just the right amount of spices to offset any tomato taste. It is a good blend like a good mixed drink. Not too fiery, the sauce has some sweetness and just enough spice not to be bland or acidic.

The slaw is a tart, tangy red slaw with a bit of jump. The finely chopped and crisp cabbage taste goes perfectly with the red Lexington-style dip and the wonderful meat. It makes a delicious sandwich or side.

The hushpuppies are about three inches of crisp, brown shell surrounding a very moist cornbread center. They aren't heavy or greasy.

I normally don't eat desserts but I had some more coarse chopped brown this time.

Hours are 10:45 a.m. to 8 p.m., Monday through Thursday, and 10:45 a.m. to 8:30 p.m., Friday. It's closed Saturday and Sunday. Telephone number: (704) 482-1998.

Bridges Barbecue Lodge, Shelby

On U.S. Highway 74 Bypass, across from Cleveland Mall and about one mile west of Buffalo Creek, sits Bridges Barbecue Lodge. A large sign on a brick post tells you that this tiny, cottage-sized restaurant has been specializing in barbecue for more than 50 years.

This is another Shelby/Warner Stamey story. It seems that while Warner Stamey was in Shelby, he not only taught Alston Bridges the fine art of slow cooking pork shoulders over hickory coals, but he imparted these skills to another Bridges as well. After his tutelage with Warner Stamey, Red Bridges (no relation to Alston) established his legendary barbecue restaurant in 1946. Red's first barbecue place was in the old Dedmons building; Red called it Dedmons Barbecue. In 1948 Red and the other redheaded Bridges, Red's wife Lyttle, opened a restaurant uptown that they call Bridges Barbecue. In 1953 the restaurant moved to its present site. Lyttle has been carrying on the business since Red's death in the late 1960s.

With Red gone, Lyttle has sole dominion over the title "The Redhead." The other name by which she is affectionately known is "Mama B." Red and Mama B's only daughter Debbie Bridges-Webb now manages the restaurant. Debbie said Mama B, now 85 years young, makes only a cameo appearance at the restaurant about once a week to make sure Debbie is doing everything like her mama taught her. When Mama B, the grande dame of barbecue in the Shelby area, holds court, everyone vies for her attention.

Mama B has been the driving force behind this restaurant since it opened. This is reflected in the restaurant's appearance and the inside décor. If the little neon pigs on the roof and the sign were removed, leaving the immaculate cottage surrounded by the white picket fence, you would probably think you were pulling into a charming little antique shop

Mama B and her daughter Debbi

or boutique run part-time by a wealthy lady as a hobby. Nothing could be further from the truth. Despite its gingerbread appearance, if you peep over the back fence you will see enough wood neatly stacked in long rows to heat 50 homes all winter. A further look would reveal a big smokehouse with 11 vents and chimneys that say "serious barbecue spoken here." No, this is not a boutique, despite the appearance of its present overseer.

Debbie Bridges-Webb is a stunning-looking woman who looks as though she may have just stepped off the cover of Vogue magazine. Despite her good looks, Debbie is not window dressing for a business her daddy and mama built. Debbie knows barbecue.

Debbie said there was little turnover in employees at Bridges Barbecue Lodge and that people seeking employment there were on the waiting list for years.

Phil Schenck has been the pit master at Bridges Barbecue Lodge for more than 16 years. Phil cooks at night from around 8 p.m. until about 4 or 5 a.m. This is long, hot demanding work. The coals have to be freshened every 15-30 minutes in just the right amounts and at just the right places. Phil does not use a fork or a thermometer. Phil does his cooking by sight and feel. The shoulders that Phil cooks go on the pits at about 13-15 pounds and, when trimmed and hand chopped, produce about seven pounds of delicious barbecue.

The barbecue is served minced, chopped or sliced. The minced is finely chopped (too fine for my taste) and comes generously sauced.

The chopped barbecue pork with sauce is moderately coarse and moist with deep, rich brown-roasted pork flavor. There's enough outside brown to kick in the smoky, woodsy, roasted-over-an-open-pit taste that we barbecue aficionados seek. This 'cue with the sauce (served hot at the table) is simply delicious.

The outside brown barbecue pork is absolutely the best outside brown you will ever eat. The woodsy, smoky, nutty-flavored pork is tender to a fault and, with sauce, it is THE BEST.

The sliced barbecue pork is tender, tender, tender. The moist pork flakes with a fork and has good roast pork taste with hints of smoky, nutty brown flavor. It's absolutely wonderful.

The tangy brownish-red sauce is tart with sweetness. The sweet and sour makes your tongue and taste buds tango and your soul happy. I love this stuff.

The slaw is classic red Lexington style. It's tart, tangy, vinegar taste goes well with the crisp fresh cabbage. At 5 inches long, the hushpuppies are large and crisp. The outside shell is not hard however and the center is moist with hints of onion.

Enjoy the best in causal food at a Shelby icon.

Hours are 11 a.m. to 8 p.m., Wednesday through Saturday. It's closed the rest of the week. Telephone number: (704) 482-8567.

Carolina Bar-B-Q, Statesville

Congenial hosts Gene Medlin and his wife, Linda, started the business in 1985 at its present site. Gene and Linda impart real down home feeling in their restaurant. In fact, there are balloons for the little people and Gene can make balloon animals. Gene and Linda are well traveled and have eaten barbecue in a number of places. They seem to have found the right cooking methods and sauces in their journeys and have brought them to Statesville.

Carolina Bar-B-Q is off the interstate and has no signage on either I-77 or I-40. But in barbecue circles, word gets around to the famous and not so famous. When Charles Kuralt visited Gene and Linda, he told them how much he enjoyed their pork product but he said, "it was too refined." Mr. Kuralt said that they needed more fat and gristle. Gene told Charles Kuralt that he would save him some fat and gristle for his next visit.

Carolina Bar-B-Q serves barbecue pork dinners, barbecue beef dinners, barbecue beef or pork ribs, barbecue chicken, barbecue salad and brunswick stew. If you see a pattern here, you are correct. This is a barbecue place. They also serve dinners of flounder, shrimp, fried chicken, hamburger steak and country ham. The sides include french fries, baked beans and coleslaw.

Carolina Bar-B-Q uses only whole shoulders. Sometimes they add hams, but usually stick with just shoulders. In the kitchen, the shoulders are stripped of all fat and gristle. Everything else is ground. The meat is cooked on a pit with hickory wood. The pit is brick with a cover. The coals are shoveled from the firebox under the pit like most pit cooked barbecue operations.

Linda said they used to chop the meat by hand, but because they had older employees that had been with them for many years, they turned to a grinder to prevent the employees from getting carpal tunnel syndrome.

I found the barbecue products produced by Carolina Bar-B-Q to be mouth-watering good.

The chopped barbecue is sauced in the kitchen with the kitchen marinade. It has a good smoky flavor and is not chopped too fine to cause dryness. With either the Eastern Carolina sauce or the Lexington-style dip, it is delicious.

The sliced barbecue has a good, strong, smoky flavor. The outside brown gives it a good, rich nutty taste. It's very tender and moist, not at all dry. With the mild sauce ,it has a sweet smoky taste and with the hot sauce, it's soooo good!

Carolina Bar-B-Q has three different sauces – one for pork barbecue, one for barbecue ribs and one for barbecue chicken. They have an Eastern North Carolina-type sauce and a Lexington-style dip. The chicken is sauced in the kitchen. The barbecue only has marinade and you choose your sauce at the table.

The mild sauce is thick, brown, peppery and tomatoey with lots of spices. It tastes like more of an A-1 type sauce to my palate. The hot sauce is an Eastern North Carolina vinegar-pepper blend that was more to my liking. I tried both on all the meat and the hot sauce gets my vote.

Carolina Bar-B-Q has red and white slaw. I found the red slaw to be tangy, crunchy, crisp, moderately sweet and slightly tart. The white slaw had a good cabbage flavor – a hint of carrot gave it lightness and it does not compete.

Carolina Bar-B-Q also has a catering service called Carolina Catering and Entertainment. Linda shared some pictures of their catering gigs – beautiful spreads – ice sculptures, the whole bit.

Carolina Bar-B-Q lies in the southwest quadrant between I-40 West and I-77 South. From I-77 northbound, take Exit 49B (Salisbury Road). Turn right at the end of the exit ramp and a go a little more than a mile. Traveling from I-77 South, take Exit 49B. At the bottom of ramp, turn right and travel a little more than a mile. From I-40, take Exit 150 (Highway 21). Go to downtown, turn left on Main Street and travel several blocks to Front Street. Turn left onto Front Street, go several blocks and Carolina Bar-B-Q will be on the corner on the left. Can't miss it.

Carolina Bar-B-Q is open 10:30 a.m. to 9 p.m., Monday through Saturday. It's closed Sunday. Telephone number: (704) 873-5585.

Little Pigs Barbecue, Statesville

Little Pigs was originally a chain barbecue franchise that originated in Memphis. Fred and Faye Sears opened Little Pigs of Statesville in July 1963. Within a month or so, Fred and Faye's daughter Sherry, along with her husband Lynn Daniels, joined the operation. Lynn and Sherry continued operating the business after Fred died in 1977.

Little Pigs cooks over hickory wood and charcoal on pits. They cook only pork shoulders. It is served hand chopped, coarse chopped and sliced with sides of coleslaw, barbecue beans and hushpuppies.

The beans are good and served hot. The hushpuppies are made from scratch and are very good. They don't put sugar in their hushpuppies. The pups have a good crunch outside, a moist center and a good cornbread taste.

Little Pigs cooks its meat eight to 10 hours. Lynn does the cooking along with his son Ricky. They don't baste while cooking but do add sauce after cooking in the kitchen.

The sauce is tomato base with not a whole lot of vinegar. It is a bit thicker than the usual Lexington-style dip. It comes in three varieties: mild, hot and extra hot.

The chopped barbecue without sauce is smoky, tender, slightly moist and lean with a good rich flavor. Specks of outside brown are mixed throughout. It is not chopped too fine. The chopped with the mild sauce is slightly sweet and very mild with only a slight spicy taste. The chopped with the hot sauce is tangy while the reddish sauce imparts a rich taste with plenty of fire. The chopped barbecue with the extra hot sauce was too much sauce for the meat.

The coarse-chopped barbecue was densely chopped with large pieces. The good smoky flavor really shines. With the mild sauce, I found it kind of bland. With the hot sauce, it had a good, rich nutty taste. The coarse chopped with the hot sauce was my choice here.

The sliced barbecue without sauce was a bit dry for my taste. The meat was tender and had a good, light, smoky flavor. With the mild sauce, I found the sliced barbecue less than exciting. Stepping up to the hot sauce, the meat and sauce became a good combo. To my taste, the sliced barbecue with the extra hot was too much heat. The sliced meat does not absorb the sauce, therefore you get the sauce first. This proved to be overpowering to the meat. With the extra hot sauce, I couldn't taste the smoky flavor of any of the meat. Those who are from India or Thailand and are accustomed to hotter dishes may enjoy the extra hot sauce; it just wasn't my ticket to ride.

They also serve cheeseburgers, hamburgers and hot dogs for children and those who have not yet acquired the taste for the wonderful dish we call barbecue.

From I-40 West, take Exit 150 (Highway 21) and turn left under the bridge. Go three stoplights and you will be at a five-point intersection. Go straight through the intersection. A Food Fair is on your right. The Little Pigs sign is on the curb. Little Pigs is located behind the Food Fair. From I-40 East, take Exit 150, turn right and follow the same directions. Hours are 11 a.m. to 8 p.m., Monday through Thursday, and 11 a.m. until 9 p.m., Friday and Saturday. It's closed Sunday. Telephone number: (704) 872-3741.

Scotz BBQ and Diner, Taylorsville

Scotz BBQ and Diner in Taylorsville is a relatively newcomer to the barbecue scene having been in business only since 2000. However, Carol Scotz has worked in restaurants since she was 17. Owners Joe and Carol Scotz have made Scotz BBQ and Diner into the place to eat in Taylorsville.

Scotz chopped barbecue was very moist, moderately chopped and had a good pork flavor. The 'cue comes from the kitchen with a slight vinegar taste but it's not spicy. With the vinegar-base red sauce, the 'cue has a slightly spicy, slightly sweet taste even though it has no sugar. With the brown sauce (Cattleman's Smoky), the 'cue steps up a click. Cattleman's was my choice.

The sliced barbecue has a good, rich, roast pork taste. It is tender, moist and not dry at all. It has a slightly tangy barbecue flavor as it comes from the kitchen. It's a good choice and, to my taste, does not need added sauce.

Scotz homemade barbecue sauce is red and tangy with a pronounced vinegar taste accompanied with peppers and spices. It is very mild for its color and tastes best on the chopped barbecue.

Scotz brown sauce is Cattleman's Smoky barbecue sauce. It has that wonderful, rich, brown, twangy, Texas and Kansas City-type taste for which Cattleman's sauces are best known. The Cattleman's sauce is best on the sliced 'cue and almost as good on the chopped 'cue. Cattleman's sauce is better on sliced or pulled meat than it is on chopped meat. I find it a little heavy for finely chopped 'cue but wonderful with larger pieces of meat.

Joe Scotz said that he cooks only Lundy hams. These delicious pork products are cooked on a homemade wood-fired cooker that Joe refers to as a 20-ham cooker. Whatever he's doing, he's doing it right.

Scotz BBQ and Diner is located in downtown Taylorsville on Highway 90. The locals refer to it as being behind the old hotel. Turn northeast off the main drag on Main Avenue. Scotz BBQ and Diner is about 50 yards from Highway 90.

Hours are 10:30 a.m. until 8 p.m., Monday through Saturday. It's closed Sunday. Telephone number: (828) 632-8999.

Stamey's Barbecue, Tyro

Stamey's Barbecue in downtown Tyro is not a satellite restaurant of the Stamey's Barbecue giant in Greensboro. In fact, owners Dan and Nancy Stamey are not even related to the Greensboro Stameys.

Dan Stamey used to own Hog City in Lexington. He, along with many others, trained at the feet of some of Lexington-style barbecue's most noted figures. In 1973, Dan moved his barbecue operation to its present site in downtown Tyro and named it Stamey's Barbecue after his own surname.

The restaurant is not large, but has a warm atmosphere inside. Today, Dan "Scoot" Stamey, Jr. and Matt, Dan and Nancy's two sons, run Stamey's. The two young men oversee the pit cooking and daily management of the restaurant.

The Stamey brothers cook only shoulders. The pork and chicken is pit cooked over hickory wood on site. The meat is not basted while cooking but is sauced in the kitchen before serving.

The hand-chopped barbecue is medium coarse, very tender and very moist. It is sauced in the kitchen, you don't need any at the table. All of the shoulder is chopped and mixed together. It has a good smoky taste. A slightly tomatoey Lexington-style dip is a nice compliment. It's not hot but has a sub-tle zip that is more apparent in the finish.

The coarse chopped barbecue is very, very tender. The dip tastes a little more peppery on this barbecue and it was my favorite. The juicy red slaw with the coarse chopped barbecue is the perfect blend of texture and taste for me.

The dip tastes a little more peppery on the sliced barbecue, which I found to be tender with light smoky taste. The outside brown was the best. It has good flavor and is not mushy or too soft. When the smoky flavor of the outside brown kicks in, you have arrived.

The small, acorn-sized hushpuppies were good.

The red slaw is chopped medium coarse with a juicy, tart, vinegary and slightly peppery fresh taste. The white slaw is also chopped medium coarse and is fresh, crisp, slightly peppery and also very juicy.

In addition to barbecue pork and chicken, Stamey's Barbecue in downtown Tyro serves the usual drive-in selection of sandwiches, wings, vegetables and steaks and also seafood on Thursday, Friday and Saturday.

The desserts are pies, cakes, cobblers and, on occasion, I am told Nancy provides a homemade banana pudding.

While the brothers run the kitchen and overall operation, Scoot's wife oversees the staff. Nancy comes in from about five to 8 a.m. while Dan drops by when his hobbies permit.

This is a simply a good place to eat barbecue.

If you are traveling from Winston-Salem on Highway 150 toward I-85, Stamey's Barbecue is about two miles east on 150 after you cross Highway 64. It's on the right, two doors down from the Tyro United Methodist Church. Hours are 6:30 a.m. until 9 p.m., Monday through Saturday. It's closed Sunday. Telephone number: (336) 853-6426.

Smoky Mountain Barbecue, West Jefferson

Smoky Mountain Barbecue was started in West Jefferson in 1990. Byron Jordan and wife Nancy built a stick building on a mobile home frame because they knew they would have to move it. It was mostly a take-out place. They couldn't use the outside seating because they didn't have public restrooms. As business grew, Byron and Nancy realized they needed a larger place and that moving the old place was not the answer. Byron said that with some assistance from the bank, he and Nancy built the present building that is quite attractive, large, rustic and looks like it ought to be in the mountains.

Byron is from Lexington. He and Nancy got married in Raleigh and lived there for 14 years so Byron has been exposed to both Lexington-style and Eastern North Carolina- style barbecue. Byron chose to go with the Eastern North Carolina style. He cooks whole hogs with an Old Hickory cooker for 20-24 hours, depending upon how many pigs and what size they are. He chops the whole hog for his chopped barbecue.

The chopped barbecue pork is moderately coarse and comes sauced from the kitchen with good vinegar-base sauce with peppers. It has a good twangy taste. The red slaw makes for a great combo. With sugar-free slaw, it's a classic Eastern Carolina combo. With white slaw, it's also very good. This barbecue is very, very lean. Byron says they only get a 30 percent yield because they trim away all fat and gristle. Most barbecue places get a 55-60 percent yield.

The fried chicken has a crisp brown skin that is ever so slightly greasy and ever more than slightly delicious. The chicken is very tender, very juicy and cooked to the bone. This is good stuff – juicy, juicy, juicy, good, good, good.

The ribs are exceptionally tender with a good glaze. The pork taste is very good and it's cooked just right or, as they would say in this area, "jus rite." You will suck the bones and lick your fingers.

Byron has an Eastern North Carolina vinegar-base sauce that has a strong vinegar prominence and peppers, but it's not as hot as some Eastern Carolina sauces. He also has a rib sauce that is reddish brown, sweet and tangy. It's good on ribs and on chicken.

The golden brown hushpuppies have a nice strong cornbread flavor and go well with the meal.

Byron said that to be able to feed the locals something other than barbecue, he introduced fish in 1992 and served whiting. The people in the area were not used to whiting and were not ordering the fish very much. One day the food distributor mistakenly left a case of flounder. In order to have something to sell, Byron tried the flounder and the locals loved it. It has been on the menu ever since.

A few years ago, people started asking for ribs, so Byron introduced Danish baby-back ribs. Byron cooks them a special way to get them really tender and not too messy because a lot of his orders are carryout and people are eating in their cars. The ribs are very, very good.

Byron said that because they were cooking Eastern North Carolina-style pork, they used Eastern Carolina white slaw for many years. When Jefferson Landing Golf Course opened, there were a lot of people playing the course from the Charlotte and Piedmont area. They preferred red slaw, so Byron introduced a Lexington-style red slaw and now serves both white and red.

Byron thought he needed a winter soup. Coming from Raleigh, he introduced brunswick stew to the area. He said that for many years he could only sell it in the winter at the old location but at the new location he sells the brunswick stew year round.

Byron and Nancy have been at the present site at 1008 S. Jefferson Ave. since June 8, 1998.

Hours are 10 a.m. until 9 p.m., Monday through Thursday, and 10 a.m. until 10 p.m., Friday and Saturday. It's closed Sunday. Telephone number: (828) 246-6818.

Hill's Lexington Barbecue, Winston-Salem

Started by Joe Allen Hill in 1951, Hill's Lexington Barbecue in Winston-Salem is the first to have the name "Lexington Barbecue," thus their claim to being the "original" Lexington barbecue. At the time they opened, there were a few small side street barbecues in Lexington operated by Stamey, Beck and Swicegood. But none called their barbecue place "Lexington Barbecue."

Joe Hill, who came from Lexington, conceived the idea to bring Lexington-style barbecue cooking to Winston-Salem. Joe, along with his wife Edna, started the business on its present site. At the time, it was a drive-in restaurant like many others in the 1950s. But Hill's was different. The difference was Edna Hill. No one in the family contests that Edna's efforts and endless hours built this business. Her portrait is proudly displayed behind the cash register today. It was through her tireless efforts that Hill's acquired the reputation that causes the cash register to ring as often as it does.

Gene, Joe and Edna's son, ably assisted them. Gene grew up in Lexington and had been exposed to good barbecue since childhood. When Gene finished high school in 1950, he worked with his mom and dad. Like many children of prominent barbecue family businesses, Gene started at the bot-

tom. He hopped curb, cleaned and learned to cook, slice, chop and make the sauce. Gene also learned one of the important lessons of every good barbecue place. In addition to a good product, you need good service and the ability to remember names and make people feel welcome.

Gene Hill with fork and Terry K. Myers, Pit Master

Gene is a master. Gene is the "Toots Shors" of barbecue in this area.

During the late 1930s and World War II, probably the biggest name in barbecue in Winston-Salem was Paul Myers. Paul had a big barbecue business and, for various reasons, came to work with Joe and Edna to help start Hill's Lexington Barbecue. Gene said Paul's wife Virginia is still a regular customer at Hill's today.

Another asset to Hill's was a black cook named Joe Johnson. Gene said Joe Johnson knew more about food than any man he had ever known. Joe's banana pudding recipe is still used by Hill's Barbecue today. Gene remembers one time they ran out of yellow food coloring. Joe went out back, gathered some green walnuts and made a yellow food dye. Gene was impressed. Joe retired after 30 years in the business.

The method of cooking barbecue, the sauce and the banana pudding have not changed in 50 years.

Gene said that in the 1970s, the Forsyth County Environmental Department advised them that they did not want to see any visible smoke from the pits. In order to stay in business, Gene had to go to electric cookers. Gene said *The Winston-Salem Journal* ran an article about pit-cooked barbecue being imported from Davidson County and showed a cartoon of cars driving from Winston-Salem to Davidson for barbecue cooked over coals. Gene said that article really hurt his business. Eventually, the Environmental Department relaxed a bit and permitted cooking 40 percent over hardwood and 60 percent over electricity.

Today, Gene cooks the old style. The shoulders are cooked over live hickory coals from a firebox between the two pits. Once cooked, they are kept in electric cookers until the time they are needed to be converted by hand chopping into some of the best barbecue you will ever hope to eat.

Gene said that in the early 1950s when "Fuzzy" Nelson wanted to start a barbecue business in Madison, he came down and talked with Gene about how to proceed with this venture. Gene said he showed him the ropes and wished him well. Get Gene to tell you the story about Gene's barbecue dip recipe.

Gene shared that when Adam Scott of Goldsboro came to Winston-Salem at the request of RJ Reynolds, Jr. to be his personal barbecue cook, Adam had Gene cook his meat. Adam used his own sauce, he never used Gene's.

Now, Gene's son, Eugene S. Hill Jr., known by many as "J.R." or "Slugger," carries on most of Hill's day-to-day management. J.R. makes the sauce for the business today. It's another one of those closed-door things.

The sauce is hot, peppery, spicy, thin (Gene says it penetrates the meat better), light reddish brown and has strong finish by itself, but not so on meat. It just fits.

The chopped barbecue consists of generous pieces that are not basted while cooking. It's very lightly sauced in kitchen. It's a good mix of outside brown and has a good smoky taste, a rich flavor and nice texture. It's perfect with sauce and slaw.

Gene's second barbecue offering is pig pickin' barbecue. This consists of large two-finger pieces of meat pulled from the pig. It sooo tender and with sauce, oh my. It's smoky and tangy – you will think you have died and gone to heaven.

The sliced barbecue is full of flavor with a good smoky taste. It's some of the best barbecue you're apt to find. With the sauce, Gene says its better than a steak. I agree.

The red slaw is tart, tangy, peppery and slightly hot. It's got a good zing but not too much so. The white slaw is crisp, crunchy with some carrot and mayo. It holds together well and is good. The potato salad is also special.

The hushpuppies are made from scratch and will be the best you ever had, bar none.

Gene shared that he was the first to introduce barbecue salad to this area. In addition, he tried beef barbecue but Gene said that just didn't catch on as well.

For many years I have carried Gene's barbecue to Nebraska on my pheasant hunts and put on barbecue dinners for my farmer friends. It was only their attachment to their land, family, friends and some large bank notes that prevented a mass exodus from Ruskin, Nebraska to Winston-Salem, North Carolina.

Hill's Lexington Barbecue is located at 4005 North Patterson Ave. in Winston-Salem. On Highway 52 North from Winston-Salem, take Exit 114 and follow the signs. It's open daily 6 a.m. to 9 p.m. Telephone number: (336) 767-2184.

Little Richard's Bar-B-Que, Winston-Salem

Little Richard's Bar-B-Que on Country Club Road is the original Little Richard's Bar-B-Que as founded by Richard Berrier in 1991. There are other restaurants named Little Richard's Bar-B-Que in this area but they are not the same.

Richard Berrier has been in the barbecue business since he was 13 years old. To many in this area he is known as "Mr. Bar-B-Que." Richard's brother, Clint Berrier, manages the Little Richard's on Country Club. Clint oversees the cooking and the kitchen. Gail Shaw, a long-time

Clint Berrier and Gail Shaw

employee, mixes the sauce every morning.

The meat is cooked on site over pits with hickory wood. Clint only uses shoulders. The meat is hand chopped on a wooden block as in days of yore. I asked Clint if he knew how much meat he cooked daily and he replied, "*a biiiiggg pile*." The meat is not basted while cooking; the sauce goes on prior to serving. Clint's wonderful offerings are smoked all the way to the bone. Clint said he chose to cook only shoulders because they are juicy, tasty and don't dry out as quickly as hams. He said that Boston butts, though tasty, are too small to deal with for the volume that he produced. Clint said that hams are okay if you eat them as soon as they are ready or certainly within the day.

Little Richard's Bar-B-Que had a fire in the fall of 2000 and the business was closed for three months. They rebuilt and refurbished the building just the same as it was before the fire; they didn't change a thing. Clint said the net result of the fire was a cleaner attic.

In addition to chopped and sliced barbecue, Little Richard's offers the usual sides: potatoes, slaw, french fries, baked beans and onion rings. Little Richard's also has an extensive drive-in menu of sandwiches, from hamburgers to corn dogs. Little Richard's barbecues chicken on the weekends and is considering adding ribs on the first of the week.

The chopped barbecue is chopped to a medium consistency with outside brown meat mixed in with the regular meat. This blend produces a tender offering with a

152

good smoky taste. The outside brown kicks in to add even more flavor. The chopped barbecue is slightly moist and is delicious without sauce. With Richard's secret sauce added, it is stuff fit for kings.

The coarse-chopped barbecue was in good chunky-size pieces and was very tender and moist with a good smoky flavor. When sauced, you have a marriage made in heaven.

The sauce is thin and brown with a very tangy vinegary taste. It's peppery and slightly hot, but not too much so when applied to the meat. The sauce has tomato ketchup but does not taste of tomatoes. It is more like the consistency of Eastern North Carolina Sauce and despite the ketchup, it tastes different from Lexington-style dip. When I asked Clint if he would share some

of the basic ingredients in the sauce without divulging the recipe, he smiled that big smile of his and pointed to the label on the bottle. It reads: vinegar base with tomato ketchup, water, spices and salt. No secrets pass Clint's lips.

Little Richard's Bar-B-Que is located at 4885 Country Club Road in Winston-Salem. To reach Little Richard's, exit U.S. Highway 421 at the Jonestown Road exit and go east on Jonestown Road until it "T's" Country Club Road. Turn left onto Country Club Road and go down a long hill. Little Richard's is on the right just as you start up the next hill. Roll your window down and follow your nose. You can't miss it. Hours are 11 a.m. until 9 p.m., Monday through Saturday. It's closed Sunday. Telephone number: (336) 760-3457.

HAVE BEEN INFORMED THAT RESTAURANT
HAS CLOSED SINCE FIRST PRINTING OF BOOK

Hall's BBQ Restaurant, Yadkinville

The affable owner of Hall's BBQ Restaurant in Yadkinville is Governor Hobart Hall Jr. His father, Governor Vance Hall, was named after the North Carolina governor. Hobart, who is in his mid 70s, has been in the barbecue business for about 45 years. He originally started barbecuing in Wilkesboro where he sold barbecue at a tavern he ran. He had two other places in Yadkinville – Hall's Truckstop and Hall's Restaurant – before deciding to go into the barbecue business full time.

Hobart cooks the old-fashioned way on open pits with hickory wood. He cooks only shoulders but will cook hams on customer orders. He says that he separates the skin and fat from the shoulder and takes out the big muscle to serve sliced. This center part of the shoulder is placed in a container and cooled for two or three days. After it has cooled, it can be sliced just like a ham but is tastier and certainly less dry. Ham tends to dry quickly unless eaten immediately, Hobart said. He also cooks ribs about every other week. Hobart allowed that the country people in the area did not eat ribs as much as city folks.

Hobart's sauce is what he calls "Hall's Style." It is a thin, brown, vinegar-base sauce with a small amount of ketchup mixed with his own special spices.

His chopped barbecue is ground in a Hobart grinder (not named after the owner). Hobart only puts the meat through twice. It looks like moderately coarse hand-chopped 'cue. The pieces are large enough to have bite and taste. The chopped barbecue was very moist and sauced, but not too heavily, in the kitchen. The meat with sauce tastes smoky and vinegary with a mild spicy taste. The secret is that it has no tomato taste at all like most Lexington-style dips.

The sauce is thin like Eastern North Carolina sauces and is slightly sweet but mildly tangy. Hobart said he did not like to make the sauce too hot because a lot of people did not prefer it that way. He serves Texas Pete on the table for those who want to ratchet the sauce up a notch or two.

The sliced shoulder was very, very tender and moist. Sauced, it was slightly tangy. The sliced pork shoulder looked for all the world like ham, but tasted more tender and was much less dry than most barbecue hams.

The white slaw was tart with a good cabbage taste. Hobart says he makes his white slaw with red vinegar so the two do not compete. The red slaw is great. Hobart uses distilled white vinegar for his red slaw. He also adds tiny bits of carrot to the moderately chopped cabbage. If it is not the best red slaw I have ever eaten, it's certainly among the best.

Hobart gets his pigs from Orrells Packing House. He buys portion packs, which have a shelf life of approximately two weeks and generally are Lundy's and Smithfield brands. He serves his meals on china with real silver, no paper or plastic. He believes his food tastes better served in this manner.

With a twinkle in his eye, Hobart shared with me that he is Andy Griffith's first cousin. They are a month apart in age. He said that Andy was always eating hot dogs on the old *Matlock* television show. Hobart said if Andy ever ate one of his hot dogs, he would never eat any other.

Hobart's talents do not end with his skills at the barbecue pit. Hobart is an accomplished singer and sings with a gospel and country group called the Senior Chorus of Yadkin County. Hobart said that once, while at a meeting in Raleigh dealing with Gov. Jim Hunt's "Work First Welfare Program," the governor asked if anyone knew the words to "How Great Thou Art." Hobart did, and the governor asked him to lead the group in this song. Hobart sang the verses and the group sang the course. It was right after the Oklahoma bombing. Hobart said it was a very uplifting experience and that he is now the only man in Yadkin

County who has played the grand piano in the state Capitol building.

Despite being outside the town of Yadkinville, Hall's BBQ has been found by those going to and from the metropolitan areas to the mountains on U.S. 421. Hobart says that Wilber Scott, the CBS weatherman, stops by from time to time along with Billy Packer, the CBS sports announcer. Dolly Parton's bus, along with the buses of other noted country singers, have found the way to Hall's parking lot. In addition to being a frequent stopover for the autumn leaves traffic, Hall's is also on the bus tour list of places to go.

Hobart's small restaurant, which was closer to the road, burned about five years ago. Hobart moved his operation into a large cinder-block building behind his restaurant which had been used for automotive repair and welding. This building has been refurbished and made into the restaurant's present site. Its exterior is cinder block painted charcoal gray. The familiar black-and-white pig that stood in front of Hobart's old restaurant is still present to those passing on Highway 421.

Generally, there is gospel and bluegrass music on Friday and Saturday nights. It is a family atmosphere.

Hall's BBQ Restaurant is two and a half miles north of Yadkinville on the left and 26 miles south of Wilkesboro on the right. Hall's BBQ sits approximately half way between Winston-Salem and North Wilkesboro. The hours are 7 a.m. to 8 p.m., Monday through Thursday, and 7 a.m. to 9 p.m., Friday and Saturday. Telephone number: (336) 468-4449.

Notes

Notes

SECTION III

The Flatlands

Location

Ralph's Barbecue, Angier **1**

Henry James Barbecue, Asheboro **2**

Hop's Bar-B-Q, Asheboro- **3**

Hamilton's Barbecue, Biscoe **4**

Wells Pork Products, Burgaw **5**

Hursey's Barbecue, Burlington **6**

Bon's Bar-B-Q, Carrboro **7**

Williamson's Barbecue and Seafood, Chadbourn **8**

Allen & Son Barbecue, Chapel Hill **9**

Farmhouse Restaurant, Clinton **10**

Lewis Barbecue, Clinton **11**

Southern Style BBQ and Chicken, Clinton **12**

Ron's Barn, Coats **13**

Bob's Barbecue, Creedmoor **14**

Bud's Place, Cumnock **15**

Ernie's Barbecue, Dunn **16**

Bullock's Barbecue, Durham **17**

Fuller's BBQ, Elizabethtown **18**

Cape Fear Bar-B-Que and Chicken, Fayetteville **19**

Chason's Famous Buffet, Fayetteville **20**

Location

McCall's Barbecue and Seafood, Goldsboro **21**

Wilber's Barbecue, Goldsboro **22**

Stamey's Barbecue, Greensboro **23**

Evan's Famous Barbecue and Chicken, Henderson **24**

Gary's Barbecue, Henderson **25**

Nunnery-Freeman Barbecue, Henderson- **26**

Skipper's Forsyth Barbecue, Henderson **27**

Knightdale Seafood and BBQ, Knightdale **28**

Ken's Grill, LaGrange **29**

General McArthur's Original Pig Pickin', Laurinburg **30**

Howard's Barbecue, Lillington **31**

Fuller's BBQ, Lumberton **32**

Village Inn Barbecue, Lumberton **33**

A&M Grill, Mebane **34**

Eddie's Barbecue, Newton Grove **35**

Smithfield's Chicken 'n Bar-B-Q, Newton Grove **36**

Clyde Cooper's Barbeque, Raleigh **37**

Don Murray's Barbecue and Seafood, Raleigh **38**

Short Sugar's Drive-In, Reidsville **39**

Gardner's Barbecue, Rocky Mount **40**

Location

Bob Melton's Barbecue, Rocky Mount **41**

Ron's Barn BBQ and Seafood, Sanford **42**

Holt Lake Bar-B-Que and Seafood, Smithfield **43**

White Swan Restaurant, Smithfield **44**

John's Barbecue and Seafood, Southern Pines- **45**

Annette's Bar-B-Q Troy **46**

Bland's Barbecue, Wallace **47**

Cavenaugh's Family Supper House, Wallace **48**

Pink Supper House, Wallace **49**

Bland's Barbecue, Warsaw **50**

Ralph's Barbecue, Weldon **51**

Jordan's Barbecue, West End **52**

Joe's Barbecue Kitchen, Whiteville **53**

Sutton's Barbecue, Willow Springs **54**

Stephenson's Barbecue, Willow Springs **55**

Flip's Bar-B-Que, Wilmington **56**

Bill Ellis Barbecue, Wilson **57**

Cherry's Barbecue, Wilson **58**

Mitchell's Barbecue, Wilson **59**

Parker's Barbecue, Wilson **60**

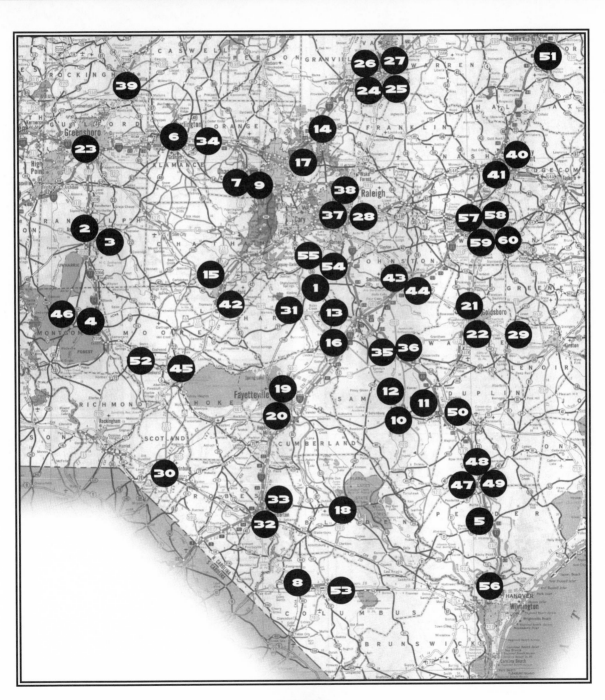

Ralph's Barbecue, Angier

This tiny barbecue establishment has been at its current site for more than 35 years. Chuck Griffen has owned it for the last six of those years. Ralph's barbecue looks like a barbecue place, smells like a barbecue place, it is a barbecue place. Ralph's serves barbecue pork, barbecue pork ribs, barbecue chicken and, for a change of pace, flounder on Friday. There's nothing fancy here, just a nice clean place to eat good barbecue if you are in the Angier community. If you are not, you may want to make an effort to make it happen.

Ralph's chopped barbecue is moderately chopped and comes sauced from the kitchen. It has a fiery Eastern North Carolina vinegar taste. It's plenty hot for me and doesn't need more sauce at the table. It's a good mix of brown and white that produces a rich pork flavor with a tart taste. Good stuff.

If you want to try the sauce, it is a reddish Eastern North Carolina vinegar-base sauce with red peppers and just the right amount of fire. The peppers perform a nice dance on a vinegar stage.

The hushpuppies have a light brown shell, are crisp outside, have a very moist center and have a really good cornbread taste. The slaw has that fresh and crunchy traditional taste of white cabbage with chips of pickle and a hint of sugar. It is a good accompaniment to the 'cue.

To reach Ralph's Barbecue from Highway 421 South, take Highway 210 North to Angier. At the intersection of Highway 55 and Highway 210, take Highway 55 West. Ralph's is located two miles west of Angier and about 100 yards into Wake County. Ralph's is housed in a small white building on the north side of the road. The sign is small also. Pay attention or you will blow by this one.

Hours are 10 a.m. until 8 p.m., Monday though Friday. It's closed weekends. Telephone number: (919) 639-2575.

Henry James Barbecue, Asheboro

James Shelton of Greensboro and his partner, Henry Rogers, began Henry James Barbecue in Asheboro in the mid-'70s. Later, the two opened another restaurant in High Point. Subsequently, they ended the partnership and James Shelton assumed ownership and management of the Asheboro place and Henry Rogers took over the High Point place. Being the "James" of Henry James Barbecue, James Shelton left the name the same.

James Shelton used to work at Warner Stamey's barbecue, where he learned his barbecuing skills. Ward Ireland, manager of Henry James Barbecue for the last 12 years, is from Toledo, Ohio. Ward, a graduate of Kurtz's National School of Meat Cutting of Toledo, came on board in August 1988. The combined skills of James Shelton and Ward Ireland have brought Henry James to the forefront of good barbecue in the Asheboro area.

Henry James cooks only Lundy pork shoulders. The shoulders are cooked electrically on a rotisserie cooker for eight hours and then are slow cooked in an electric warmer at 200 degrees for another 12 hours. Then this wonderfully slow-roasted pork is hand chopped and sauced with the house secret sauce.

The sauce from the kitchen has a mild vinegary taste with hints of black pepper. The sauce at the table is made of vinegar, ketchup, salt, red pepper, black pepper and spices.

The chopped barbecue pork has a coarse chop and a very good, fresh roast-pork taste. It is moist and lean with no fat. My serving was a bit over sauced from the kitchen for my taste; even so, it was good. With the sauce from the kitchen, the chopped barbecue has a mild vinegary taste with hints of black pepper.

The sliced barbecue pork was oh so tender and moist, not dry like most sliced pork. It was not moist from the sauce but from the cooking method. Sauced in the kitchen, it had a light vinegary taste with tangy peaks from peppers and spices in the sauce. You can taste the sauce more on the sliced than on the chopped from the kitchen. It has a very good roasted-pork flavor.

The barbecue beef ribs were equally tender and nicely cooked so that the meat almost fell off the bone. The ribs come sauced in the kitchen with a tomatoey, thick Kansas City-type sauce. It's mildly tangy, slightly sweet and has a good smoky flavor.

The brunswick stew consists of crushed tomatoes, corn, lima beans, peas,

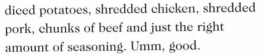
diced potatoes, shredded chicken, shredded pork, chunks of beef and just the right amount of seasoning. Umm, good.

The sauce at the table is a brown, vinegar-base sauce with more fire than the sauce from the kitchen. It is very good on the chopped and sliced 'cue.

The slaw is a red Lexington-style that is moderately fine chopped. It's very crunchy, tart, spicy – a good accompaniment to the 'cue.

The hushpuppies are light with a golden-brown outside and a moist inside. It's very good and not greasy.

Henry James Barbecue is located at 2004 South Fayetteville St. in Asheboro. To reach Henry James Barbecue, follow Route 220 business to Highway 64 East, turn right on Park Street (South Asheboro Middle School is on your left). Follow Park Street to Fayetteville Street, turn right onto Fayetteville Street and proceed a half mile. The restaurant is on the right. Hours are 11 a.m. to 9 p.m., Monday through Saturday. It's closed Sunday. Telephone number: (336) 625-1649.

Hop's Bar-B-Q, Asheboro

B.A. Hopkins opened Hop's Bar-B-Q in 1948 and ran the establishment for 32 years. Joe Turner took over the reins and ran it for the next 10 years. Joe was followed by Hop's present owners, Jerry and Lila Stouthard who have run the place for the past 11 years along with Kathy, Lila's sister.

Unless specially ordered, Hop's cooks only hams. This wonderful pork product is cooked on an electric rotisserie and hand chopped and sliced. The hams are cooked slowly at low temperatures for 12 hours. Jerry said that he does not chop ahead to prevent drying. The meat is pretty much chopped as ordered.

The chopped pork barbecue was very moist and very tender with a rich, slow-cooked pork flavor. The sliced barbecue was very moist and oh so tender. You could cut the sliced barbecue with a fork like a hot knife through butter.

The coarse chopped is like pulled chunks at a pig pickin'. These wonderful morsels are about the size of tennis balls. This stuff is so good you don't want to swallow. It's my favorite here.

The hushpuppies are the size of acorns and have a golden brown, crunchy outside and moist, cake-like inside with a hint of onion.

The slaw is an Eastern Carolina white cabbage variety with vinegar, sugar and salt. This slaw is very good, crisp and fresh. It is the perfect companion to the to delicious pork.

The sauce is Hop's original recipe, which is a hybrid Eastern Carolina/Lexington sauce. It is sweeter because Jerry only uses Hunt's Ketchup with his vinegar base and spices.

Located on the corner of Sunset and Church Streets in downtown Asheboro, Hop's is a small, gray stone building and looks like everything you would expect a classic '50s barbecue place to be.

To reach Hop's, follow Route 220 business to Highway 64 East and turn right on Park Street (South Asheboro Middle School is on your left). Follow Park Street to Fayetteville Street, turn left onto Fayetteville Street and proceed 1.3 miles to downtown Asheboro. Turn left onto Sunset Street, cross the railroad tracks and Hop's will be on your right at the intersection of Sunset and Church.

Hop's is open 6 a.m. until 6 p.m., Monday through Thursday, and 6 a.m. until 8 p.m., Friday. Hop's is open 6 a.m. until 3 p.m., Saturday. It's closed Sunday. Telephone number: (336) 625-2710.

170

Hamilton's Barbecue, Biscoe

Hamilton's Barbecue opened for business in 1990. It was the dream of Don Hamilton and his wife Phyllis. Don was born in Montgomery County and Phyllis was born in Smithfield. Don's parents used to cook at White Swan Barbecue in Smithfield. When Don's parents retired, they helped Lynwood Parker for awhile and Don picked up his barbecue skills from his parents.

Don cooks the barbecue pork. Phyllis, with a big smile and a wink, said she does everything else. When they first opened the business serving Eastern North Carolina barbecue and Eastern North Carolina vinegar-base sauce and white slaw in an area that was accustomed to Lexington-style barbecue, dip and slaw, people were slow to accept their offerings. Phyllis said that when they served the plate with the white slaw, people looked at it and said they did not order potato salad. She then watched with horror as people dumped ketchup over the barbecue. She said that she and Don thought they would have to close the doors. But, they're still here and have a good following. The locals have adapted well to a different style of barbecue.

Hamilton's cooks only shoulders electrically on a Nunnery-Freeman Kook Rite Kooker. The meat is ground on a Hobart chopper.

The chopped barbecue comes moderately coarse chopped and is basted when cooked. Nothing is added in the kitchen. It has a good Eastern North Carolina vinegar taste with enough flecks of red pepper peeking at you to be interesting. The meat has a good rich pork taste and a slightly nutty flavor, which is interesting, as it is not heavily smoked. The sauce on the moist white inside meat and brown outside meat mixed together produces a very pleasing treat.

The hushpuppies are a light golden color. They have a thin and crisp outside and a moist, almost cake-like inside and are so light they will float off your plate. People 20 miles away had already told me about the famous hushpuppies.

The slaw comes in two colors. The red is crisp with a fresh cabbage taste. It's finely chopped with pickles and carrots. This is a nice change of pace. It is not a Lexington slaw or an Eastern Carolina slaw. The yellow slaw has a good fresh cabbage taste complemented with tiny chips of carrot and pickle, vinegar and spices. The addition of mustard creates a really good Eastern Carolina slaw with a twist.

The sauce is vinegar, red and black pepper, spices, no tomatoes or ketchup or tomato puree. It is not a Lexington-style dip.

171

This sauce without meat is fiery – lots of pepper. On the 'cue, it calms down and behaves. You don't need much added at the table unless you want to risk cauterizing your taste buds.

To reach Hamilton's Barbecue from Highway 220, take the Highway 24/27 exit toward Biscoe/Troy. Hamilton's is about two miles from the only stoplight in Biscoe on the left. It is a brownish building and looks like a barbecue place. Hours are 6 a.m. until 3 p.m., Monday, and 6 a.m. until 8:30 p.m., Tuesday through Saturday. It's closed Sunday. Telephone number: (910) 458-9730.

Wells Pork Products, Burgaw

After talking to a half dozen or more locals in and around Burgaw, I was advised that there are no restaurants in that area that still cooked their own barbecue and made their own sauces. They don't need to. Wells Pork Products does it for them. If you approach Burgaw from any direction and do not see a Wells Pork Products billboard or large sign, you should not be on the road driving. They are everywhere.

Legendary pork producer Earl Wells has been marketing pork products in this area for more than 20 years. Earl buys and processes hogs. He owns a slaughterhouse, processing plant and state-of-the-art facilities for processing pork products into every type desired by man, including barbecue. Earl processes 500-600 hogs per week. Wells Pork Products processes every thing about a hog but the oink. Pork can be bought fresh, cured or smoked, and they make delicious barbecue on-site.

Barbecue pork can be purchased in bulk at Wells Pork Products Store. Though Wells Pork Products is not a restaurant, it will heat your barbecue for you. In addition to delicious chopped barbecue, Wells has its own line of sauces that can be purchased at the store. Scott Wells, son of the owner and manager, says for catering events they will barbecue and serve the whole hog, pig pickin' style.

Wells does not serve sliced barbecue. They chop the whole hog for their delicious 'cue. It is moderately course and sauced in the kitchen with a good hot Eastern North Carolina sauce. This delicious barbecue has lots of outside brown mixed with the white. It has a great slow-roasted pork flavor and is pleasantly chewy.

Wells Pork Products makes a number of their own sauces. Pick your favorite. The sauces range from Eastern North Carolina vinegar-base sauce with red pepper spices to a ribs and chicken sauce that is tomato base and much thicker. The Wells Pork Products Retail Store is an emporium of all the best "other white meat" products. If you want it and a hog can grow it, you can find it here. This is a Pork Palace. Pig out!

Hours are 7:30 a.m. until 5:30 p.m., Tuesday through Friday, and 6:30 a.m. until 4 p.m., Saturday. It's closed Sunday. Telephone number: (910) 259-2523.

Hursey's Barbecue, Burlington

Charles Hursey started the present Hursey's Barbecue in 1960. While Charles is still prominent on the scene, a large part of the management has been turned over to Charles' two sons, Chuck and Chris. Their mother Ellen and sister Carey ably assist the two sons.

Charles Hursey's grandfather started the Hursey men in the direction of cooking hogs many years ago. It was originally a hobby and part of festive occasions for the family.

Golden Chicken Award 1993

Charles' father, Sylvester, whom everyone I met described as a "character," learned to cook hogs from his father as a child. The hog cooking remained pretty much a family event until Sylvester reached his 30s. Most in the area have heard the stories of the party that Sylvester and some of his friends had in the backyard, at which time a little drinking and some coincidental successful hog cooking launched Sylvester into the commercial barbecue business.

From a meager beginning of a little tin building in the backyard and a recipe given him by his father, Sylvester founded Hursey's Barbecue. His production was not enormous: one hog per week. It was about this time, as the story goes, that Sylvester won a competitor's barbecue sauce recipe in a poker game. Sylvester combined the competitor's sauce with his father's and created the present day Hursey sauce.

The sauce as served on the chopped barbecue and sliced ham is a very tasty blend between the Eastern North Carolina vinegar-base sauce and the Lexington-style (sugar, tomato-added) dip. This sauce is used for cooking and basting. A sauce at the table, which leans more toward the Lexington-style dip, is for customers who want more. The sauce at the table sticks on meat better but Chris said they use a different type in the kitchen. Only Charles Hursey and his sons know the ingredients for the secret sauce. An employee knows part of the recipe. He mixes his part and one of the Hurseys adds the other part after he is gone. It's one of those "lock the doors, pull down the shades and put out the dog" operations.

The big, white Hursey's Barbecue trucks have emblazoned on their sides,

"Hursey's National Award-Winning Barbecue." The Hursey family has every right to be proud of their barbecue. It won them the 1984 North Carolina/ South Carolina cook-off competition in Washington, D.C. The barbecue is shipped to all 50 states and several foreign countries. It brings people from Greensboro, Lexington, Raleigh, Durham and even one couple from West Virginia.

Hursey's secret sauce, applied to the hams and shoulders from Hursey's pit, has been the delight of Lyndon B. Johnson, Ronald Reagan, Bill Clinton and George Bush Sr., as well as Sen. Jesse Helms and Gov. Jim Hunt. Other celebrities, such as the Harlem Globetrotters and numerous show-business personalities, also have enjoyed barbecue at Hursey's. The sons said with pride that their barbecue was one of Dale Earnhardt's favorite meals.

Hursey's Barbecue is such a draw that people from distant places come in, eat, and leave unannounced only to be realized when the Hurseys receive a letter. Such is the case with a U.S. Congresswoman from New York. This gives the family immense pleasure to know that their product is enjoyed by so many in so many different walks of life.

The two sons were equally proud of having won the Golden Chicken Award in 1993, which is the national award for the best "broasted" chicken in the nation. I have eaten broasted chicken at various truck stops across the country in my travels. It always appeared to be a battered piece of chicken that had been dropped into a deep fat fryer in the same grease that had cooked french fries, battered shrimp and any other frozen foods that had come out of a cardboard box. I was not impressed. To me, good fried chicken was something that was done with fatback drippings or Jewel lard in a black iron skillet on the stove. The Hursey broasted chicken is, in fact, fried chicken cooked in a pressure cooker that keeps it from getting as greasy as chicken fried in a pan. Though skeptical, I tried it. I stand a convert. Hursey's broasted chicken is absolutely delicious. It does not taste as greasy as fried chicken, but still has the flavor that good fried chicken imparts. Hursey's sells up to 3,500 pounds of chicken per week. Chuck told me that their supplier told him that they cook and sell more chicken than their local nationally known chicken-cooking competitor.

Hursey's cooks about 200 pork shoulders, or 3,000 pounds, per week at its downtown location. Their wholesale operation cooks about 8,000 pounds per week.

I found their chopped barbecue to be medium coarse, slightly sweet, slightly peppery, slightly vinegary with an Eastern North Carolina taste. It has a slightly hot taste, but not too much so. It is tender, moist and sauced just right. It is very, very good – one of the very best.

The sliced ham was very moist and not overcooked, as you sometimes find. It was slightly peppery and absolutely wonderful with Hursey's original sauce.

The meat is cooked over open pits with approximately 75 percent hickory wood and 25 percent oak. They cook about 80 percent shoulders and mix with 20 percent ham.

The coleslaw is white, crisp, crunchy and juicy with light mayo. It's good stuff. The baked beans are slightly sweet with a slight tomato taste, a hint of chili powder, onions and mustard. The onion rings are good. The brunswick stew is good and meaty with tomatoes, lima beans, chicken, a little beef and a little pork. Chuck said the customers wanted it thinner, so they made it thinner than he likes.

Cooking meat slowly over coals is long, hard and tedious work and has pretty much been the domain of men. I was pleased to learn that Hursey's had employed the only woman that I have yet encountered in North Carolina that worked with the men at the firebox and the pits. Leola, a black lady, started working with Sylvester Hursey

and remained with the business at the pits for many years. Chuck Hursey said that Leola was fiercely independent and very proud of what she did and wouldn't let anyone touch her shovel.

It is this kind of employee and old-school work ethics, passion and the fierce pride of doing something the best it can be done that has enabled Charles Hursey to pass on to his sons a benchmark barbecue operation.

Charles and his brother Larry are partners in the wholesale side of the business. Larry's son Kent serves as general manager. This operation is about five miles north of Burlington on Highway 87. There is also a Hursey's Barbecue satellite store on Highway 87, which is much smaller than the downtown location but serves the same good food.

To reach Hursey's Barbecue from Interstate 85/40, take exit for N.C. Highway 62. Follow Highway 62 (also called Alamance Rd.) north to its intersection with U.S. Highway 70 (South Church St.). Hursey's is on the left. Hours are 11 a.m. until 9 p.m., Monday through Saturday. It's closed Sunday. Telephone number: (336) 226-1694.

Bon's Bar-B-Q, Carrboro

The front of the menu reads "Food with an Attitude." Of course it does, this is Tar Heel country, home to the Sultans of Strut. Everything in the Chapel Hill area has a little "attitude." Bon's Bar-B-Q, nestled in little Carrboro, a suburb of "blue heaven," is no exception.

The tall lady that gives Bon's wonderful morsels its "attitude" is Julia Smith, daughter of Mildred Council (the legendary Mama Dip of Chapel Hill). Julia has been cooking since age 7 when she helped her mama fry chicken and box it to go, long before there was a KFC. Now, approaching 50, Smith has her own place in Bon's Bar-B-Q.

"Bon" is what family, friends and customers call Julia. Mama Dip used to call Julia by her middle name, Yvonne. Her brothers and sisters could not pronounce it, so they called her Bon and it has been Bon ever since. Bon's mother got her nickname "Mama Dip" because she too was tall, had long arms and could reach down into the barrel with a dipper to get water when the other siblings could not.

It seems all of Bon's family has been in the food business in one way or another. Her grandfather ran a barbecue place called Bill's Barbecue in the 1960s. One of his specialties was a "Stack Burger" which was two hamburgers sandwiched in between three slices of bread with 1000 Island dressing. Sound familiar?

Bon worked with her mother until approximately age 22. Since then she has worked on her own. She ran her grandfather's place for a year and a half. Eighteen of the past 20 years she worked at one of the UNC fraternities, Pi Kappa Alpha, as a cook and housemother. In the summertime, she ran a sandwich shop. She realized her dream on Oct. 16, 1999 when she opened Bon's Bar-B-Q.

When Bon cooked for Pi Kappa Alpha, she often fed 500-600 people on a home football weekend. She also fixed barbecue for others. Bon said people liked her barbecue. They still do. Bon now cooks and sells 600-700 pounds of barbecue per week. Bon's barbecue has been voted Best Barbecue in the Triangle. Bon is equally proud of her string of 100 percent sanitation ratings from the Orange County Environmental Health Department. Several quarters she got 102 percent, getting extra points for putting on safety classes for her kitchen.

Bon goes pedal-to-the-metal 16 hours a day. In addition to her restaurant, she spends many of her discretionary hours on the Chapel Hill Community Cuisine

Committee. This is a group of food people who help those who have fallen on hard times to find jobs in the food business. These Good Samaritan restaurant folks teach the various aspects of the restaurant business to nonfood people. Some of the people that take these courses have been on drugs and/or alcohol. Many turn their lives around. Every three months the committee puts on a fundraiser to help fund the efforts. The committee teaches people coming out of jail or halfway houses how to dress, interview and prepare food. It teaches them the needed skills that will enable them to get a job in the food business and have a second chance. Bon also teaches high school students the food business so they can have a good skill base and be able to get a job anywhere in the country.

Never one to follow the main stream, Bon cooks her scrumptious barbecue in a convection oven and then removes all fat, gristle and skin. The wonderfully slow-roasted pork is then chopped by hand. Bon said they usually cook the meat four and a half hours at 325 degrees.

I find it incredible that Bon, who has been a vegetarian for 30 years, cooks barbecue. She makes her own sauce, seasons her barbecue and produces an excellent product that she has never tasted. She relies on those she trusts to tell her what tweaking needs to be done, and then she does it. The

steady stream of customers and the continuous bouquets thrown by food critics say she must be doing something right.

The chopped barbecue pork at Bon's is a moderately fine chop, moist, nutty flavored and sauced in the kitchen. Bon's barbecue pork tastes more like Lexington style than Eastern Carolina, but is different from any other Lexington style that I have eaten. The lean, slow-roasted pork shines and the light sauce makes it into a gastronomical delight. There's no fire here – it's slightly sweet and rich. Bon's barbecue is different and delicious.

The sauce is vinegar, ketchup, Worcestershire, mustard, sugar, water, seasoning salt and a bit of Texas Pete. Bon said she did not use peppers as most Eastern North Carolina sauces have because a lot of her customers bring their children and she did not want her barbecue to be too hot for the children to enjoy. Bon is planning a "baby wall" for her customers' new babies. Bon calls her customers "guests." She says that she spends 16 hours a day at the restaurant. It's like her home and she prefers to think of the people who go there as her guests. Big on family, Bon's walls are covered with family pictures of Bon, Mama Dip, Bon's husband Milton, brothers, sisters, nieces, nephews, etc.

Another crowd favorite at Bon's is the hushpuppies. These wonderful golden nuggets melt in your mouth. This is hushpuppy perfection. Trailing cornbread taste gives a first impression that this is not a hushpuppy. It is light as a feather, not greasy or heavy. It's positively wonderful. Many people refer to Bon's as "hushpuppy heaven," she said. Some of her customers come just to eat the hushpuppies.

The slaw at Bon's is fresh (as you might expect from a vegetarian) with finely chopped cabbage, tiny slivers of carrot, light, light mayo. It is juicy and delicious – the freshest tasting slaw ever.

Bon's brunswick stew contains tomatoes, corn, butter beans and lots of chicken and pork. It is spiced just right and has that wonderful blend that creates a unique fla-

vor. It's a composite of its parts, the benchmark of a good brunswick stew.

In addition to barbecue pork, Bon's serves delicious barbecue chicken, pulled chicken, sliced barbecue beef, babyback ribs, pork chops, fresh fish and shrimp, brunswick stew, 15 sides and eight desserts including banana pudding. The sandwiches at Bon's are named after her family members. Check out Milton's Favorite and Roy Roy.

Bon's Bar-B-Q is located in the Carrboro Plaza Shopping Center on Highway 54 in Carrboro. Hours are 11 a.m. until 9 p.m., Monday through Saturday, and 12 p.m. until 8 p.m., Sunday. Telephone number: (919) 960-7630.

Williamson's Barbecue and Seafood, Chadbourn

Chadbourn is the home of the North Carolina Strawberry Festival. Its other claim to fame is Williamson's Barbecue and Seafood. Williamson's, as is the practice in this area of the state, serves a combination of barbecue, seafood and country vegetable buffet.

Owner Kurt Williamson, who had no history in barbecue whatsoever, built at the present site 16 years ago. He said he felt cooking barbecue was his calling. It was. This is a family-run affair with Kurt's son, daughter-in-law and granddaughter all working there.

Williamson's Barbecue and Seafood serves barbecue pork, barbecue pork ribs, fried chicken, a host of seafood and 19 different sandwiches. It is well worth the two-mile trek off of Highway 74 to sample their delicious fare.

Williamson's cooks shoulders and hams with gas. The sliced barbecue comes from shoulders and hams, not just hams alone. The chopped is a mixture of hams and shoulders. The chopped is ground with a Hobart chopper.

The chopped barbecue is moderately fine and very moist with a good roast-pork flavor. It is sauced in the kitchen and is a nice ham and shoulder mix that gives the barbecue a nice flavor and a fine texture.

The 'cue needs a little added house barbecue sauce at the table because it is only lightly sauced in the kitchen. Because the house barbecue sauce is not a fiery as most, you may wish to add a few drops of Texas Pete if you want a bit hotter taste. That was the ticket for me.

The sliced barbecue pork has a rich, roasted-pork flavor and is moist. It's so tender you can flake it with a fork. This is ham at its best. Chunks are as big as pulled pieces at a pig pickin'. Add a little house sauce at the table to make it sing. Hot sauce is too much on this offering.

The white cabbage slaw has a fresh taste that is just good Eastern North Carolina slaw. This slaw has light mayo and no pickles, carrots or onions. It complements the 'cue.

The hushpuppies are light and airy, almost a cake-like texture. The pups have a golden skin with a little tail and have a slightly sweet, moist center.

Vinegar and Worcestershire Sauce highlight the red sauce. It also has soy sauce but no peppers. It is moderately hot and tangy with lots of zip but no lasting aftertaste.

From U.S. Highway 74 South, take the Chadbourn exit (Business 74). Go two miles and cross U.S. Highway 64. Williamson's

Barbecue and Seafood is on the immediate left.

Williamson's is open 9 a.m. until 8 p.m., Monday through Thursday, 9 a.m.

until 9 p.m., Friday and Saturday. It's open 9 a.m. until 2 p.m. on Sunday. Telephone number: (910) 654-3106.

Allen & Son Barbecue, Chapel Hill

Allen & Son looks like a barbecue place. It has vinyl tile flooring, wooden tables, checkered oilcloth table-cloths and slat back chairs. Keith Allen is a hunter and the walls are covered with pictures of ducks, pheasants and intermittently a stuffed large mouth bass or two. The walls are painted cinder block and paneling. This place has the right feel.

A walk out back quickly tells you that this is a "serious" barbecue place. Large brick barbecue pits on either side of a sizeable firebox billow with gray smoke and good smells. Outside, whole hickory logs await the chain saw and a splitting maul. Keith Allen still does this Paul Bunyan-thing himself. There are few Eastern North Carolina-style barbecues still using wood or charcoal. Allen & Son is the only place that I know of that splits its own wood.

In 2001, Allen & Son catered the pig pickin' for my daughter and son-in-law's rehearsal dinner in Chapel Hill. Both daughter and son-in-law attended UNC- Chapel Hill for four years. Each had exposure to lots of good barbecue in the area. Allen & Son was the restaurant of choice for their special occasion. Need I say more?

The barbecue only comes chopped. It has a tangy, rich, brown taste with smoky overtones. The outside brown mixed in gives it a great flavor and more body. Sauced at the smokehouse, none is added in the kitchen. This rich (not fat) tasting 'cue has a wonderful peppery taste and good zip without adding sauce at the table.

The sauce at the table is a thin, reddish, vinegary, spicy blend that imparts tartness. The peppers bring on the heat when tasted alone. On the 'cue, it is the perfect combination. The slow smoked over live coals barbecue and the tart, peppery, vinegar-base sauce really do the tango.

The slaw was slightly tart with vinegar and pepper and a good fresh taste of cabbage. It is not overwhelmed with spices or mayo. It's good.

The hushpuppies were slightly over-cooked and slightly greasy.

The barbecue chicken was also good.

Tomato, vinegar and pepper flavors leap up. You can see black pepper. It's hot and tasty, but not as impressive as the pork barbecue.

Pork barbecue, barbecue chicken, brunswick stew, flounder, shrimp and catfish round out the entrees. There are the usual sides plus fried okra. There are 11 sandwiches of choice.

The desserts are homemade pies and cakes, cobblers, bread pudding and homemade ice cream. The bread pudding was the one chosen by my waitress as her dessert of choice. It is rich with lots of raisins and a brandy taste. It was flavorful but kind of dry. Keeping it covered airtight and some kind of sauce would kick it over the top.

Six large vans and as many large portable cookers let you know that Allen & Son are into barbecue catering in a big way. The vans have Allen & Son and a coy girl pig on the side.

Allen & Son is on Route 2 in Chapel Hill. It is located one and a half miles north on Highway 86 from I-40. You will find Allen & Son Barbecue on the left, tucked back in the woods. You will see a Farmhouse Restaurant sign before you see the Allen & Son sign. It's a good stop!

Allen & Son is open at 7 a.m. for breakfast on Saturday. Hours are 10 a.m. until 8 p.m. Tuesday through Friday. It's closed Sunday and Monday. Telephone number: (919) 942-7576.

Farmhouse Restaurant, Clinton

The Farmhouse Restaurant sits about six miles east of Spivey's Corner. This appears to be just about the right distance to enjoy wonderful cooking and not be disturbed by the National Hollering Contest in Spivey's Corner the 3rd Saturday in June of each year.

The owner of the Farmhouse Restaurant is James R. Van, a nicer man you will never meet. Helen, his wife, ably assists him. James is a member of the Dunn Clowns, Sudan Temple, A.A.O.N.M.S. and the Southeastern Clown Association. When in paint and costume, James is a sad sack hobo named "Robin." Get James to show you the pictures.

In the '60s and early '70s, James was running a truck stop across the road that was a fueling station for the Highway 421 traffic. Heeding the pleas of truckers and others to build them a place to eat in this area, James took bit in teeth and built the present Farmhouse Restaurant in 1973. It opened on Mother's Day. James said he just built a big restaurant out in the country and started cookin' and servin'. Word spread and they came. The restaurant seats 550 people and, on many occasions, this is not enough.

The pork shoulders are cooked electrically for 12 hours at 200 degrees and then are hand chopped. They do not slice. The meat is not basted while cooking but is sauced in the kitchen.

The sauce is an Eastern North Carolina vinegar-base sauce with a little ketchup, no sugar, salt, dried mustard, lemon juice and pepper seeds.

The chopped barbecue is VERY moist and has a good mix of outside brown and inside white. The vinegar taste is fiery enough to make your taste buds burst. It's just delicious 'cue. It's moderately chopped with enough tartness and zip to make this a very interesting barbecue.

The moderately chopped slaw is white and green cabbage parts with tiny carrot bits and light mayo. It's a nice mix and a very good slaw.

The hushpuppies are moderately large pups with a delicate, gold shell and a moist cake-like inside.

All of this is surrounded by a multitude of other good country food offerings that is crowned by a fresh coconut cake that has been made by the same lady for 300 years. I am not a dessert fan but, at James' insistence, I tried the coconut cake. Right there in his presence, I unashamedly asked for her hand in marriage.

Farmhouse Restaurant is located on Highway 421, 12 miles west of Clinton and

LOCATION
10

17 miles from Dunn (I-95) or for hollering fans, six miles east of Spivey's Corner. Hours are 4:30 p.m. until 9 p.m., Thursday, Friday and Saturday, and 11 a.m. until 2 p.m., Sunday. It's closed Monday, Tuesday and Wednesday. Telephone number: (910) 564-6250.

185

Lewis Barbecue, Clinton

Lewis Barbecue is located on Highway 701 on the northern skirts of Clinton. This small, gray cinder-block building located on the west side of the road, houses the only purely barbecue place in this area.

Founded by Rooster and Doris Lewis on June 11, 1948, this tiny barbecue treasure has constantly produced wonderful barbecue. A dozen or so years ago, Samson County started a "Samson's Best." Rooster and Doris' creation has been voted the best barbecue in Samson County for the past 12 years. The business is now owned by their son Jimmie and is managed by Barbara Mattocks.

This scrumptious roast pork (shoulders) is slowly cooked on a Nunnery Freeman Kook Rite Kooker and hand chopped with lamb spreaders. Jimmie said that with the volume and the hand chopping, he wears out two chopping-block tables a year.

The chopped barbecue is served moderately coarse chopped and sauced at the kitchen. It has a good Eastern North Carolina vinegar-base taste with red pepper flakes throughout. It is mildly hot and has a tangy taste with a good finish. You know you've had some good 'cue. The taste does not linger too long to be unpleasant but it does have a strong finish. It is very, very moist from the cooking method, not from the sauce. It's slightly greasy, but not too much so. I like it!

The golden-brown hushpuppies are light with a delicate skin and a good, moist cornbread center.

The slaw is a white cabbage, Eastern North Carolina type that is fresh and crunchy with light mayo. It goes well with the 'cue.

Lewis Barbecue is located on Highway 701, just north of Clinton on the west side of the road. Hours are 11 a.m. until 2 p.m., Tuesday and Wednesday, and 11 a.m. until 8 p.m., Thursday, Friday and Saturday. It's closed Sunday and Monday. Telephone number: (910) 592-3215.

Southern Style BBQ and Chicken, Clinton

The founder of the business is George Monroe, a former pork producer. Samantha Dipento, his daughter, said that about 12 years ago, the government paid George and a few others to stop raising hogs. George suddenly found himself fairly well off, retired and holding a golden parachute. George decided to cook and sell what he had formerly fed and tendered (pigs).

Southern Style BBQ and Chicken, Inc. started in March 1989. At this time, Samantha (Sam) had just graduated from college with a degree in education. Instead of teaching children about the three little pigs, Sam decided to help her father cook and serve them. Armed with ambition and Raymond Bedsole's (Barbecue Hut fame) sauce recipe, George and Sam set out on their new venture. It proved to be a good move for both.

As I sat talking to Sam, cars pulled over to the side of the road to exit into Southern Style BBQ and Chicken and pass by the take-out window. This steady stream of traffic never stopped while I was there and they were still cued up when I left. Sam said it was like this all the time. A good product gets good business.

Southern Style BBQ and Chicken has been voted the best fried chicken in Samson County for the past dozen years and the runner-up in barbecue for the same period.

Southern Style cooks whole hogs with gas. Then, this nice pork product is carefully hand pulled and hand chopped.

The sauce consists of vinegar, brown sugar, Worcestershire, lemon, hot sauce but no peppers.

The chopped barbecue pork comes in good meaty pieces. It's slightly tart with a mild vinegar taste. The good outside brown and inside white mix produces a wonderful pork flavor and good texture. The outside brown gives it a rich, woodsy taste. This 'cue is moist and lean with no fat and gristle. Sam said they went to extra lengths to hand pull the meat and separate all fat and gristle before chopping the pork. She said this is what their customers wanted and expected, and this is what they got.

The fried chicken is the best damn chicken you ever tasted. The crisp outside brown skin is not hard or overcooked. It has moist beads of juice and the inside is perfectly cooked to the bone. Slightly salty, it tastes like fat back drippings – mmm, good.

The golden hushpuppies have a thin shell and a light, cake-like inside with a good cornbread taste.

The slaw is good Eastern North

187

Carolina white coleslaw that tastes good with the chopped 'cue. The slaw consists of crisp cabbage, flecks of pickle and light mayo. It's not too runny.

From Highway 701 in Clinton, turn left on Highway 24 West and Southern Style BBQ and Chicken is on your left. Hours are 11 a.m. until 8 p.m., Monday through Saturday. It's closed Sunday. Telephone number: (910) 592-6212.

Ron's Barn,
Coats

Take 50 Jolly Green Giant helicopters, attach to Ron's Barn in Sanford, lift gently, move eastward and set lightly on the side of the road five miles east of Angier. You have just produced Ron's Barn in Coats.

The menu at Ron's Barn in Coats, like the exterior and interior of the building, is pretty much like Ron's Barn in Sanford.

Ron's Barn is on Highway 55 East, just outside of Coats and about five miles east of Angier on the right, corner of Highway 55 and Pig Out Lane. Hours are 5 p.m. until 9 p.m., Thursday through Saturday, and 11 a.m. until 2 p.m., Sunday. It's closed Monday, Tuesday and Wednesday. Telephone number: (910) 897-6750

Bob's Barbecue, Creedmoor

Many years ago, Bob Whitt, founder of Bob's Barbecue, had a little building behind his house not much bigger than a one-car garage that seated 25 or 30 people. Bob cooked barbecue in his backyard and sold it in his little building. Eventually the food business lured Bob away from his job as a deputy sheriff for Person County. Bob ran a barbecue place in Roxboro for 14 years. In 1970 Nita, Bob Whitt's only child and her husband Robert J. Whitfield opened Bob's Barbecue at its present site. Nita ran the business as general manager for many years.

Paula Whitfield Ellington and Carla Whitfield Mangum, twin daughters of Nita and her husband, bought the business from their parents in 1996. Paula is a former real estate broker and Carla, who has a master's in education, is a former schoolteacher.

Louise Blevins, an employee for more than 25 years, still makes all of the pies except the sweet potato pie. Ruby Goss makes the sweet potato pie. Mary Chappell has been manager for Bob's Barbecue for 27 years.

The barbecue is cooked on Nunnery Freeman electric cookers.

I found the chopped barbecue, sauced in the kitchen, to be very good. It had a rich spicy taste that came on strong at the finish. It is medium chopped, slightly dry and plenty peppery. I would prefer it a bit more moist.

The mild sauce without meat will open your sinuses. The reddish sauce has a strong vinegar and pepper taste with just the right amount of spices. The hot sauce with crushed red peppers and spices really had some heat. This one by itself will create perspiration under your eyes. It's really good stuff. On the 'cue, the hot sauce was my choice over the mild. Paula said that normally the mild was golden in color and the hot red in color, but not always. I could not see any difference in color and neither bottle was labeled. I suggest you taste first.

The lightly golden hushpuppies were tender and moist with a good cornbread taste. The pups were slightly greasy, but good nonetheless.

The white slaw was finely chopped and ever so slightly sweet. It is juicy, has no carrots and is not heavy on mayo.

The brunswick stew is thick and contains pork, beef and chicken in addition to potatoes, tomatoes, lima beans, corn and a bit of onion. It has a rich, slightly tomatoey taste with plenty of meat. It holds together nicely. It has the right amount of spices for a middle-of-the-road brunswick stew taste. A few drops of Texas Pete hot sauce makes this dish sing.

To get to Bob's, take Exit 191 off I-85 North and turn right at the top of the ramp. It's less than half a mile on the left. Going south on I-85, take Exit 191, turn left and

Bob's is less than half a mile on the left.

Hours are 10 a.m. to 8 p.m., Monday through Saturday. It's closed Sunday. Telephone number: (919) 528-2081.

Bud's Place, Cumnock

A hundred years ago Cumnock was a coal-mining area in Lee County. One of the big mines was the Egypt Coal Mine. Another large company operating at the time was Enden Iron Works. John Kennedy of Cumnock operated the Old Egypt Mines Store, a sort of general store for the miners. Mules were used to pull the carts in the coal mines. The mules would go blind. In the 1920's an act was passed requiring that the mules be taken out at night.

There is a poem written about this area that goes like this:

*Fifty-five men rode down the track
and only two of them came back.
The sun was shining, it was late in May,
none in Deep River could forget that day.
There was a big blast then a second came,
it was a dynamite charge that got the blame.
There were two men injured and fifty-three dead;
one man smothered, a sheepskin on his head.
There were seventy-eight orphans, and thirty-eight wives
left without support when the miners died.
Not much is left at Coal Glen
after that day, mining was no good, not ever again.*

Despite Lee County's loss of its underground treasures of gold, iron and coal, the county can still boast of treasures above ground like Bud's Place.

Bud's Place looks like everything you would expect a retro barbecue place to look like. It has that wonderful timeworn, gener-

ously used patina of 50 years of serving good barbecue. Inside there are plastic chairs and tablecloths and an old Coke machine. The gray carpet hides wear well. There are framed newspaper clippings about the mines adorning the walls. The place is warm and shop worn. This is a barbecue place.

J.B. "Bud" Burns and wife Eleanor started Bud's Place in the late 1930s in Sanford. The Burns occupied an old building in Sanford, lived upstairs and sold barbecue downstairs. The Burns moved to Cumnock in 1950. They built Bud's Place on the present site. Despite the loss of his left arm below the elbow in a cotton gin accident, Bud Burns could not only tie his shoes but could cook pork with the best of them on open pit with wood. In addition, he was an avid coon hunter. Phil, Bud's son, said his dad could do anything a man with two arms could do.

Phil has been running the business for the past 25-30 years. Phil, as most second- and third-generation barbecuers have done, now cooks with electricity on a Nunnery-Freeman Kook Rite Kooker. Phil cooks wonderful pork shoulders and hams. He chops the shoulders and slices the hams.

The chopped barbecue pork is sauced in the kitchen and is coarsely chopped. It has good chewy pieces with a light vinegar roasted-pork flavor. The 'cue is very moist and tender. This is just good ol' Eastern North Carolina barbecue.

The sliced barbecue ham is very tender as well and comes in generous thick slices that have a good roasted-pork flavor. It is moist with vinegar and pepper sauce at the table. This succulent offering is classi-cally roasted Eastern North Carolina barbecue pork.

The slaw is white cabbage that produces a crisp clean fresh taste with light mayo and tiny chips of sweet pickle.

There are two sauces at the table. One is an Eastern North Carolina vinegar and pepper sauce that is fairly mild. The second is a reddish-brown Kraft barbecue sauce tweaked by Phil. This sauce has a prominent vinegar and pepper taste, hotter than the Eastern North Carolina vinegar-base sauce.

Proceeding south on Highway 421 about four miles south of the little community of Gulf, look for a state sign on the median showing that Cumnock is one mile away. This sign is located at the intersection of Highway 421 and a country road to Cumnock. Turn left, go about a mile and Bud's Barbecue is on the left. Proceeding north on Highway 421 about one and a half miles north of Sanford city limits, turn right at the sign to Cumnock. Go one mile and Bud's Place is on the left.

Hours are 7 a.m. to 2 p.m., Monday through Friday. It's closed Saturday and Sunday. Telephone number: (919) 776-1424.

Ernie's Barbecue, Dunn

In June 1992, Ernie Starling opened Ernie's Barbecue in Dunn. Ernie was not a stranger to the barbecue business, having worked for Bill Ellis in Wilson for 13 years and having managed Abram's in Smithfield for a period of time. However, Ernie had never owned and operated his own barbecue establishment. He said he just opened and learned everything as he went along. His plan was to try it for six months, leasing the building and equipment. The business caught on so well that at the end of his self-imposed time period, Ernie bought the equipment and continued to lease the building.

As with most barbecue places in this area, Ernie's is a barbecue, seafood and country cookin' buffet-style restaurant. The pork is cooked on Nunnery-Freeman Kook Rite Kookers, and Ernie only cooks whole hogs. His pork product is served pig pickin' style and chopped, all done by hand.

The chopped barbecue is moderately chopped and slightly fiery. It is sauced in the kitchen with an Eastern North Carolina vinegar and pepper sauce which, combined with the good roast pork, was just right for me.

The slaw was a white Eastern North Carolina style with cabbage, carrot, spices and relish.

The golden hushpuppies are light with a crispy outside and a good cornbread taste with a hint of sugar.

From I-95, take the Highway 421 Dunn exit and go north on Highway 421 for three and a half miles. Look for Wayne Shopping Center's sign. Ernie's is in this center. It is a long, white building that is easily seen if you are looking for it and easily missed if you are not. There is no signage at the street. Hours are 11 a.m. until 9 p.m., Monday through Saturday. It's closed Sunday. Telephone number: (910) 892-2225.

194

Bullock's Barbecue, Durham

Bullock's was the barbecue place in the Research Triangle Park area chosen by UNC-TV to cater its Spring Festival when they started this event. Bullock's did this event for a number of years. The festival committee subsequently decided to spread the businesses among other barbecue places in the area.

When Bullock's does a pig pickin', they pull the meat from the whole hog, filet, and then re-stuff the pulled meat into the pig like a twice-baked potato. For pig-pickings, Bullock's uses their special pig picking sauce, which is slightly sweet and mild.

Bullock's Barbecue originally started its barbecue operation cooking with wood over a pit. Then they went to gas with lava rocks. Now they cook with an electric/wood smoker called a Barbecue Slave. After the meat is cooked, it is put through a Hobart chopper with a special blade and run through only one time. It is not finely chopped, nor is it dry. Bullock's cooks shoulders and hams and blends both into the chopped barbecue. Bullock's has found the shoulders to be moister and the hams to be drier. Blended together they form the perfect union. They do not water down their product, and serve only lean meat.

They offer only sliced and chopped barbecue at the restaurant but advised they are going to offer hand-pulled barbecue.

Tommy Bullock, who has been in the barbecue business for 50 years, owns Bullock's Barbecue. From 1952 to 1970, Bullock's was housed about a half mile from the present site. Since 1970, Bullock's has been at its Quebec Street location in Durham.

Glenn and Lillian Bullock started Bullock's Barbecue business on Aug. 1, 1952. However, Glenn had cooked barbecue in his backyard for more than 10 years before starting Bullock's Barbecue restaurant. He sold his barbecue out of his house for 35 cents per pound. Lillian, who was a great cook, helped Glenn get the restaurant up and running. They started out very small. Hard work and stick-to-itiveness helped them build the business that Bullock's is today.

Tommy worked for his mom and dad from age 7. He helped his dad cut open the pigs and put them on the pit. He helped fire pits with hickory wood. He worked in the restaurant busing and waiting on tables as well as washing dishes and cleaning up.

Tommy says that his parents taught him the old-school work ethic. Tommy is very proud of the business his parents started and is proud to carry it on today.

Tommy, who wanted to be a doctor,

said he could not walk away from the business his parents had started. He knew the tremendous effort they had expended to start and grow the business. His family values and pride in his parents' accomplishments won out over medicine. Judy, Tommy's wife, works with him just as his mom worked with his dad. In addition, all three of their children have masters' degrees but all three came back to the barbecue business to work with mom and dad. Strong family ties are the supporting bricks of Bullock's Barbecue. Tommy beamed as he talked about his children and how proud he is of their character. His daughter-in-law and son-in-law also work in the business.

It's obvious from his big smile and twinkling eyes that Tommy loves his work. He said that much to the chagrin of his staff he always brings in a customer who arrives at or shortly after closing. He said that he knew what it was like before they had customers and how hard his parents struggled to make a go of the business. He said he would never turn away a customer at any reasonable time and that his hat still fits his head.

Tommy said that when customers buy barbecue to take home, he never serves them barbecue that is on the line to be served in the restaurant. That barbecue has been kept warm and should not be allowed to cool and be reheated, lest it dry. Tommy

gives take-out customers cool barbecue so that it is only heated once.

Tommy also does a lot of catering. Bullock's does all the catering for Jefferson Pilot Communications. Jefferson Pilot televises all ACC games, both basketball and football for the triangle area, Duke, State and UNC Chapel Hill.

Bullock's also does the catering for ABC, CBS and NBC when national televised games are in the area. Bullock's provides the barbecue on their buffet.

Bullock's catering took an avenue that Tommy said he never envisioned. Bullock's walls are covered with signed pictures of celebrities who have had the good fortune to partake of Tommy's barbecue including Waylon Jennings, Dolly Parton, Jimmy Buffett and Robert Duvall. Tommy said that when Duvall was making the *Handmaiden's Tale* with Faye Dunaway, he ate at Bullock's often and made a special effort to eat his last meal in Durham at Bullock's before leaving the shoot. Tommy beamed as he told the tale of how he served the New York Yankees when owner George Steinbrenner's daughter was at UNC in the late '70s. The Yankees won the World Series in 1978 and Steinbrenner brought the team to Chapel Hill to play an exhibition game against the Tar Heels because of his daughter's connection to the university. Catfish Hunter, the Yankees' pitcher from Hertford, recom-

mended that Bullock's cater the event. Based on Catfish's recommendation, Steinbrenner employed Tommy to feed the Yankees, his daughter and his friends. Tommy's barbecue was so well received that the following year, Steinbrenner brought the Yankees back to Chapel Hill for a second helping.

Good food and good service at a reasonable price has taken Bullock's from its humble beginnings to its position as one of the premier barbecue places in the Triangle area.

Tommy related a tale about a customer who came to his door one morning at 9:30 a.m. and wanted seven pounds of barbecue to go. Though the business did not open until 11 a.m., Tommy provided the man his barbecue. Two weeks later this same scenario occurred again. Two weeks later, again. It turns out that the man was in the secret service and worked in the White House. His son was at Duke hospital receiving skin graphs. The man heard about Bullock's Barbecue. He continued to purchase barbecue from Tommy every time he brought his son to Duke. The man said that one day he asked President Ronald Reagan if he liked barbecue. Reagan said he did and the man shared a pound of Bullock's barbecue with the president. The president was so impressed with the barbecue that he asked his secret service agent to bring him a

pound or two every time he went. This went on for two years. President Reagan personally signed a picture for Tommy and sent it to Tommy at his house. Needless to say, this is one of Tommy's treasures.

The chopped barbecue at Bullock's is moist and a good mixture of ham and shoulder. The chopped comes seasoned from the kitchen. It has a mild vinegary taste, accentuated with red pepper; they play off of each other nicely. The chopped barbecue is somewhere between most restaurants' chopped and coarse chopped. It is not fine and has good, meaty pieces. The outside brown of the shoulders and hams, mixed with the total blend, gives it a good smoky flavor and great texture.

The sliced barbecue is tender, moist and sauced in the kitchen with a tangy original sauce that is slightly reddish-brown. It's tart with a hint of sweetness but it's not a Kansas City molasses rib kind of sauce. There is an occasional pique of pepper that, with the slight sweetness, makes a nice mild explosion in your mouth. The meat is fall-off-the-bone tender. The sliced barbecue has more sauce than I would prefer from the kitchen. You might ask them to let you sauce it at the table.

Tommy says he has three kinds of sauce – one for the chopped barbecue, one for the sliced and one for pig pickings.

The slaw is fresh and crisp with hints

197

of carrot, vinegar and mayo. It is very juicy and very good. The hushpuppies are crisp outside, moist inside and look like jumbo shrimp.

At the table, they have a reddish-brown hot sauce. There's definitely some heat here. It is tangy, peppery and spicy. It's not the widow-maker, but definitely an attention-getter. Surprisingly it doesn't have a long aftertaste. You know you've had a visitor but it was a friend.

I found that the hot sauce coupled with the sweet sauce really cranks the sliced barbecue up a notch or two to a level that I like.

The hot sauce sprinkled lightly on the chopped barbecue was a perfect union for me. It gave the slight vinegary tasting sauce applied in the kitchen just the zing I wanted to make my taste buds dance. Hot, spicy and tangy, this sauce is Bullock's barbecue at its best.

The chopped barbecue with the hot sauce and slaw is a festival of flavors. It is well balanced and makes a great plate or sandwich. The sliced with the slaw was not enough contrast unless you added hot sauce to the sliced. Then the slaw became a good side. The chopped barbecue with the hot sauce at the table is the ticket for me.

Bullock's also serves a full menu with 39 entrees including seafood, but barbecue is their name and barbecue is their game. They also have 24 sandwiches and 12 desserts. You will not leave Bullock's hungry.

To reach Bullock's going south on I-85, take 15-501 South and immediately take the first exit onto Hillsborough Road. Turn left, go to the second traffic light and turn left on LaSalle Street. Go 100 yards and turn right onto Quebec. You are in Bullock's parking lot. Going north on I-85, exit at Colemill Road. Turn right, go to the first traffic light and turn left onto Hillsborough Road. Then turn left at the third traffic light and you are there. Bullock's hours are 11:30 a.m. to 8 p.m., Tuesday through Saturday. It's closed Sunday and Monday. Telephone number: (919) 383-6202.

Fuller's BBQ, Elizabethtown

Fuller's BBQ in Elizabethtown opened in October 1999. It is a large, gray cinder-block barn with a gray roof and a long red awning extending from the front door to the parking lot. This country setting sits amidst a large front yard that's immaculately kept and shaded by pecan trees. A white fence and horses separate this lovely setting to the left. It has a very appealing curb appearance.

Run by Fuller Locklear's (Fuller's BBQ in Lumberton) son and daughter-in-law, Fuller's BBQ of Elizabethtown serves a buffet that replicates all the good offerings of Fuller's BBQ in Lumberton.

Fuller's slow-roasted barbecue is hand chopped and served as part of his extensive buffet which includes barbecue, seafood and country cooking items typical of this area.

The barbecue pork is medium chopped with smoky nuances throughout. The delicious white meat mixes with the outside brown (they chop the whole hog). Sauced in the kitchen, this barbecue comes moist yet pleasingly chewy. It has a brown nutty flavor and has no fat or gristle. This is a good Eastern North Carolina barbecue. With some additional drops of the house sauce at the table, this is "very good stuff".

The vinegar-base red sauce is filled with peppers and spices that stand up and salute.

The slaw is an example of good Eastern Carolina coleslaw. It's white, medium-coarse chopped cabbage with carrots, pickles and light mayo.

The hushpuppies are small, light cream-colored puffs.

The fried chicken has a good crisp outside and a tender inside.

Fuller's BBQ is located across from Westgate Plaza, beside Winn-Dixie on Highway 41 West (Hwy 87 Business North). Hours are 11 a.m. until 9 p.m., Monday through Friday, and 11:30 a.m. until 9 p.m., Saturday. It's open 11:30 a.m. until 4 p.m. on Sunday. Telephone number: (910) 872-0122.

Cape Fear Bar-B-Q and Chicken, Fayetteville

This barbecue emporium has been at its present site only since 1999. It is as clean as a whistle and sports an A health rating at 99 percent. Oh, and the food is good. June Massengill is the owner and Rene Lewis ably manages the business.

The chopped pork barbecue is a good coarse chop that comes sauced from the kitchen. There are lots of red pepper flakes that have a zippy taste accentuated by vinegar and peppers. It's pretty hot stuff but it's good. The nice roasted-pork taste dances with the fiery licks laid down by the peppers. This is real 'cue.

The slaw is a mix of white and green cabbage with flakes of pickle. It has a nice crunch, a fresh taste and is lighter than most slaws.

The light tan hushpuppies have a crunchy shell, a moist inside and good cornmeal taste – a good pup.

The amber-peachy colored sauce has a prominent vinegar taste accompanied by red pepper, black pepper and spices. The sauce at the table does not taste as hot as the sauce in the kitchen. I think this is because whoever filled the bottles didn't shake the container before filling. My bottle had mainly vinegar with little pepper. If you want hotter sauce than you find at the table, ask them to share some from the kitchen.

From I-95, take Business 95 South (Hwy 301 becomes Eastern Blvd.) to Grove Street. (which is the intersection of Highway 23 and Highway 53). Turn right on Grove Street and Cape Fear Bar-B-Q and Chicken is approximately 100 yards on your right. Hours are 10 a.m. until 10 p.m., Friday and Saturday, and 10 a.m. until 9 p.m., Sunday through Thursday. Telephone number: (910) 483-1884.

Chason's Famous Buffet, Fayetteville

The parent of Chason's Famous Buffet in Fayetteville was the Chason's Barbecue that originated about 20 miles south of Fayetteville in Lumber Bridge. Chason's Barbecue was enshrined in an old wooden building with a large door and an oversized handle and a brick chimney. Formerly a general store and barbecue wholesale building, Chason's of Lumber Bridge offered pit-cooked, hand-chopped barbecue as well as fried chicken, fresh seafood, vegetables and pies. This was Fred Chason's baby. Red-and-white checked plastic tablecloths, Cyprus wood imparting wonderful aroma, and brick floor made for good ambiance. Fred opened Chason's in Lumber Bridge in April 1981. Fred came to the area to retire and lower his blood pressure from his previous fast-paced business life. Retirement quickly took a back seat. People for miles around talk about the good country cookin' and the killer chocolate cream pie.

Fred learned barbecuing from his father who cooked 10 years for the public.

As a child, Fred and his friends would put 25 cents each in a hat to buy a pig. Then as boys are prone to do, they would take the pig to the woods, cook it over open fire and eat their prize. Fred has cooked pigs all of his life. Fred and his pals would also have a big fish fry when they had caught enough fish. Thus, it was only natural for Fred to return to his hometown of Lumber Bridge at his retirement. This was the place that held the memories. Fred died in 1995.

Deborah Chason, Fred's daughter, has run the business since Fred's death. The business in Lumber Bridge burned down in January 1997. Because so many of the customers in Lumber Bridge were from Fayetteville, Deborah reopened Chason's in Fayetteville in October 1997. The new Chason's has the same red-and-white plastic tablecloths and the outstanding buffet that gave it its legendary reputation that had people driving for 50 miles one way to eat the fine barbecue and seafood.

When the occasion calls for celebration and only a pig out, pig pickin' or pig party will do, Chason's is still the place.

Now the barbecue is cooked with gas but it is still whole hog and chopped by hand. It's not basted and is sauced in the kitchen.

The chopped barbecue is moderately coarse chopped with a good mix of brown and white meat. The tangy vinegar taste gets mild heat from red peppers and seeds. It has a good Eastern North Carolina twang.

201

The fresh, white slaw is chopped daily. It's moderately coarse with chips of carrot and light mayo. It's not runny and it's just good.

The reddish-brown sauce is an Eastern North Carolina vinegar-base variety with no shortage of red peppers and seeds. This sauce will light your fire by itself. Have lots of water close at hand if eaten alone. It is delicious on the 'cue. Use sparingly at the table until you reach the right degree of Fahrenheit.

From I-95 take Business 95 South (301 South) to the intersection of Highway 24 and Highway 53 (Grove Street). Proceed through the intersection and continue south on Eastern Boulevard (I-95 Business) for a half mile. Chason's is on the left beside Howard Johnson's. Hours are 11 a.m. until 9 p.m., Wednesday through Saturday, and 1 p.m. until 8 p.m., Sunday. It's closed Monday and Tuesday. Telephone number: (910) 486-0016.

McCall's Barbecue and Seafood, Goldsboro

Randy McCall worked in sales with Purina and was on the road quite a bit back in 1984. Martie, his wife, was an RN and working erratic hours at the hospital. Both wanted more quality family time and more time for Martie to be at home during the day with the children. What to do? Buy a barbecue place. Elmer and Tempy Davis of Pikeville had a tiny backyard mom-and-pop operation that cooked only on Friday and sold their good barbecue Friday night and Saturday. The answer to a prayer.

Elmer and Tempy were ready to retire so Randy bought their equipment and recipes and cooked at home for five years. Randy and Worth Westbrook, one of his cohorts at Purina, decided to go into business together. In 1988, they saw a building, leased the building, quit their jobs at Purina and have been cooking pigs ever since.

When Randy and Worth first opened McCall's Barbecue and Seafood, the plan was for Randy to continue to cook the pigs at home and transport them to the restaurant until the cooking pits could be completed on site. Randy said the local health department granted him a 90-day period to complete the construction of his barbecue pits at the present location and begin cooking his pigs on-site. No problem. Randy and Worth opened McCall's and the very next day Randy experienced a pit fire at home that burned his pits to the ground. Problem! Ever-resourceful Randy got the local fire department to let him use the pits that they use for their Annual Firemen's Barbecue for 90 days so he could complete construction at the new restaurant. No problem. Neighbors helping neighbors has deep roots in rural communities.

Randy, with just a little bit of pride, said that McCall's had grown in business every year since it has been open. It's small wonder. Build a better mouse trap and ...

McCall's serves barbecue pork, barbecue chicken, fried chicken, and Calabash-style seafood. All barbecue items are cooked in an Old Hickory Pit Cooker and finished over open pits with wood.

The chopped barbecue is moderately coarse and is sauced in the kitchen. It has a good smoky flavor accented by peaks of vinegar flavor from the Eastern North Carolina sauce. This 'cue really has a good open-pit, woodsy flavor that is hard to come by in the east these days.

You get the feel of a fall day as you taste the barbecue beef ribs. They have deep, rich smoky taste and are just mouth watering.

The barbecue chicken's crisp skin conceals a melt-in-your-mouth moist offering that's tender and pink to the bone with good smoke penetration. The chicken is done, but not overdone. It's a taste sensation.

The slaw is fresh, crisp and slightly sweet with a good, bright taste. It's finely chopped and not runny.

The hushpuppies have a golden outer shell that's slightly crunchy. The moist center has a good, slightly sweet cornbread taste. This is a nice puppy.

McCall's uses a vinegar-base Eastern North Carolina-style sauce that has a dark peach color. The peppers are at play here. Moderately hot by itself, the sauce is wonderful on the barbecue. Add the slaw and bread and you have a great sandwich.

McCall's is located on Highway 70 at the intersection of Highway 70 and Highway 111 in Goldsboro. The building is set back from the road. Going east approaching the intersection, McCall's will be on your left. Going west on Highway 70, pass through the intersection and McCall's will be on your right. Hours are 11 a.m. until 9 p.m., daily. Telephone number: (919) 751-0196.

Wilber's Barbecue, Goldsboro

There are a number of good barbecue places in Eastern North Carolina. There are a number of good barbecue places in Eastern North Carolina that have been in existence for many years. There are a number of good barbecue places in Eastern North Carolina whose founders played a prominent part in establishing Eastern North Carolina-style barbecue. But I would venture to say there is no name associated with Eastern North Carolina barbecue as familiar to as many people as the name Wilber's. For many people the name Wilber's and Eastern North Carolina barbecue are synonymous. Some people even refer to Eastern North Carolina barbecue as Wilber's Barbecue. Wilber Shirley did not invent Eastern North Carolina style barbecue but he has certainly served it on site to perhaps more people than any other single barbecue operation east of Raleigh.

Wilber's is located on Highway 70 just east out of Goldsboro. Over the years, thousands and thousands of people from across the state who travel to Morehead City, Beaufort, Harkers Island and other points east have stopped at Wilber's to eat or to take his delicious barbecue with them to the coast.

Owner Wilber Shirley learned how to cook barbecue at an early age from his daddy. He later worked at Griffin Barbecue in the Goldsboro area for 13 years. He has been cooking pigs since July 24, 1962.

Wilber's is one of the very few barbecue places in Eastern North Carolina still cooking whole hogs over pits with wood. Wilber's Barbecue burns about 15 cords of wood per week, mostly oak mixed with some hickory. Cooking with wood adds a tremendous expense to Wilber's operation. Eddie Ward has been supplying Wilber with wood for the past 30 years and he doesn't know what he would do if anything ever happened to Eddie. Another long-time fixture at Wilber's was Ike Green. Ike had run the pits and cooked the pigs at Wilber's for 30 years until his death in February 1997. Since that time Jackie Martin, who had worked with Ike for 15 years, has continued cooking Wilber's wonderful pork products.

Wilber Shirley said that today people want their barbecue drier and lighter with no fat.

I found Wilber's barbecue pork to be absolutely delicious. The chopped pork has a smoky flavor and is not heavily sauced from the kitchen. It was chopped in fairly large pieces but not too coarse. The high quality of the meat along with the slow cooking over pits with live oak and hickory coals imparted a delightful woodsy, smoky flavor and a lasting finish. The chopped barbecue was reasonably moist, but a bit dry for my taste. I readily admit prejudice for pulled pig that is more moist with a teeny bit of fat and tiny bits of skin. But for most of the world, Wilber's wonderful pork product is exactly the barbecue they're seeking. Wilber Shirley certainly knows his customers.

The white slaw had a very crisp, fresh taste and was a bit more tangy than most Eastern North Carolina-style coleslaw.

The barbecue chicken was unlike most any other barbecue chicken I have tried. The barbecue chicken tasted a bit more like baked chicken in a slightly creamy sauce with hints of barbecue spices. It was ever so tender, delicious and different.

The brunswick stew taste more like a really good vegetable soup. The stew has a tomatoey taste and was kind of bland. This problem was easily cured with a few drops of Texas Pete. Having raised the spiciness of the stew a click or two, I found it most enjoyable.

My dinner plate did not have slaw. It had potato salad instead. Wilber's is the only place that I have visited that serves potato salad with its barbecue. The potato salad had a creamy texture and a mustard flavor. It's just plain scrumptious. It is the kind of potato salad you seek out at a church picnic.

The hushpuppies were golden with a crisp outside shell and a moist center. They are just plain good pups and a perfect accompaniment to Wilber's yummy barbecue.

The interior of Wilber's is stained pine paneling and has the ambiance we all seek when we're lucky enough to find a retro barbecue place that still serves great barbecue. Weather permitting, I prefer to eat my barbecue sandwich and drink outside. I like to wander about and look at the various items on the fruit and vegetable stands in front of Wilber's. I like to stretch my legs as Wilber's is about halfway from Winston-Salem to Harkers Island (300 miles) and I'm tired of sitting by the time I get to this area.

If hard pressed, I would confess that the real reason I take my lunch on the tailgate of my Blazer is the air show. The kid in me thoroughly enjoys seeing the F-15 and F-16 fighter planes from Seymour Johnson's Air Force Base suddenly appear in the sky. Their landing approach takes them tree-top level directly over Wilber's to a runway that must start in the back parking lot. The planes are so low that you can actually see the pilots' faces and wave. The high-pitched whine of jet engines, the acrid smell of aviation fuel, a bright crisp October day and Wilber's good barbecue – who could ask for anything more?

A visit to the beach is not complete without a stop at Wilber's Barbecue. If you can't stop, honk your horn to show your appreciation to Wilber Shirley for the time, effort and expense he expends to continue to offer the public great barbecue prepared in the classic Eastern North Carolina style. Better yet, honk twice, this delightful man deserves it.

Wilber's is open 6 a.m. until 9 p.m., seven days a week. Telephone number: (919) 778-5218.

Stamey's Barbecue, Greensboro

Located immediately across the street from the coliseum in Greensboro, Stamey's Barbecue is a barbecue mecca for tens of thousands of people who have enjoyed its fine product while attending the ACC Tournament and other events at the coliseum.

Jess Swicegood and Sid Weaver taught the Lexington-style barbecue cooking to Warner Stamey while he was in Lexington. Warner, in turn, has taught numerous others the Lexington style of cooking pork, including his brother-in-law Alston Bridges and Red Bridges (no relation to Alston) while he lived in Shelby. Warner later moved back to Lexington and then to Greensboro.

Warner Stamey was an entrepreneur. He not only knew how to cook the best barbecue in the area but he also knew how to make it a profitable business venture. Ever on the cutting edge, Warner carried Stamey's Barbecue to the pinnacle of the barbecue business in North Carolina. He was indeed a legendary figure in the barbecue world and an astute businessman.

Warner later turned the reins of Stamey's barbecue empire over to his sons, Keith and Charles. Keith was an impassioned Wake Forest University Demon Deacon fan and remained so until his recent death. He left his entire estate to Wake

Forest (more than $7 million). Keith graduated from Wake Forest in 1959, two years after its move to Winston-Salem from the old campus at Wake Forest. Charles graduated from Wake Forest at the old campus in 1956. Both were Sig Eps'. Continuing the tradition, Charles Keith "Chip" Stamey, Charles's son and the owner and operator of the Stamey Barbecue empire, also graduated from Wake Forest University in 1989.

Chip has been in the barbecue business since he was 10 years old. He started mowing grass around the building, picking up bottles and working in the kitchen. He learned how to do the cooking and at one time or another has done everything there is to do related to the business.

On the day that I interviewed Chip, I found him with a dustpan and broom sweeping up a small mess on the restaurant floor. I was immediately impressed. The new owner and operator still had the common touch. Stamey's Barbecue is in good hands.

Chip was pleased to give me a tour of the facilities, including the smokehouse. This is a very large building which houses the fireboxes and 12 huge pits that give Stamey's the single largest barbecue cooking capacity in the state. On the far edge of the parking lot, there is a pile of hickory

pieces that are the by-products of a local manufacturer. This pile of wood is about the size of a railroad boxcar. A front-end loader carries wood from this pile to the huge custom wrought-iron firebox that feeds it into the interior firebox, producing a constant stream of hot hickory coals for shoveling under the pits. Most everything in the smokehouse, even the shovels, is custom-built for Stamey's. There is a separate cooler the size of a small house just for cabbage. Another cooler of similar size houses the meat. Stamey's buys its meats in large cardboard containers or pallets that hold 2,000 pounds of meat each.

Stamey's cooks only shoulders and hasn't cooked hams in more than 20 years, Chip said. They don't break out the shoulder into different parts as do many restaurants. They commercially cut (grind) the entire shoulder. Chip said they were always after speed in their business while rendering good value, an excellent product and good service. Like his father, uncle and grandfather, Chip believes in chopping the entire shoulder and mixing all of the meat into one uniformly good product. With 12 pits, Stamey's has the capacity to cook every three days, but Chip chooses to cook fresh daily. He said this produced a better product.

Chip told me that he would continue to cook with wood until he was made to stop. Chip's take is that a lot of people who quit cooking with wood were not made to do so but chose the easier, less-labor-intensive, less-expensive way of cooking pork. Cooking with electricity or propane does not entail the skill required to cook with coals. Moisture in the wood, moisture in the pig, a 10-degree variance in temperature, a change in humidity, the height of the coal bed from one day to the next, and a number of other variables are all things that impact the final product. It takes more than a year to teach a person how to run a pit. It is much easier to teach them how to set a timer and flip a switch.

Warner Stamey was always looking for things to improve the business of barbecue cooking and marketing. He produced new ways to write the tickets, improve the construction and the production of the pit, and was one of the first to go into the drive-in restaurant business. Chip said he was proud that his granddad was always on the cutting edge, always pushing the envelope. Chip, like the other Stamey men, continues to push the envelope and improve Stamey's product, service and bottom line.

At one time, Stamey's had four locations – two in Greensboro, one in Asheboro and one in High Point. Now they run the two in Greensboro. Chip said they were getting too stretched out to get good hands on management in four different places, especially with two out of town. Chip strives to preserve the old and embrace the new.

Warner Stamey had a place in Lexington called the Snack Shop. The slaw recipe used at Stamey's Barbecue is the recipe from the Snack Shop. They had an employee, a Mrs. Dell, who made the slaw since 1930 until her death approximately 25 years later.

The chopped barbecue is ground, medium fine, and comes sauced from the kitchen. It has brown mixed with lean white and regular meat. It has a good, fresh smoky flavor but it's not strong. When sauced with dip at the table, it perks up to become a nice offering. The dip, meat and slaw form a nice combination.

The sliced barbecue was very tender, not overcooked and lightly sauced in the kitchen. It's not sauced as heavy as the chopped barbecue and probably needs some dip at the table. It has a good fresh taste. When sauced with the dip at the table, it's the ticket.

The dip is reddish-brown and thin with a good tangy, vinegary and peppery taste.

It's slightly hot by itself but it's not a torch. On the meat, it's a smile.

The red slaw is crisp, fresh, moderately fine chopped and slightly vinegary with a hint of pepper. The hushpuppies are good too.

The desserts are homemade cherry and peach cobblers. I am not a dessert person, per se, but had heard enough about Stamey's cobblers to feel that I would be remiss if I did not try a tablespoon of each. The cherry cobbler is very good. It has a great flaky crust and a rich, tart cherry taste that's not too sweet. The peach cobbler – oh, mamma – you'll write home about this. It is perfect, so damn good you don't want to swallow.

To reach Stamey's from any direction entering Greensboro, follow the signs to the Greensboro Coliseum. Stamey's is across the street from the coliseum at 2206 High Point Rd. Hours are 10 a.m. until 9 p.m., Monday through Saturday. It's closed Sunday. Telephone number: (336) 299-9888.

Evans Famous Barbecue and Chicken, Henderson

In my hometown of Henderson, during my youth, there lived a black man named Warner Evans. Warner Evans was Henderson's counterpart to Goldsboro's Adam Scott of legendary barbecue fame. Warner Evans' original place on Raleigh Road, that I knew so well, burned. Warner's sons run the operation today on a new site across the road from the original.

Warner sold barbecue in bulk for taking home and provided catered pig pickin's. Warner Evans was a household name in Vance County and surrounding areas. Every afternoon, except Sunday, produced game day-like traffic around Warner's place as mill workers, farmers, businessmen and landed gentry picked up supper for their families.

Among barbecue places, Warner coined the word "clean." Warner and all the black ladies that worked with him were dressed totally in white. Inside the cinder-block building, the ceilings, walls and floors were painted and spotless. It did not end there. Warner was fastidious. After the meat-packing company had butchered and "dressed" the pig (*dressed* means completely cleaned, scraped free of bristles and head removed), Warner gave it his special touch. Warner would hand wipe the pig with cooking oil and shave it all over with a straight razor. When Warner finished, the pig was as smooth as a baby's bottom.

Warner's cooking was a bit different too. As a child, Warner let me "help" him add corncobs to his hardwood coals for his barbecue flavor. But these were not corncobs to me. They were bombs released from my imaginary P-51 Mustang or Hellcat (hands) at just the right moment to strike their target and cause showers of red coals and plumes of smoke as I banked steeply and climbed into the clouds to make my escape. Warner not only cooked great barbecue but also had infinite patience with a certain small redheaded freckled-faced boy with a vivid, war film-stimulated imagination.

When a whole pig is cooked to perfection (golden brown, no charred spots and uniform glaze) locals refer to it as a "pretty pig." Warner Evans, like his legendary counterparts, cooked a pretty pig.

Today, Warner's sons Daniel, Lafayette and Warner Jr. carry on the tradition Warner started so many years ago. A portrait of Warner hangs in the restaurant. When you look at Daniel and he smiles, you think Warner has been reincarnated.

Evans Famous Barbecue and Chicken uses the same recipes started by its founder. Like most of the barbecue places in the

211

east, the pork is no longer cooked over coals on pits but instead, electrically with a Nunnery-Freeman cooker and hickory inserts. Following tradition, Evans Famous Barbecue and Chicken cooks whole hogs and shoulders.

The chopped barbecue is moderately chopped and comes sauced from the kitchen. It has a hot, peppery, vinegary taste that epitomizes the best in Eastern North Carolina barbecue flavor. This is good stuff. It needs nothing at the table to enhance its wonderful flavor.

The tomato-base brunswick stew includes corn, butter beans, potatoes, chicken and beef. This stew is thick and has just the right amount of spices to give it a good flavor and just enough fire. It is not too bland nor is it too hot. As Billy Joel sang, "I love you just the way you are."

The slaw has a very clean, crisp, cabbage taste that's moist, not runny and goes well with the 'cue, playing off the pepper and vinegar acidity of the sauce.

The hushpuppies are golden brown with a good crispy outside and a moist, yet slightly heavy inside. It's slightly greasy and has the country cornbread taste like your grandma used to make.

In addition to its barbecue pork (chopped and ribs), Evans Famous Barbecue and Chicken has barbecue chick-

en, fried chicken, brunswick stew, fish, oysters and shrimp. Evans also serves 15 side items including collard greens. Yes, they have chitlins. The desserts are pecan pie, sweet potato pie, peach or apple cobbler and ice cream.

Evans Famous Barbecue and Chicken is located on Old Highway 1 (Raleigh Road). From U.S. Highway 1 North, take Business Highway 1 into Henderson at the first Henderson exit. Proceed through Kittrel and Bear Pond (one stoplight). It is not advisable to approach Bear Pond during rush hour, as the traffic (both cars) is tremendous. Evans will be on your left as you reach the Henderson city limits.

From the I-85 North exit at Dabney Drive, turn right and continue on Dabney Drive until you cross Highway 158. At the next light, turn right on Old Raleigh Road (U.S. Highway 1 Business) and go about three-quarters of a mile. Evans Famous Barbecue and Chicken is on the right at the stoplight. There is a BP oil station on the left at this light. Evans is on the corner of Miriam and Raleigh, just a few feet outside Henderson's city limits.

Hours are 10 a.m. until 9 p.m., Monday through Wednesday; 10 a.m. until 10 p.m., Thursday through Saturday; and 11:30 a.m. until 6:30 p.m., Sunday. Telephone number: (252) 438-6155.

Nunnery-Freeman Barbecue, Henderson

Founder O.H. Freeman was born in Henderson on Christmas Eve in 1923. He and his business partner, J.E. Nunnery, started this landmark barbecue in 1957. It was originally across the road from its current site. When the state widened the road, it took the precious little parking space they had. So, they moved across the street in 1972.

In the late 1990s, O.H. turned over management of Nunnery-Freeman Barbecue to Gary, his son. Gary's Barbecue on I-85, just outside of Henderson, is part of this operation. Although Gary owns all of the stock in Nunnery-Freeman, Inc., O.H. comes in early in the morning and gets things going and then goes home to rest. He says he wants to die with his shoes on.

Nunnery-Freeman invented the Kook Rite Kooker. This electric cooker with the hickory wood insert is probably used by more barbecue places in North Carolina than any other make. Gary said that they ship Kookers all over the nation and to the South Sea Islands, London, Stockholm, Saudi Arabia, Denmark and Paris, among other places. Wherever people are cooking good barbecue today, it is generally done on a Nunnery-Freeman Kook Rite Kooker.

As O.H. Freeman and J.H. Nunnery experimented with design and development of various cookers, Gary said he hauled more discarded designs to Perry's Junkyard in Henderson than one could ever imagine. He said that he felt they kept most of the sheet metal men in Henderson living high on the hog for a number of years until they finally settled in on the present design.

Gary chuckled as he said that a lot of the barbecue places that claim to cook over pits are really using Kook Rite Kookers in the back. He said they throw some wood in the fireplace and throw a few pork skins and fat on the grill to get the chimney to smoke and emit that good barbecue smell in the air.

Nunnery-Freeman chops its barbecue with a Hobart chopper. However, they have added a wrinkle or two. They cut off two blades, leaving one blade, and they run the meat through one time only. Thus, they can chop 350 pounds of barbecue in a matter of minutes and it looks and tastes like its been hand chopped.

O.H. said that they served the first hushpuppies in this part of the state. Because O.H. and J.E. were particular in the way they wanted their meal ground for their special hushpuppies, the miller that prepared their hushpuppy mix has a custom blend just for Nunnery-Freeman.

213

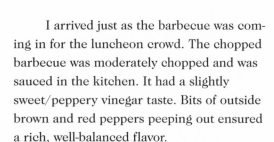

I arrived just as the barbecue was coming in for the luncheon crowd. The chopped barbecue was moderately chopped and was sauced in the kitchen. It had a slightly sweet/peppery vinegar taste. Bits of outside brown and red peppers peeping out ensured a rich, well-balanced flavor.

The kitchen sauce is brownish-red with a tart vinegar taste and a light pepper flavor.

The yellow mustard sauce (for chicken) is moderately thick and has rich, sweet taste that is not vinegary at all. It is unlike any store-bought mustard you ever tasted. The reddish-brown mild sauce is thin with hints of sweetness and a moderate amount of fire for a good balance and a spicy finish. The brown hot sauce is thin with lots of fire. It's pretty stout by itself but the peppers cease to shout on the meat. The hot sauce is my favorite.

The hushpuppies are light, non-greasy with a crisp outside and a moist inside. These are the absolute best you will ever eat.

The brunswick stew (they make 35 gallons per night) is rich, thick, well balanced and not overly tomatoey. It has the usual ingredients of tomatoes, corn, butter beans, potatoes and lots of meat. Like a good mixed drink, you don't taste the component parts. It is not sweet and is moderately spiced.

In 1997, an article in the *Charlotte Observer* newspaper rated Nunnery-Freeman Barbecue #1 in "The 10 Great Barbecue Places in North Carolina."

To get to Gary's Barbecue (part of the Nunnery-Freeman operation) from I-85, take Exit 212, turn left onto Emergency Room Drive. Proceed about 10 feet and turn down Zeb Robinson's Service Road. Gary's is open daily 10 a.m. to 9 p.m. Telephone number: (919) 430-7144.

To reach Nunnery-Freeman Barbecue, exit I-85 north on exit 215. At top of the ramp turn left onto Hwy 158 and Nunnery-Freeman Barbecue is on your immediate right. Nunnery-Freeman's hours are 10:00 a.m. to 8:30 p.m., Tuesday through Sunday, closed on Monday. Telephone number: (919) 438-4751.

Skipper's Forsyth Barbecue, Henderson

When Marshall Henry Forsyth returned home to Henderson after 18 years in the U.S. Army, he worked as a delivery-man for Henderson Laundry. Because of his fast pace, one of the locals nicknamed him "Skipper." He's been Skipper ever since. Skipper and Mrs. Skipper, the former Flora Kelly, opened their service station on Norlina Road in 1942. A local doctor and frequent customer suggested that Skipper and Flora make and sell barbecue and brunswick stew. When Flora said she didn't know how to cook these items, Dr. Upchurch offered to share his recipes and help Flora with her skills in preparing some of the South's favorite casual food dishes.

Skipper's original barbecue place was a simple affair. Customers sat on nail kegs or drink crates to eat the delicious pork product. It was the only place in the area in the early 1940s to serve barbecue and brunswick stew.

By word-of-mouth, Skipper's fame spread quickly. The original building burned after 32 years and the Forsyths opened the present Skipper's Forsyth Barbecue facility in 1974.

The address changed but the recipes did not. Almost 60 years later, Skipper's is still using Dr. Upchurch's recipes for barbe-cue and brunswick stew.

Ferebee and T.H. Weldon, Skipper and Flora's daughter and son-in-law, took over management of the busi-ness after the original owners retired.

Regina Ellis, the Weldon's daughter, began working in the restaurant along side her grandfather Skipper in 1971. She con-tinued with the business and is now the manager. The restaurant currently has 34 employees including Patsy Newman and Mary Hilliard, Regina's able assistant man-agers, and Allen, Regina's son, who is the fourth generation of the family that built this landmark barbecue place.

Skipper's caters throughout the area but their tasty morsels have been shipped over the country to former Henderson resi-dents and people who have discovered Skipper's on their jaunts up ol' 158 and the new I-85.

Regina's husband, Charles Ellis, is a long-distance truck driver. Sometimes cus-tomers as far away as Pennsylvania will call Regina and ask that Charles bring barbecue the next time he is headed their way. Charles does. These customers meet Charles at a truck stop in their area to pick up their prize.

I've not only had the pleasure of eat-ing Skipper's wonderful products when visit-ing family in the area, but I have hunted

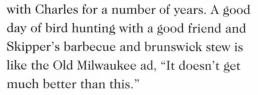

with Charles for a number of years. A good day of bird hunting with a good friend and Skipper's barbecue and brunswick stew is like the Old Milwaukee ad, "It doesn't get much better than this."

Regina said that Skipper's cooks mostly pork shoulders and some ham. The two are mixed with the outside brown and inside white included. Skipper cooks with Nunnery-Freeman electric cookers and the 'cue is chopped with a Hobart commercial chopper. Barbecue sauce and salt are added in the kitchen. A hot barbecue sauce and a mustard sauce for the chicken are available on the table.

I found the chopped barbecue to be brown in color, not gray, with a good, strong vinegar/pepper taste. You see tiny flakes of crushed red pepper. It has nice zip and is very moist. The 'cue is moderately chopped. Adding the hot sauce at the table gives the barbecue a little more fire and a stronger finish. I like it as it comes from the kitchen for plate barbecue but I like it with the hot sauce when eaten on a bun with slaw.

The sliced barbecue looks more like pulled barbecue. It is very moist, flavorful and just a nice roasted-pork taste.

The rib sauce is brownish-red or red-dish-brown (you decide). It's tangy, moderately thin and very spicy. It starts nicely and has a strong finish. It is especially good on the ribs and sliced barbecue.

The white slaw is crunchy and flavorful with specks of pickle and light mayo.

Hushpuppies are golden on the outside with a pleasant cornmeal taste and moist texture on the inside.

The mustard sauce is a golden liquid with a spicy, slightly hot mustard taste. It is best on chicken, for which it was designed.

The brunswick stew is thick and well balanced with tomatoes, butter beans, corn, potatoes and chicken. A hint of sweetness goes well with the tomatoes' acidity. Skipper's uses both kernel corn and cream corn. Skipper's also uses hens and frying-size chicken to impart different flavors to the stew. In addition to chicken, the stew includes stew beef, pork shoulder and bacon. Spices include crushed red pepper, black pepper, sugar and salt. Skipper's makes one of the best commercial brunswick stews I have ever tasted.

Hours are 10 a.m. until 9 p.m., Monday through Saturday. It's closed Sunday. Telephone number: (252) 438-5228.

Knightdale Seafood and BBQ, Knightdale

Knightdale Seafood and BBQ was housed for many, many years in a one story cream colored building on the north side of Highway 64 in Knightdale. This place had a shop worn patina that looked like an old barbecue place nestled in some trees with a dirt parking lot. It was just that. For the past fourteen years Knightdale Seafood and BBQ was owned by Larry and Phyllis Addelton.

I tried to stop here many times on my barbecue journeys to the eastern part of the state but the parking lot was always packed and I figured I would catch it the next time. In November 2001 to my chagrin, I passed by and the place looked deserted. It was. Larry and Phyllis built a large brick place across the road in a mini shopping mall on Money Street. Going east on Highway 64 the front of this place was partially obscured by trees and going west on Highway 64 you would not see it at all.

On my most recent visit to this area I had the good fortune to pit stop at the BP Station and saw the new establishment when I came out to my car. It was approaching dinnertime and seemed like the perfect opportunity to see if this small barbecue place that had been such a treasure had lost anything in its upgrade in size. I can happily report that it has not lost a step. The only

significant change from the old to the new Knightdale Seafood and BBQ is that they now have room for more people to enjoy their delicious pork and seafood products.

When Knightdale Seafood and BBQ was housed across the street 14 years ago they cooked with open pits. Later that method of cooking was abandoned in favor of a barbecue cooker. Now Knightdale Seafood and BBQ cooks with hickory wood on a Southern Pride cooker. The meat products are being produced by the same pit master that has been with Knightdale for the past 14 years.

Knightdale Seafood has one of the few Southern Pride cookers I have found in Eastern North Carolina. This cooker is most often found west of Asheville. Meat cooked in this fashion is never in contact with direct heat but is cooked slowly with hot air and smoke that blows through a filter into a convection type chamber for 22 to 24 hours. This slow roasting, indirect heat method causes the meat to appear pinkish in color all the way to the bone, the sign of good smoke penetration. The meat is completely done. It just does not have the color to which Easter North Carolinians are accustomed. This is especially true with the chicken. The chef shared that people were

217

so concerned about eating chicken that had a good brown skin and was pink to the bone that they had to put a disclaimer on the front of the menu advising that the meat was in fact done. It is not only done, it is done really well. I shared with the chef that a number of barbecue places west of Asheville are using a Southern Pride cooker fired with pecan logs from Georgia and the chef indicated he may well try this himself. If he does the good people of Raleigh, Knightdale, Fuquay-Varina area will be introduced to yet another delightful barbecue flavor.

Knightdale's sliced pork barbecue is a wonderful robust, smoky, woodsy pork dish that is delightful. It comes sauced from the kitchen with a rich tomato based sauce with a sweet and sour flavor.

The chopped pork barbecue offering has good brown and white mixed with a hint of vinegar sauce as served from the kitchen. With a dash of the homemade Eastern North Carolina sauce at the table, this little piggy struts its stuff. Mighty good 'cue.

The barbecue chicken is cooked tender to the bone and then coated with a mouth watering sweet and sour sauce that is a symphony of flavors on your palate. The

meat of this bird is pink showing good smoke penetration. It is very moist and ever, ever so tender.

Knightdale's sauce is a vinegar-base Eastern North Carolina classic. Reddish in color, this sauce is full of zip and ready to dance. It is mildly hot by itself on a teaspoon and is the perfect accompaniment to Knightdale's chopped barbecue pork.

The slaw is fresh white cabbage coleslaw at its best. This treat is a bit juicy with mayo but oh so good. Tiny chips of pickle are a nice touch.

Knightdale Seafood and BBQ serves chopped pork barbecue, sliced pork barbecue, fried chicken, barbecue chicken, brunswick stew and a large variety of fresh seafood plus frog legs. Fourteen vegetables plus steaks and babyback pork ribs round out the fare.

Knightdale Seafood and BBQ is located on Highway 64 in Knightdale. The address is 706 Money Ct. It is across the street from the BP Station at the stoplight on Highway 64. Don't miss this one. Hours are 11 a.m. until 10 p.m., Monday through Saturday and 11 a.m. until 8 p.m. on Sunday. Telephone number: (919) 266-4447.

Ken's Grill, LaGrange

I knew the barbecue at Ken's Grill must be good when it took three visits before I got any. My first two visits were on trips to Eastern North Carolina while working on this book. Somehow each visit found me at the door of Ken's Grill about five minutes before closing.

On the first visit, David Eason, who owns the grill along with his brother Ken, fixed me a plate of potato salad, some beans and a couple of pieces of bacon. They were sold out of barbecue and the grill had been shut down. With an infectious smile, David said "I'll never let a hungry man leave hungry." The food was good and filled a void but it was not memorable. The visit with David was special. Both David and his brother are rightfully proud of their barbecue place. Ken's Grill is another second-generation barbecue operation. Their father Kenneth, nicknamed "Skins," started a barbecue place called Skins' Drive-In down the road. He sold barbecue only on Saturdays. When Kenneth passed away in 1974, the boys were too young to own and operate a business. Skins' was sold and Ken worked for the new owner. Later, Ken bought the business back.

Ken built the now 70-seat restaurant on the present site in 1980. Ken and David have pretty much continued in their father's footsteps. The barbecue is no longer cooked over a wood-fired pit but is cooked on an electric cooker. Their dad's secret sauce recipe is still the same. The boys talk about it in hushed tones. The barbecue is chopped by hand.

On my second visit, I again arrived at the bewitching hour. Chairs were being turned up on tables and staff was mopping the floor. David, bless his heart, recognized the face pressed against the window and let me in. This time my meal consisted of some warmed-up beef barbecue, some slaw and bread. Again the food was good (not something to write home about) and a hungry man was fed. The memorable part was another good visit with David while he cleaned the grill and counters. David was kind to share many stories about his and Ken's childhood, their father, learning to cook barbecue and some of the ingredients in the family secret sauce.

On my third visit, I intentionally left Harkers Island early so I could get to Ken's Grill before the barbecue ran out. By this time I had become pretty determined that I was going to have some of that barbecue that the locals told me about. The third visit was a charm. I hit the mother lode. The barbecue had just been cooked the night before and was fresh, hot and scrumptious. This time I got the whole nine yards: barbecue, slaw, hushpuppies and a big glass of sweet tea. The gods were smiling. I found the chopped barbecue (whole hog) to be moist, tender with a good mix of outside brown and inside white. It had a rich, robust, savory barbecue flavor that many do not accomplish with an electrical cooker.

The slaw is traditional Eastern North Carolina white slaw and the hushpuppies are delicious. The white slaw was fresh, crisp, with a prominent cabbage flavor, light mayo and a hint of sweetness. The hushpuppies were little golden bars with a crisp outer shell, a nice moist center and a lingering cornbread taste that made them just about perfect. They are formed in a different way than most pups. Get the cook to make some while you're there. Interesting.

Ken's Grill still only serves barbecue on Wednesday and Saturday. It is cooked

the night before and served until it runs out.

In addition to barbecue, Ken's offers a host of side items and drive-in-type sandwiches including hand-patted hamburgers. On Friday nights, Ken's serves the one thing that, in my mind, surpasses the barbecue – fish stew. Come early. They always run out of the fish stew.

Ken's Grill is a small place located on the right as you are traveling east on U.S. Highway 70 and enter the little community of LaGrange, south of Kinston. You will have to look carefully since the signage is not large. Unless you're particularly fond of potato salad and bacon, I suggest you call ahead. Hours are from 5 a.m. until 3 p.m., Monday and Tuesday; 5 a.m. until 8 p.m., Wednesday through Friday; and 5 a.m. until 3 p.m., Saturday. It's closed Sunday. Telephone number: (252) 566-4765.

General McArthur's Original Pig Pickin', Laurinburg

In the 1980s, owner Colon Shallot McArthur, (owner) was still a farmer. Brent, his son and manager of General McArthur's Original Pig Pickin', said that a lot of the farmers (his father included) were having a hard go and his father decided to go into the barbecue business full time. Going into the barbecue business was not a new experience for Colon as he had been catering barbecue parties in the area for 25 years. Colon took two tenant houses and a tobacco barn and built his rustic restaurant on the edge of a rural road in a bean field. The seats are well-worn pews from an old church in the area.

Brent said when his father served in Vietnam, he was unable to go into combat areas because he was deaf in one ear and had poor hearing in the other. His father was put in the kitchen. Because of his cooking skills and presence in the kitchen and his last name, Colon picked up the handle "General McArthur." Colon and Brent had to apply to Washington to get permission to use the restaurant's name. It was subsequently approved because the five-star general, Douglas MacArthur, spelled his name differently.

Brent told of catering in Scotland. It seems that this came about as part of a student exchange program between schools in the area. Brent said it was a neat experience.

General McArthur's is a buffet-style restaurant with an extensive list of meats, vegetables and seafood. There are many pig parts from which to choose. The barbecue pork is cooked on electrical cookers and ground with a chopper.

The chopped barbecue is ground fairly fine like a minced barbecue. It was a bit dry for my taste. I believe this to be due to being ground too fine (which allows more air to get to the pork), coming off a buffet board, and being under heat lamps. The chopped barbecue comes sauced in the kitchen with an Eastern North Carolina vinegar-base sauce that has a mild peppery taste. The sauce gives the 'cue some moisture and makes a palatable dish with a lingering pepper aftertaste.

The pulled barbecue is like a pig pickin', much richer in pork flavor than the chopped barbecue. It is not smoky, but does have a good roasted-pork taste that is not heavy or greasy. With the sauce, this little piggy lights up. The peppery red sauce has this pork singing. It's my favorite offering here.

The red sauce is tomatoey and vinegary with black and red peppers that dance with the spices to create a carnival of flavors. Peppers are the stars here but are well behaved and do not steal the show. Apply lightly at the table.

The fried chicken has that tasty Southern-fried chicken taste that good Eastern Carolina cooks mastered so many years ago. It's just greasy enough to be delicious.

The slaw is finely chopped and has a good cabbage taste with fine chips of carrots and pickles. It's a bit more tart than most Eastern North Carolina white slaws.

General McArthur's has cornbread fritters that are some kind of good. The slightly crunchy golden crust encases a wonderfully moist cornbread center that has a delicious light corn taste. It's slightly greasy, but only to the extent that good cornbread

should be.

General McArthur's is located just off of U.S. Highway 74. Take Exit 15/401 South, go less than two miles to Hasty Road and turn left. Go a mile and a half to Barns Bridge Road. Turn right on Barns Bridge Road, go less than half a mile and the restaurant is on the right. The restaurant is a brown board and batten, unpainted rustic building. See the picture of a pig in a general's uniform with white scarf, sunglasses and corncob pipe out front.

Hours are 11 a.m. until 2 p.m., Wednesday through Friday for lunch, and 5 p.m. until 9 p.m., Wednesday through Saturday for dinner. It's open for Sunday brunch from 11 a.m. until 3 p.m. Telephone number: (910) 276-1498.

Howard's Barbecue, Lillington

Located on Highway 421 in Lillington overlooking the Cape Fear River, Howard's Barbecue has one of the most picturesque settings you will find among barbecue places in the east. Inside, a combination of burgundy and green wallpaper and rich paneling gives the place a nice, warm ambiance. The side of the restaurant located next to the river has a former patio now encased in glass for an outside seating feeling and an uninterrupted view of the Cape Fear. It's very tranquil and very nice.

The restaurant's owner, Howard Avrette, has been barbecuing pork most all of his life. He used to cook pigs for his family and friends. Friends encouraged him to quit CP&L (Carolina Power and Light) and open a restaurant. In 1971, Howard did just that. Howard ran Howard's Barbecue for 20 years and then David, his son, took over in 1991. Howard's started as a small barbecue that sat only 20 people. His first business was out toward the Old Farm community. The business then moved across the road and, in 1993, moved to its present site. Howard's now seats 100 more people than the original.

The wonderful cooked pork is accomplished on a hand-crafted, custom-built electric cooker that holds approximately 1,000 pounds of shoulders. After the meat has been slowly cooked for many, many hours at low heat, it is machine chopped with an adjustable chopper that has been tweaked to produce a chop that looks like hand chopped.

The chopped barbecue is sauced in the kitchen as soon as it's cooked. The whole shoulder is chopped, producing a mixture of brown and white moderately coarse chopped pork with lots of good outside brown flavor and a slightly chewy, wonderfully delicious taste. Tiny peppers dance on your tongue.

The hushpuppies are light with a crisp shell and a good moist center.

The slaw is finely chopped, fresh, crisp cabbage with light mayo, sugar and some pickle. It's slightly sweet and very good.

The reddish vinegar-base sauce has no tomatoes but it does have red peppers, seeds and spices. It's mighty fine.

Hours are 10:30 a.m. until 8 p.m., Tuesday and Wednesday, and 10:30 a.m. until 9 p.m., Thursday, Friday and Saturday. It's closed Sunday and Monday. Telephone number: (910) 893-4571.

Fuller's BBQ, Lumberton

Owner Fuller Locklear has cooked pigs all of his life as a farmer. Fuller extended his family pig pickin's to doing fundraisers for schools in Robeson County. With the black hair, black mustache and tan, Fuller looks more like a lead star on a daytime television series than a farmer.

Fuller has no family history of "my grandfather did it, my father did it and now I'm doing it." About 11 years ago, Fuller decided to go into the barbecue business. He built his present restaurant (large) at that time. Fuller said he pit cooks the barbecue on his farm, using only whole hogs and hickory and oak wood. The roasted hogs are brought to the restaurant and are chopped and sauced. Fuller does not do catering but will sell in bulk.

Fuller's slow-roasted barbecue is hand chopped and served as part of an extensive buffet which includes barbecue, seafood and other country cooking offerings typical of this area.

The barbecue pork is medium chopped with smoky nuances throughout. The delicious white meat mixes well with the outside brown (they chop the whole hog). It's moist with sauce from the kitchen. It's nutty and chewy but has no fat or gristle. This is a good Eastern North Carolina 'cue. With some additional drops of the house sauce at the table, my, oh my, this is some kinda good.

The vinegar-base sauce is red with peppers and spices that stand up and speak to you.

The coleslaw is white, medium-coarse chopped cabbage with carrots, pickles and light mayo. This is good Eastern Carolina slaw. The hushpuppies are small, light, cream-colored puffs.

The fried chicken has a good crisp outside and a tender inside, especially for a buffet line that had been out awhile. I got there just before closing time.

From I-95 South, take Exit 20 and turn right. Go a quarter of a mile and Fuller's BBQ is on the left. It is a large building and you can't miss it. There is a sign at the end of the exit ramp. Hours are 11 a.m. until 9 p.m., Monday through Friday, and 11:30 a.m. until 9 p.m., Saturday. It's open 11:30 a.m. until 4 p.m. on Sunday. Telephone number: (910) 738-8694.

Village Inn Barbecue, Lumberton

Village Inn Barbecue began as Hayes Barbecue 30 years ago in a location across the road. In the late '70s, the restaurant moved to its present site and changed its name to Village Inn Barbecue. At this time, they started serving seafood along with their barbecue treats. Dewey Stone bought half interest in the late '80s and started into the barbecue business from scratch. Dewey took to the business like a duck to water. He bought out the other owner about four years ago.

I knew this would be a good place to eat when I stopped at a pizza place outside of town encircled with Highway Patrol cruisers. I asked three of the patrol officers about good barbecue and they said they all got together at the Village Inn for barbecue on Friday nights.

The Village Inn cooks its pork shoulders electrically for 80 percent of the cooking time and then the slow-roasted meat is finished over an open pit with charcoal. The meat is served minced and sliced.

The minced barbecue is ground fine and tastes of vinegar and black pepper. It's tart, moist and sauced in the kitchen. It has a slight charcoal flavor, but is not heavy and is certainly pleasing.

The sliced barbecue is moist and has a good roast-pork flavor. The outside brown pieces mix in to add flavor. With the sauce at the table, this is my favorite.

The slaw is a white Eastern North Carolina variety with fresh cabbage, flecks of carrot and light mayo. It's moist but not too juicy.

The hushpuppies are light and have a cream color. The thin shell houses a moist center with good cornbread taste.

The vinegar-base sauce is red and very tart with lots of spices. There are just enough peppers to be interesting but not overly hot. It has no lasting aftertaste. It's moderately hot but not fiery.

Hours are 10:30 am. until 9 p.m., Thursday, and 10:30 a.m. until 9:30 p.m., Friday and Saturday. Unfortunately, it's closed Sunday through Wednesday. Telephone number: (910) 739-2050.

A&M Grill,
Mebane

A&M Grill, founded by Charlie R. McAdams Sr., has been in business at the same location since 1947.

Charlie was another one of Warner Stamey's (Greensboro Stamey's) barbecue protégés. Charlie started working with Warner Stamey in the 1940s. Charlie was supposed to go to Lexington and open a branch restaurant for Stamey. Instead, Charlie came to Mebane and opened his own small business called The Log Cabin. In 1947, Charlie was running a service station that had a small kitchen area, a few booths and some bar stools. From his tiny kitchen Charlie began selling his delicious barbecue.

People took notice and within a year Charlie had them lined out the door. To accommodate his ever-growing number of customers, Charlie built the dining room where one enters today. Charlie built the back dining room two years later. Charlie ran the place until his death in 1971. Charlie R. McAdams Jr., who had been working at his dad's side, took over the management of the grill along with his wife Donna. Three daughters, a son-in-law and a congenial staff ably assist Charlie Jr. and Donna.

Donna said that A&M cooks pork shoulders slowly and lovingly for approximately 14 hours on pits over live hickory coals. Donna said they rarely cook hams except on holidays and for special orders. All chopped barbecue at A&M is hand chopped. A&M does everything surrounding its delicious pork products in the old-fashioned method with the original recipes, and it shows.

The chopped barbecue is a moderately coarse chop that tastes as if it were sauced in the kitchen with Eastern Carolina vinegar-base sauce and then a Lexington-style dip ladled on top. The 'cue is very moist and tender. The outside brown mixed with the inside white produces a pungent woodsy flavor that gives this barbecue good balance, texture and taste.

The sliced barbecue pork is thick, tender slices of pork. It's my favorite offering at A&M. It has a wonderful woodsy, nutty, smoky flavor that's very tender like a pig pickin'. The sliced pork comes sauced in the kitchen with a tomato-base sauce. It's slightly twangy but not hot. It has kind of a sweet and sour taste and is a nice partner with the sliced 'cue. This pork has an exceptional deep, rich taste that can only come from cooking over live coals by someone who knows how to do it. In the immortal words of K.C. and the Sunshine Band "That's the way, uh-huh, uh-huh, I like it. Uh-huh."

The hushpuppies have a golden skin and a moist cornbread center with a hint of onion. They are slightly sweet – a really good pup.

The coleslaw is pink coleslaw and has a good, fresh white cabbage taste up front. There's a hint of vinegar. The addition of ketchup with the mayo turns the slaw pink. I don't know why they want to do that, but it tastes good.

Neither my business nor my curiosity had ever carried me to Mebane before my visit to the A&M Grill (my loss). After you leave the interstate and get into the little town of Mebane, you find yourself passing through a corridor of lovely restored antebellum, gingerbread homes. By the time you reach the railroad tracks that cross Fifth Street, you feel that you have stepped back into a kinder, gentler time. This mood is not broken when you enter A&M Grill. It seems reminiscent of the '40s and '50s. The next time you're riding down I-40 and see the Mebane exit, take it. You won't be sorry to have taken a moment from your busy schedule to be swept back into the comfort zone that only a small town like Mebane affords. A&M's delicious barbecue is just frosting on the cake.

A&M Grill is located on East Center Street in Mebane. From I-40, take the Mebane exit (Highway 119). It becomes Fifth Street until you cross over the railroad tracks. This is a hike from I-40, probably five miles. When you cross over the railroad tracks, turn immediately to your right onto Center Street. Go approximately one mile and A&M Grill is on your left.

Hours are 6:30 a.m. until 8 p.m., Monday through Saturday. It's closed Sunday. Telephone number: (919) 563-3721.

Eddie's Barbecue, Newton Grove

Owner Eddie Giddens grew up in the barbecue business. His dad (Henry) started Henry's Barbecue at the present site in 1956. As a 6-year-old, Eddie used to stand on pop crates to help his dad cook. Eddie said that at that tender age he also peeled 100 pounds of potatoes a day by hand. Eddie's dad ran Henry's for approximately 20 years and then sold the place to Shirley and Wayne Williams. The Williams ran the place for another 20 years. During this time Eddie grew up, moved to Raleigh and worked for Pepsi. He returned to Newton Grove 17 years ago. Upon his return, Eddie opened a barbecue place in the Old Frog Island Building. The building acquired its name because it was by a swamp in one of the lowest places in the county. Every big rain produced some flooding and frogs. Eddie got the opportunity to buy his dad's old barbecue place from the Williams in 1990 and he came full circle.

Eddie's Barbecue moved across town back to its roots. Though the ownership has come full circle and the cooking method has changed from wood to gas to electrical, the product, the hospitality and the service remains outstanding. Eddie's Barbecue transforms whole hogs into "pretty pigs." This transformation is accomplished with an electrical cooker (McClan) and slow, all-night roasting. The barbecue is then carefully chopped by hand. Eddie then cooks his pork skin and chops it up into tiny, tiny kernels and mixes it with his barbecue.

Eddie goes to great lengths to make sure that his pork product is the best available. Each week Eddie takes his truck and stock trailer and goes to a friend's local hog farm and picks out only number one hogs for his restaurant. Eddie then takes his hogs to a slaughterhouse where they are processed and kept for Eddie until needed on a daily basis. After cooking his pretty pigs, Eddie separates the pig into six distinctive parts and chops each part separately. Portions of all six parts of the hog, along with some tiny skin sprinkles, produce Eddie's wonderful barbecue product.

The chopped barbecue is moderately coarse and is sauced in the kitchen. The zippy vinegar highlights, couched with a rich roasted-pork flavor, make a dynamic duo. Flakes of red pepper dance with good outside brown. This 'cue starts mild and finishes strong as peppers come on at the end.

Eddie's uses a red vinegar-base sauce with lots of peppers and seeds. By itself, WOW! On the barbecue, it's just the right kick but use sparingly. This sauce is so thick with peppers, you could eat it with a fork.

It's good stuff.

White cabbage is coarsely chopped to make this slaw which is very crunchy, very fresh and very good. The hushpuppies are light with a golden outside shell and a moist cornbread center. The pups are not greasy.

From I-40, take the Newton Grove exit (Hwy 701 north), go a mile or so to Newton Grove and go around the traffic circle to other side. Eddie's is a quarter mile on the right north of Newton Grove. Hours are 11 a.m. until 9 p.m., Monday through Saturday. It's closed Sunday. Telephone number: (910) 594-1144.

Smithfield's Chicken 'n Bar-B-Q, Newton Grove

Smithfield's Chicken 'n Bar-B-Q is a chain operation with 17 places located in Eastern North Carolina. Some of the places are owned by the company, which is headquartered in Cary. See the bottom of this review for a list of the locations.

I have eaten at several Smithfield's Chicken 'n Bar-B-Q places both company-owned and franchise-owned. I found the food to be uniformly fresh and good at all the locations I have visited.

Smithfield's Chicken 'n Bar-B-Q serves pulled barbecue pork like that at a pig pickin'. It is served from the kitchen in large pieces about the size of three fingers. The barbecue is very tender and moist without the sauce at the table. It is served from the kitchen with a light serving of Eastern North Carolina-style barbecue sauce. The 'cue has a good outside brown and inside white mix and a wonderfully robust roast pork flavor. I found this 'cue to have a rich brown nutty taste. It's just really good barbecue by anyone's yardstick.

The barbecue sauce is a classic Eastern North Carolina vinegar base with crushed red peppers. The vinegar taste steps to the front and is mildly hot. It has a good start and a good finish.

The chicken and rib sauce is reddish, medium hot and tastes good by itself. I found this sauce to be great on chicken and ribs but also good on the pulled barbecue pork.

The brunswick stew is rich and thick with hunks of potatoes, corn, tomatoes, green beans and lots of chicken. It tastes like a really good, thick vegetable soup like your mamma would make. I enjoyed the stew but somehow it did not reach my expectations of a brunswick stew.

Smithfield's makes an Eastern North Carolina white-cabbage coleslaw that's crisp, tart and fresh. This slaw is a nice side with the chicken and barbecue.

The hushpuppies are golden brown and moist with a good cornbread taste and just a hint of sugar. The pups were ever so slightly greasy but good none the less.

The fried chicken at Smithfield's Chicken 'n Bar-B-Q is pound the table good. This delicious offering has a crisp, crunchy outer shell and a moist tender center. This is the one your favorite aunt makes that causes you to rush to the front of the line at the family reunion. Have seconds for dessert.

Smithfield's other locations are as follows:
• Jones Sausage Rd., Garner I-40 exit 303
• 40/42 Garner, I-40 exit 312

- Newton Grove, I-40 exit 341
- Warsaw, I-40 exit 364
- Clayton, Hwy 70
- Smithfield, 924 N. Brightleaf Blvd. (Hwy 301)
- Hope Mills, 5539 Camden Rd.
- Fayetteville, Intersection of Raeford Rd. and Cliffdale Rd. (Hwy 401)
- Havelock, Hwy 70
- Zebulon, Triangle East Shopping Center (Hwy 64 exit 421)
- Dunn, Harnett Crossing Shopping Center (I-95 exit 73 – Hwy 421)
- Morehead City, Hwy 70

- Wilmington, 7300 Market St. (Hwy 17)
- New Bern, Intersection of Hwy 70 and 17
- Jacksonville, 1105 Gum Branch Rd.
- Jacksonville, 315 Western Blvd.
- Hwy 401 S., Garner McCullers Crossroads

To get to the Newton Grove location, take I-40 to Newton Grove. Take Exit 312 and it's right there. You can't miss it. Hours are 10 a.m. until 9:30 p.m., Sunday through Thursday, and 10 a.m. until 10:30 p.m., Friday through Saturday. Telephone number: (910) 594-0415.

Clyde Cooper's Barbeque, Raleigh

Return with me to those thrill-packed days of yesteryear. From out of the past comes the thunder of hoof beats and a hearty Hi-Yo Silver, the Lone Ranger rides again. Okay maybe the Lone Ranger didn't eat at Clyde Cooper's Barbeque, but some of his friends did. Check out the picture on the front of Cooper's menu showing Clyde Cooper on the left and one of his buddies on the right who has just ridden his beautiful Palomino into town for some of Clyde's good 'cue.

Clyde Cooper, founder of Clyde Coopers Barbeque, was living proof that barbecue not only tastes good but was good for you. Clyde's good pork products served him well. He lived to the ripe old age of 99 years. Good sources tell me that Clyde's cowboy friend just turned 102 and his horse placed second last month at Santa Anita at age 90. There's no end to what good barbecue can do for man and beast. And Cooper's barbecue is some of the best.

When you enter Clyde Cooper's Barbeque you enter a time warp. This is the way Barbecue Places used to look when I was a child. Two long narrow rooms, a long counter with 13 stools (one is missing), 15 four-tops and five two-tops serve the constant stream of barbecue aficionados that frequently visit this barbecue legend like it

was a pilgrimage. All with good reason as the food here is tops.

Established in 1938, Clyde Cooper's Barbeque has been a fixture in downtown Raleigh and played a large part in the eating habits of its citizenry. Clyde Cooper's Barbeque is a barbecue man's barbecue place. It looks like a barbecue place from the outside. It looks like a barbecue place from the inside. It smells like a barbecue place. It is a barbecue place.

Clyde Cooper's Barbeque serves pork barbecue (chopped or sliced), pork barbecue spareribs, barbecue chicken, chopped barbecue chicken and fried chicken. These mouth-watering items are accompanied by succulent sides of collard greens, steamed cabbage, corn, butter beans, boiled potatoes, potato salad, coleslaw, french fries and brunswick stew. The beverages of choice are iced tea or lemonade and canned soft drinks. If you still have room for dessert, the offerings are lemon pie or carrot cake.

All of the above listed wonderful items can be purchased in bulk including whole cooked shoulders or whole pigs. In fact, you can rent a pig cooker and buy an uncooked pig to round out your barbecue plans.

The chopped barbecue is moderately chopped, sauced in the kitchen with an Eastern Carolina vinegar-base sauce, hot with peppers, perfect marriage with the 'cue. The chopped barbecue is very moist and nicely spiced. If one adds additional sauce at the table I would suggest adding it sparingly as it comes just about perfect from the kitchen.

The coarse-chopped barbecue is tender roast pork with a delightful flavor. With a hint of vinegar sauce and woodsy overtones, it's absolutely delicious.

The meat on the barbecue spareribs falls right off the bone. Even the bones are tender. The ribs have a good roasted pork taste and are slightly spicy.

The slaw is a yellow variety with a strong green and white cabbage flavor. With the chips of carrot and mustard, the slaw goes nicely with the 'cue.

The hushpuppies have a brown outer shell and a moist center with a nice, rich cornmeal taste. It's slightly greasy, just enough for great taste. It's a very light, tasty pup.

The sauce is an Eastern North Carolina vinegar-base sauce that is tannish-brown in color. It has a strong vinegar beginning with notable pepper presence. This classic Eastern North Carolina barbecue sauce is just hot enough with no lasting aftertaste.

The brunswick stew has lots of vegetables, corn, butter beans, green beans, carrots and tomatoes. This offering is fairly thick for a stew and tastes more like a good, rich vegetable soup. I had never had carrots in a brunswick stew before. This and the taste, to me, makes it more like a soup.

You can't help but enjoy yourself at Clyde Cooper's Barbeque. The walls are covered with pictures of old Raleigh including those of downtown buildings with horses in front, Model A Fords and early construction of what are now Raleigh landmarks. In addition, there's a pig over the door. The men's bathroom is marked Boars and I assume (I did not seek it out) the woman's bathroom is marked Gilts (young girl pigs). Sows would be rather unflattering.

Cooper's Barbeque is located at 109 East Davie St., one block east of Fayetteville Street Mall in downtown Raleigh. There is an hourly parking lot directly across the street that generally has space even during lunch.

Hours are 10 a.m. until 6 p.m., Monday through Saturday. It's closed Sunday. Telephone number: (919) 832-7614.

Note: The above introduction is the best I can recall of the beginning of the *Lone Ranger* radio program I listened to as a small child sponsored by Merita Bread. It was one of my favorites along with *The Shadow, The Green Hornet* and *Johnny Dollar*.

233

Don Murray's Barbecue and Seafood, Raleigh

Don Murray's Barbecue and Seafood is a large, white-framed building located almost on the corner of the 440 belt-line and Capital Boulevard. The sign is a large dollhouse looking replica of the restaurant itself. The restaurant sits back off the road and it's a bit difficult to see if you're not looking for it carefully.

Don Murray's has an extensive buffet much on the order of the barbecue places east of I-85 and south of U.S. Highway 70. Good barbecue appears on the menu in a number of forms: chopped barbecue pork, barbecue chicken and barbecue pork ribs. These items are served separately or in combination as dinners and they appear on the buffet along with a host of seafood items and vegetables.

Don Murray's menu offers at least 20 different dinners and at least that many side dishes. Breads come in the form of hush-puppies or cornsticks – both are delicious. Sinfully rich desserts include a cobbler of the day, various cakes, pecan pie and the star dessert of any good barbecue place – banana pudding.

Don Murray's barbecue products are cooked electrically and chopped with a Hobart Chopper.

The chopped barbecue was moderately chopped and sauced in the kitchen with a good Eastern Carolina vinegar-base sauce. It's slightly hot and seasoned well with lots of flecks of red pepper.

The barbecue comes from the kitchen with ample sauce if you actually want to taste the 'cue. If you add sauce at the table, I suggest you do it a few drops at a time. It won't take much additional sauce to raise the heat. This is good 'cue.

The cornsticks are a light golden tan. They're crisp but not crunchy and have a wonderful cornmeal taste, more so than the hushpuppies. The hushpuppies have a good crisp golden outer shell and a moist center. They're slightly sweet and are not greasy.

The coleslaw is white and tart with a predominant cabbage taste. Tiny celery seeds and mayo produce a very fresh, light-tasting slaw with hints of sweetness.

The basting sauce is a red-colored Eastern North Carolina vinegar-base sauce. It's hot with peppers – not for ice cream. The sauce is great with the barbecue.

The red, tomato-base dipping sauce is thick with vinegar and a host of spices. I found it to be delicious. It is more a sauce for the chicken or pulled pork than a sauce designed for the chopped 'cue. It has both a slightly sweet and spicy taste which works well. To my palate it was more like a good sweet and sour dip.

Don Murray's hours are 11 a.m. until 9 p.m., Monday through Saturday, and

Sunday, 11 a.m. until 8 p.m. Telephone number: (919) 872-6270.

Short Sugar's Drive-In, Reidsville

Short Sugar's Drive-In opened in June 1949. Located on Scales Street in Reidsville, it had the typical 1950s drive-in look. Even today, it has no curb. A painting inside depicts its configuration before the expansion on the left side of the building. It originally was a glass front drive-in with twin chimneys for barbecuing and a lunch counter with stools. You expect the Fonz to step out at any moment.

Since adding more seating capacity with booths and tables, Short Sugar's is larger but still has the old '50s drive-in look.

Short Sugar's was originally the dream of the Overby brothers Johnny, Clyde and Eldridge. However, Eldridge was killed in an auto accident a few days before its opening. The two surviving brothers, Johnny and Clyde, decided to name the restaurant in honor of their brother and called it by his nickname, "Short Sugar." There are varied tales around town as to how Eldridge acquired that nickname. All agree he was not tall. It stops there. Local folk with a twinkle in their eye will tell you a myriad of tales about the "sugar" part of Eldridge's nickname. In any event, the restaurant that bears his nickname is a landmark in Reidsville.

Louise Whaley who oversees the breakfast preparation has been arriving at Short Sugar's at 3 a.m., six days a week, for more than 40 years. Louise's husband, Bill, was the overseer of cooking the meat until 1999 when health caused him to throttle back. He still comes by to check on the operation and to make sure that his trainees are carrying out their tasks. Short Sugar's only chops or slices pork as ordered to ensure the meat is fresh and moist. This task puts added pressure on those chopping and slicing, but from all observations, it seems to be in good hands.

Out of 35 employees, about a dozen have been there 10 years or longer. Bill and Louise have been there since 1949 while George Clinton worked for owners of the place before it was Short Sugar's. George kinda came with the building. He's a delightful man.

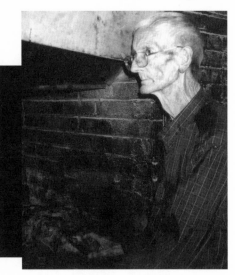

George Clinton

236

Short Sugar's pit cooks its pork over open pits using hickory coals. The pit and firebox are located behind the counter and immediately next to the drive-in window. This makes for what one could only describe as a "hot corner," not only in terms of heat but also in activity. When the cover to the pits is open, coals are shoveled from the firebox on the right, under the meat. The wonderful aroma that only comes from meat slow cooking over coals wafts across the restaurant causing you to want to order again when you have already eaten.

Johnny Overby developed the sauce used at Short Sugar's when they were only a hot dog and hamburger stand. David Wilson, Johnny Overby's son-in-law, is the keeper of the sauce. David oversees its mixing from the original recipe. David said they use and market approximately 72 gallons per week. David said that they do not baste their meat at all when cooking. He said that mostly they use hams and some shoulders. There is more net product from the hams than from the shoulders that have more fat, he said. The meat is cooked over a raised pit using only the hard woods oak and hickory. David said they use slabs, not split logs, since slabs produce coals faster.

In 1981, some political figures in Washington, D.C. came upon the idea to have a barbecue bowl or cook-off between North and South Carolina barbecue restau-rants. The event was held with much fanfare. After the cook-off, in typical political fashion, the judges declared a tie. The following year a barbecue bowl was held and Short Sugar's was one of the invitees. Short Sugar's had just closed for remodeling and expansion. Short Sugar's won the 1982 Barbecue Bowl and was the first restaurant from either North Carolina or South Carolina to be crowned champion. This happened at the same time that Short Sugar's reopened its restaurant after remodeling. David said that on the day they reopened, a TV news crew, *Stars and Stripes* and others came over to interview the new champion. He said that from a media/publicity standpoint one could not have planned the event any better.

Short Sugar's sauce is a brown, smoky liquid that imparts memorable flavor to the chopped and sliced barbecue. The sauce is more akin to Eastern North Carolina sauce in texture as it has less tomato paste or ketchup, but it does not taste like a Lexington-style dip. I found the sauce thin, dark brown, vinegary, peppery and slightly sweet. There was some presence of sugar and Worcestershire that gave the sauce zip. David said that all of the sauce was made with Garner Food Products. He said that changing any one item to another brand would change the overall taste of the sauce. I agree.

The barbecue was chopped by hand. I had the coarse-chopped barbecue, which was pleasantly moist with a good smoky flavor. It came lightly sauced from the kitchen with the original Short Sugar's sauce. The sliced ham with Short Sugar's sauce was very moist and tender with a light smoky taste – an absolute joy.

Short Sugar's also cooks ribs. David said these pre-cooked and pre-smoked ribs were packaged by Bryan. Short Sugar's heats the ribs in their special rib sauce for an hour or more. The ribs were very tender and had a delightfully smoked flavor with piques of tanginess from the sauce. Because the rib sauce is one-half Kansas City original and one-half Short Sugar's sauce blended, the ribs are not as sticky as some of the rib sauces I have encountered in other states. It's very tasty.

Reidsville is off of U.S. Highway 29, north of Greensboro. From the south, take U.S. 29 Business into Reidsville and bear right on Scales Street. Short Sugar's will be on the left. From the north, exit U.S. 29 onto N.C. Highway 87 and follow it into Reidsville. Turn onto Scales Street. After several blocks, you will see the restaurant on the right. Hours are 12 p.m. until 9 p.m., Monday through Thursday. It's closed Sunday. Telephone number: (336) 342-7487.

238

Gardner's Barbecue, Rocky Mount

This well known Rocky Mount barbecue icon has a large following locally and around the state. Originally founded by Jim Gardner, Gardner's Barbecue is now owned by Jim's brother Jerry. Though the torch has been passed, in the minds of its faithful followers Gardner's Barbecue still produces mighty fine 'cue.

Gardner's Barbecue has three locations in Rocky Mount. The home base and larger of the three being on Highway 301. The fare here is much like many of the restaurants east of I-85 and south of Highway 70. It is a buffet replete with good barbecue, fried chicken, country vegetables and mounds of delicious seafood. The offerings can be purchased in the form of a buffet (all you care to eat) by plates or combination plates.

The barbecue pork comes only in the form of chopped 'cue. It is sauced at the kitchen. This barbecue like many of its eastern neighbors is moderately fine chopped and slightly dry with flecks of red pepper peeking from within. The chopped barbecue has a hint of vinegar as served. For my taste this offering was a teeny bit dry (I admit prejudice for hot pulled pork from a whole hog, pig pickin' style). It has a delicious roast pork flavor as a result of being cooked on gas grills. The 'cue has no hints of smoki-ness but the outside brown mixes well with the inside white to produce a good robust pork flavor that satisfies the most demanding aficionado.

I found the fried chicken breast golden brown and moderately moist on the inside. The outside was neither greasy or moist. It was good chicken.

The brunswick stew was tomato based with lots of corn, some baby lima beans, green beans, some meat and tastes to me like a good homemade vegetable soup. This brunswick stew is cooked the way most eastern folks like it.

The house sauce was a reddish colored vinegar base Eastern North Carolina style sauce with lots of zip. This one is a bit fiery. I liked it.

Gardner's barbecue slaw was a green colored coleslaw consisting of finely chopped cabbage that produced a bright fresh taste that goes well with the 'cue. This one has a hint of mustard. I find this a nice change of pace from the traditional white slaw with mayo.

The bread at Gardner's consist of cornsticks and hushpuppies. The cornsticks had a nice crunchy skin, a moist center and were to my taste a bit heavy. The hushpuppies had a golden shell with a moist center and presented as a very light, airy pup. To my taste, the hushpuppies were several clicks above the cornsticks.

If after eating any of Gardner's delicious offerings you still have room for dessert, Gardner's has a dessert bar almost 10 feet long. Enjoy!

To reach Gardner's from Highway 64 East, go to the intersection of Highway 301. Take Highway 301 approximately one mile. Gardner's is on the left. Hours are 11 a.m. until 9 p.m., Sunday through Thursday and 11 a.m. until 9:30 p.m., Friday and Saturday. Telephone number: (252) 446-2983.

HAVE BEEN INFORMED THAT RESTAURANT
HAS CLOSED SINCE FIRST PRINTING OF BOOK

Bob Melton's Barbecue, Rocky Mount

Bob Melton, Eastern North Carolina barbecue guru, began his barbecue operation on the banks of the Tar River in a wood and tin shed in 1922. Bob Melton acquired a reputation for producing outstanding barbecue. He was often mentioned in articles about North Carolina and southern barbecue. One magazine even linked him with "king." Though he was "discovered" in his later years by regional and national writers, the good people of Eastern North Carolina, more particularly the Rocky Mount area had known of his barbecuing skills for more than 35 years.

In 1924, Bob Melton opened his first sit-down restaurant on the banks of the mighty Tar. And the familiar white-frame building became a barbecue shrine for much of Eastern North Carolina. Generations of barbecue lovers would drive down the old dirt road or come by boat, depending upon the weather, for some of Bob Melton's superb barbecue. Spring rains, flooding, mosquitoes as big as buzzards, nothing deterred the faithful.

Various storms and floods contributed to the changing faces of Bob Melton's Barbecue emporium. Despite the facelifts, paved parking and vinyl siding, Melton's on the river provided a comfort zone for its patrons for 75 years. The flooding from Hurricane Floyd in 1999 changed all of this forever. Melton's was destroyed and they were unable to rebuild at that site.

Melton's new address is 501 Old Mill Rd. in Rocky Mount. The new quarters looks much like a Shoney's restaurant. It has a curved glass atrium-looking front. The interior looks very clean, bright with fresh new paint and carpet. It looks nothing like any barbecue place at which I've eaten that has been in existence for a long time. Fortunately the only thing that changed about this Rocky Mount barbecue icon was its address and its building.

Tommy Smith, the owner, said Melton's was using the same recipes, cooking style and sauces as they had at the old place on the river. He said their loyal friends still seek them out and business is good. Tommy also said that he did not miss having to carry hip waders in his car during the rainy season to get to and from the restaurant as he did at its old location on the Tar.

Bob Melton was one of the first to cook and sell at a sit-down restaurant the type of pork barbecue commonly referred to today as Eastern North Carolina-style barbecue. This style barbecue was generally produced from cooking whole hogs on rods over an open pit containing oak or hickory coals. The whole hog was then broken down, hand chopped into a fairly dry, finely chopped offering that was seasoned in the kitchen with the same sauce used to baste the roasting pig. This sauce was vinegar base plus salt, black pepper and finely ground red pepper. The sauce became known as Eastern North Carolina sauce. It's Lexington-style counterpart is called dip. It has ketchup, tomato paste or tomato puree along with brown sugar to which other spices are added. Unlike many of his counterparts, Bob Melton added a sheet of tin on top of the pig so that coals could be shoveled on top as well as under the pig providing heat from both sides. Today, Melton's famous 'cue is cooked with gas and no one seems to mind at all.

On my recent visit to Melton's Barbecue at its new location, I found the barbecue to be very tasty. Melton's barbecue is still among the best of the Eastern North Carolina-style barbecue. It has a delicious roast pork flavor and the brown and white mix of the cooked pork shoulders created a delightful flavor festival for this diner. I prefer my barbecue a bit more moist than

Melton's 'cue but legions prefer it just as it is. And if I were Tommy Smith and my choice was to please a few or legions I would definitely opt for legions.

The sauce at Melton's is just like days of yore. It is a peppery vinegar-base sauce in the best of Eastern North Carolina tradition.

The coleslaw was yellow, crisp with green cabbage prominent and a trailing hint of mustard.

The fried chicken at Bob Melton's makes strong men weak and women swoon. I could eat this chicken three times a day, 365 days a year. It is absolutely wonderful.

The address has changed and the ambiance is not the same but the product that made Bob Melton's a legend in its time, remains unchanged in the minds of the faithful. Whether Bob Melton's is a destination or a stopover for a weary traveler, you can still get some of the best Eastern North Carolina barbecue and fried chicken a fella could ever hope to find.

Bob Melton's Barbecue is open 10 a.m. until 8 p.m., Monday through Thursday, and 10 a.m. until 9 p.m., Friday and Saturday. It's open from 10 a.m. until 3 p.m. on Sunday. Telephone number: (252) 446-8513.

Ron's Barn BBQ and Seafood, Sanford

Ron's Barn is one of those new places that is made to look old. The building has a rustic clapboard outside and a rusting tin roof (just enough for patina). The entry is decorated with old farm implements and the dining area is designed to look like a tobacco pack house. The place gives you the old country store feel. Ron's serves a buffet that includes some really good barbecue. One enjoys Ron's wonderful food on tables covered by red-and-white checkered oilcloth tablecloths. This is country food served quickly in a country setting.

Ron's cooking is also a little bit of the old and a little bit of the new. The pork is cooked electrically, but Ron has held on to the Eastern North Carolina tradition of cooking whole hogs and the pork is hand pulled and hand chopped.

The chopped barbecue is served moderately coarse and sauced from the kitchen with an Eastern North Carolina vinegar-base sauce. The 'cue has good flavor, a vinegar prominence with enough red peppers to get your attention. It has a pleasant, lasting aftertaste. The whole hog barbecue presents with good outside brown mixed with inside white that provides a good texture and a nice mix of flavors. This barbecue is sauced just right for me. I don't need more. With additional sauce at the table, the 'cue really steps up to hot in a hurry.

The slaw is good, crisp, crunchy white cabbage with light mayo. It has chips of green bell pepper and pickles. The slaw is not runny. It offsets the sauce nicely and makes a great sandwich. It's good combined with the 'cue.

The hushpuppies have a golden shell, a really good cornbread taste and a moist center. But they are a bit heavy.

The sauce is a good, hot vinegar-base Eastern North Carolina-style sauce with plenty of peppers. Use sparingly.

Ron's Barn is on the southern side of Sanford where Highway 421 and Highway 87 intersect. Going north on Highway 421, Ron's Barn is just north of the little community of Seminole. Lunch hours are 11 a.m. until 2 p.m., Tuesday through Friday and Sunday while dinner hours are 5 p.m. until 9 p.m., Thursday, Friday and Saturday. Telephone number: (919) 774-8143.

Holt Lake Bar-B-Que and Seafood, Smithfield

From 1976 through 1978 James and Helen Barefoot leased the barbecue place that is now the White Swan. In 1979 they built Holt Lake Bar-B-Que and Seafood at the present site. Several years later they had the misfortune of a fire that consumed a large part of the business. James and Helen rebuilt Holt Lake Bar-B-Que and Seafood 20 years ago as it presently exists. Today this barbecue emporium is owned and run by James and Helen's sons, Terry and Kevin Barefoot.

My charming waitperson Janice Jackson has been working at Holt Lake for the past 15 years.

Holt Lake Bar-B-Que cooks whole hogs, hams and shoulders electrically on a Barbecue Slave cooker. Brothers Terry and Kevin shared that they bought their hogs from James Masengill. The cooked pork is chopped with a Hobart Chopper.

The chopped pork barbecue is moderately chopped and sauced at the kitchen with a classic Eastern North Carolina sauce. Flakes of red pepper play peek-a-boo from behind tasty morsels of delicious roasted pork. This barbecue is moist with a good mix of brown and white meat that produces a very well balanced flavor. This 'cue has a good start and a good finish with no fiery aftertaste. I found all of the Holt Lake Bar-B-Que offerings to be fine representatives of all that is good about Eastern North Carolina barbecue.

The sauce served at Holt Lake is a typical Eastern North Carolina style vinegar-base sauce. This sauce has lots of red peppers and it pretty hot stuff by itself. On the barbecue it calms down quite a bit to offer a really fine compliment to all of Holt Lake's pork products. For my palate the 'cue could use a few dashes to bring it up a click. I suggest you take a toothpick and clean your sauce bottle ports so they will pass more peppers or you can simply shake the bottle up and remove the cap and ladle some on the 'cue with a teaspoon.

The slaw offering consisted of white cabbage chopped moderately with carrot chips, flecks of pickle and celery seed, which produced a fresh cabbage taste with a bright flavor. The slaw is light on mayo and is a typical Eastern North Carolina style coleslaw.

The hushpuppies are golden brown in color and the outer shell has a slight crunch encasing a moderately moist center. The pups are slightly sweet and more than slightly good.

If the secret of Holt Lake's good Bar-B-Que was not already out, the recent article in Our State magazine spilled the beans.

244

In addition to its delicious barbecue pork, Holt Lake Bar-B-Que has yummy fried chicken that is sold separately and in combination plates with the pork. Holt Lake also has a large array of fresh seafood, sandwiches and an extensive vegetable list which includes brunswick stew. The brunswick stew here is very, very good.

Holt Lake Bar-B-Que and Seafood is located on Highway 301 South in Smithfield. From I-95 take the Smithfield exit. Follow Highway 301. Holt Lake will be on your left and Holt Lake Bar-B-Que and Seafood will be on your left just beyond the lake. Hours are 11 a.m. until 2 p.m., Monday and 11 a.m. until 9 p.m., Tuesday through Saturday. It's closed Sunday. Telephone number: (919) 934-0148 or (919) 934-5564.

White Swan Restaurant, Smithfield

The White Swan Restaurant was established more than 60 years ago. Its present owner, Linwood Parker, bought the business some 11 years ago. Linwood has carried the White Swan into four locations.

Linwood's manager, Marie Simmons, has been with him since he bought the business. She is a gracious hostess and very proud of the good pork products the White Swan produces. The White Swan cooks pork shoulders electrically with a Barbecue Slave. The meat is chopped by hand.

The chopped barbecue is a moderately coarse chop. The outside brown mixed with the inside white makes it an outstanding offering. Marie said they mix everything except the skin. They fry the skin for pork skins that are sold separately. The chopped barbecue is sauced in the kitchen and has a good Eastern North Carolina vinegar-base taste and plenty of red pepper. It has a strong start and strong finish, but does not carry a lingering hot aftertaste.

The slaw is very finely chopped, sweet and flavorful with carrot pieces.

The hushpuppies are rich, caramel brown with a nice crusty outside and a moist center. They have a very good, slightly sweet cornbread taste and are not greasy. The texture is almost like cake or spoon bread.

The fried chicken is cooked in vegetable oil. The chicken is crisp outside, but not brittle, and moist inside. It's absolutely delicious.

The brunswick stew has a Pocahontas Tomato Puree base with tomatoes, celery, onions, baby lima beans, green beans, corn, diced potatoes, beef, pork and chicken. The stew is thick, slightly sweet and does not have a vegetable-soup taste. The White Swan sells approximately 500 gallons per week.

The sauce is typical Eastern North Carolina-style sauce with the traditional vinegar, crushed red pepper, salt, etc.

The White Swan serves pork ribs everyday and fish on Friday. For the past 15 years, the White Swan has sold barbecue sandwiches for 99 cents on Thursday at 4 p.m. Lines form out the door and loop around the parking lot.

Hours are 10 a.m. to 8 p.m., Monday through Wednesday; 10 a.m. to 9 p.m., Friday and Saturday; and 10 a.m. to 5 p.m., Sunday. From I-95, take Exit 97 onto Highway 301 toward Smithfield. The White Swan is a half-mile from I-95 on the left. Telephone number: (919) 934-8913.

John's Barbecue and Seafood, Southern Pines

John White, the owner, is from Florida and formerly worked as a civil engineer for Dade County. Margaret, his wife, is from Carthage. After retirement in 1970, John and Margaret moved back to Southern Pines and John built a restaurant on the present site. About 10 years ago, he tore that building down to build the present restaurant. John said that he went into the barbecue business because he had a friend in Miami who owned Shorty's Barbecue. He said that down in Florida they serve only sliced barbecue. John had cooked barbecue for many years and had an interest in this favorite casual food.

John said that his barbecue business started very slowly in the early '70s as there was not barbecue in the area and people were slow to acquire the taste for this wonderful product. He said that he added seafood to give the restaurant more draw until the barbecue caught on. In a year or so things began to happen at John's Barbecue in Southern Pines. Now John's Barbecue feeds hundreds and hundreds of people each night. John said the sale of barbecue and seafood is about 50/50. John said the locals are his bread and butter. He shared that he gets some of the golfers of course, but the locals sustain his business.

John's Barbecue originally cooked on wood-fired pits. John said the city got so fussy with its requirements that he eventually went to gas. John, who cooks whole hams, said he used to cook Boston butts. The hams are slow cooked for 11-12 hours. John's does not baste the meat as it is cooked; it is sauced in the kitchen. It is shredded by hand, not chopped. It's pulled apart by gloved hands.

The "chopped" barbecue was finely shredded and a bit dry for my taste. There were flecks of red pepper in the 'cue sauced in the kitchen that gave it a mild Eastern Carolina taste. With sauce at the table, it tastes a little more tart and a little hot.

The pork ribs were tender, had a good smoky, woodsy flavor and were not over cooked.

The barbecue chicken was moist, sauced with the same barbecue sauce as the 'cue. It had a nice tangy flavor on chicken but does not penetrate the meat.

The red, moderately hot sauce consists of tomato, vinegar, celery seed, salt, crushed black and red pepper and seeds. It has a Texas Pete taste but is much thicker than Lexington-style vinegar-base dip or Eastern North Carolina vinegar sauce. It has a Mexican hot sauce taste, more Southwest than North Carolina.

247

The slaw is white Eastern Carolina-style cabbage with flakes of carrots, mayo and spices. It's not tangy and is a good middle-of-the-road slaw.

The brunswick stew is made up of diced tomato, chunks of potatoes, corn, lima beans, green beans, meat and spices. The stew is thick enough but has more characteristics of a good, heavy vegetable soup than stew. The predominant flavors here are tomatoes and vegetables. It does not rise to a stew that has a unique flavor all its own, like a good mixed drink.

The hushpuppies are good.

From Highway 220 exit on Highway 211 toward Pinehurst, go through Pinehurst to the traffic circle and take Highway 15/501 East. John's Barbecue is a large building with a large parking lot on your left about a mile before you reach U.S. Highway 1. From U.S. Highway 1 take 15/501 West, John's Barbecue is about a mile down the road on your right.

Hours are 11 a.m. to 9 p.m., Monday through Saturday. It's closed Sunday. Telephone number: (910) 692-9474.

Annette's Bar-B-Que, Troy

Jeff Gallimore started this barbecue establishment in 1986. It used to be A Better Burger walk-up. The present kitchen service counter used to be the front of the building.

The current owner, Annette Stutts, took over the business from her brother a couple of years ago.

Annette said about 80-90 percent of the business is local. It seems that Annette's Bar-B-Que is the social hub of Troy. A lot of her customers are older people. She said that some come in several times a day, several days a week. All of the help is local. Annette said that when family members are trying to find other family members, they call Annette's to see if they are there or to leave a message if they haven't arrived, knowing that about everyone that comes to Troy stops by Annette's.

The pork shoulders are cooked electrically for about 12 hours at 275 degrees.

The chopped barbecue is ground, with a moderate chop, and tastes like good roast pork with a mild Lexington-style dip.

The coarse-chopped barbecue was in big, generous-size tender chunks. It had a good, dark smoky flavor, the most smoked flavor I have encountered with electrically cooked 'cue. This is my favorite offering here.

The sliced barbecue was very tender, slightly pink, had good pork flavor and did not have the smoky flavor of the coarse chopped.

The slaw is red Lexington-style: fresh, crisp, crunchy, very tart, not hot but spicy. The sauce is a vinegar, ketchup, sugar, salt, pepper and water Lexington-style dip. The white slaw is typical Eastern Carolina slaw, except it's much juicier than most. The hushpuppies are a light golden color with a nice skin that's not crunchy. They are fairly moist inside and are pretty good pups.

To reach Annette's Bar-B-Que from Highway 220, take the exit for 24/27 Biscoe/Troy exit and proceed through Biscoe into Troy. When you pass the stately Montgomery County Courthouse on your left, Annette's is about a half mile further down the street on the same side.

Hours are 5 a.m. until 9 p.m., Monday through Saturday. It's closed Sunday. Telephone number: (910) 572-3565.

Bland's Barbecue, Wallace

Doug and Paulette Jones, co-owners of Bland's Barbecue in Warsaw, own Bland's Barbecue in Wallace.

The pork shoulders and hams at Bland's Barbecue are slowly cooked on a Hart Inferno (this is a gas cooker infused with wood chips). The shoulders and hams are chopped and served with an extensive list of side dishes as a part of a buffet. I found the barbecue pork to be moderately chopped with a good roast pork flavor. It is sauced in the kitchen with mild Eastern North Carolina-style sauce. The barbecue as served has a hint of vinegar, hint of peppers and needs more house sauce at the table for my taste. The 'cue has a good combination of outside brown and inside white and is tender, moist and chewy.

The table sauce at Bland's is an Eastern North Carolina vinegar sauce with lots of red pepper seeds and spices. The sauce on the barbecue from the kitchen is similar but much milder.

Bland's slaw is an Eastern North Carolina variety. It is green and white, very crisp and has a fresh cabbage taste. There are slivers of carrot with light mayo and a hint of sugar. The slaw has good color and taste.

The hushpuppies that accompany Bland's buffet have a golden crisp shell, a moist center and a hint of sugar. These are good pups by anyone's measurement.

Bland's barbecue is located on Highway 117 in downtown Wallace, a couple of blocks on the left traveling north from the intersection of Highway 117 and Highway 41. Hours are 11 a.m. until 8:30 p.m., Monday through Thursday and Saturday, and 11 a.m. until 9 p.m., Friday. It's closed Sunday. Telephone number: (919) 285- 8125.

Cavenaughs Family Supper House, Wallace

About four miles north of I-40 on Highway 41 East, a lovely old white farmhouse sits nestled in trees by the road. It has character. You just know lots of good times have taken place here. The house was built by Lib Cavenaugh's great granddaddy more than 100 years ago. Lib's mother, Sallie McClund, was born and reared in this house. More than 40 years ago, Sallie built a place across the street that is now Cavenaughs Family Supper House. Sallie ran it as a grocery store for about five years and supplemented her income by cooking barbecue the old-fashioned way on an open pit with wood.

Lib, today's lady of the manor, has run Cavenaughs Family Supper House for more than 30 years with the assistance of her son Sam. The first six or seven years of operation, Lib and Sam served barbecue pork, barbecue chicken and fried chicken. Lib said that when she first started selling plates, the small plate was $1 and the large was $1.25. Now she has a full menu. Lib said she still does about 700 pounds of barbecue per week even with a full menu. Before the full menu, Lib sold 1,500 to 2,000 pounds of her tasty barbecue pork each week.

The chopped barbecue pork is moderately coarse with that slow-roasted pork fla-

vor. It has lots of brown pieces mixed in with the white to give it a smoky flavor and a nutty taste. Tender and moist, the barbecue comes sauced from the kitchen with Eastern Carolina sauce. The 'cue has a hint of vinegar and pepper, but only enough to complement the pork. It is not hot.

The sauce at the table is called Sambo's House Special Barbecue Sauce. The recipe is Lib's own. She said she makes it weekly and it is sold in bulk to locals to cook hogs. In addition to the house sauce, Scott's Barbecue Sauce (Adam Scott of Goldsboro) and Texas Pete (Garner Foods of Winston-Salem) are also available. I would suggest one or the other but not both. Scott's sauce has plenty of fire and so does Texas Pete. Both would be too much. Be careful with your fire.

Lib also has a way with chicken. The fried chicken at Cavenaughs has a good crisp skin and is reasonably moist inside with a good fatback and black skillet flavor. The barbecue chicken is once, twice, three times tender. It has a good, smoky flavor but is slightly greasy.

Cotton candy masquerading as a hushpuppy might best define Lib's bread offering. Lib makes her own hushpuppy mix from scratch.

The slaw featured at Cavenaughs is a good example of fresh Eastern North Carolina coleslaw. It's green and white and crisp with chips of carrot, a bit of sugar and light mayonnaise. It's a perfect complement to either the wonderful chopped barbecue pork or chicken (fried or barbecued). It's delicious.

From I-40, take Exit 385 and follow Highway 41 toward Chinquapin. Cavenaughs Family Supper House is located on your right about four miles down the road. Hours are 10 a.m. until 8 p.m., Monday through Thursday, and 10 a.m. until 9 p.m., Friday and Saturday. It's closed Sunday. Telephone number: (910) 285-5248.

Pink Supper House, Wallace

More than 60 years ago, the Ladies Auxiliary of Northeast Pentecostal Freewill Baptist Church started the group that is today the Pink Supper House. These lovely ladies wanted to do something to help the community and provide funds to meet various community needs. After many years of operation, Hurricane Floyd took its toll and they decided not to reopen. In September 1999, some of the ladies got together with other members of the community and formed a nonprofit corporation called "Pink Supper House, Inc." This group's goal is the same as the Ladies Auxiliary: to provide funds to those who need it when they need it. The group has 11 directors that volunteer their services and oversee the dispensation of the group's funds. The needs could be related to health, property damage, education, volunteer fire fighters or whatever, and the Pink Supper House, Inc. tries to match funds to the needs.

The Pink Supper House is open on Saturday only and serves from 2 p.m. until 8 p.m. There is at least one volunteer director present at all times. The pretty young waitresses are high school girls and they are paid. "There's something special about this place and it's goals that cause these pretty young ladies (anyone of whom could be in the homecoming court or the queen) to spend their Saturday night as a waitperson," said Coy Carter, program director. "Most young people their age do not want to work on Saturday at all, much less Saturday night."

Like most places in the east, The Pink Supper House no longer cooks with pits and wood. The Pink Supper House now cooks its wonderful barbecue electrically with Nunnery Freeman Kook Rite Kookers. The House still clings to all the other things that are wonderful about Eastern North Carolina barbecue. They cook whole hogs. The entire hog is chopped for their delicious 'cue. The chopped barbecue pork is moderately moist, has the wonderful flavor of good slowly roasted pork and is moderately chopped. The North Carolina-style sauce is put on the meat in the kitchen. The House adds tiny pieces of chopped skin and red peppers that play hide and seek amongst the 'cue. Chopping the whole hog (they do not serve sliced) gives the 'cue a delightful mixture of outside brown and inside white. The moist shoulder, drier ham, midlins and tenderloin make for a wonderful texture and a bouquet of flavors.

The House's other meat entrée is fried chicken. Now this is not just fried chicken, this is food for the gods. The chicken is

253

crisp, has a golden brown skin, is perfectly cooked to the bone and has a moist, juicy inside. Have a napkin ready. This chicken takes finger-licking good to the next level.

The sauce used by The Pink House is Wells, "Hog Heaven Barbecue Sauce," made by Wells Pork Products in Burgaw. It is an Eastern North Carolina sauce consisting mainly of vinegar, salt, sugar, water, smoky flavoring, peppers and spices. M'm! M'm! Good!

The House slaw is Eastern Carolina white. It has a good strong cabbage flavor, bits of carrot, hints of sugar and moderate mayo. It is very juicy and very good with the barbecue – a perfect marriage.

The Pink House hushpuppies are very light with a crunchy brown shell, a moist center, and an excellent cornbread taste. All in all, it's a very, very good pup.

The Pink House desserts make good country cooks green with envy and their husbands hold their stomachs and howl at the moon. These are homemade cakes and pies like your grandma made.

NOTE: The last Saturday in September the North East Volunteer Fire Department puts on its annual "FIRE SALE" where whole hogs are pit cooked over hickory wood. It's barbecue to die for. Don't miss it. This is a once a year event that people drive from all over to attend. It benefits the community and makes the attendees smile. Smiles are good.

The Pink Supper House is located in the North East Community Building. Look for a pink building with the Rotarian symbol. The Pink Supper House is located on Highway 41 East, about six miles east of I-40 off Exit 385 and four miles west of Chinquapin.

Again, it's open only on Saturday from 2 p.m. until 8 p.m. Telephone number: (910) 285-8858.

254

Bland's Barbecue, Warsaw

Estrus Bland built this tiny restaurant at its present site in 1958. Estrus ran the business for many years before Tina, his daughter, and Bill Jones, his son-in-law, took over the business. When Tina and Bill retired in 1996, sons Wayne and Doug (along with their wives) took over the management of the restaurant.

Bland's cooks its wonderful pork products electrically. Wayne said they put the pork on at about 9 p.m. and roast it slowly all night until 6 a.m. the next day. These pork shoulders are then chopped by hand. They leave the skin out of the barbecue at the restaurant but include it upon request if they are catering.

The chopped barbecue served by Bland's is moderately coarse. It has good brown and white mixed (they chop the whole shoulder). It is sauced in the kitchen with an Eastern North Carolina sauce. It is really quite good 'cue. This slowly roasted pork has good flavor, good texture and, above all, good taste.

Bland's serves a buffet that includes the special barbecue, a host of good country vegetables, fried chicken and seafood.

Bland's slaw is an Eastern North Carolina-style white cabbage coleslaw with teeny carrot chips, light mayo and sugar – good stuff.

Bland's serves hushpuppies, not cornbread or cornsticks. The pups have a golden shell, a good moist center and a wonderfully light cornbread taste.

It is well worth your trip to leave the interstate and drive a few miles into Warsaw for some of the Jones Brothers' good food.

From I-40 take Exit 369 (Warsaw exit) and follow Highway 117 into Warsaw (three miles) to the intersection of Highway 24. Turn right at the intersection and go about a mile. Bland's is on the left. Hours are 6 a.m. until 8:30 p.m., Monday through Saturday. It's closed Sunday. Telephone number: (910) 293-4216.

Ralph's Barbecue, Weldon

Ralph Woodruff founded Ralph's Barbecue in 1941 in a small place that cooked barbecue and brunswick stew outside. Ralph moved his business to its present site on Highway 158 in 1943. At that time, Highway 158 was a dirt road. The present take-out section of the restaurant used to be the main dining room and there used to be a big oak tree in the parking lot. Ralph would sit out under the oak tree on Sundays, hoping to sell a pound or two of barbecue to passers-by.

The sauce used at Ralph's today is the same sauce originated by its founder. It is a vinegar-base sauce with crushed red peppers, salt and sugar that is boiled for about an hour. They make about 80 gallons three times a week.

The brunswick stew is also made three times a week and they sell about 210 gallons a week.

There are no fillers used in Ralph's barbecue. Some places use soy bean filler to get more weight from a "pound" of meat. Ralph's cooks pork hams and shoulders. The hams are usually 21-25 pounds and are used for the sliced barbecue.

Before 1972, the present building was the pits for the old building. Ralph used wood until 1972. Mason Woodruff, Ralph's son, used to pick up the pigs (live pigs that is) in Rocky Mount to use in Ralph's famous barbecue. Vivian Woodruff, Mason's wife, told her daughter Kim Amerson that Mason sometimes picked her up on a date with a truck full of live pigs. Vivian must have loved that man.

Mason came into the business with Ralph around 1945. Vivian came onboard around 1951. Everybody seems to agree that Vivian was the backbone of the business. Ralph and Mason were the spareribs. Vivian's presence did a lot to develop the good name of Ralph's Barbecue. Kim came to work part-time after school and went full time in 1977. By that time, Ralph had already switched to Nunnery-Freeman cookers (1972).

Ralph's caters in Richmond, Alexandria and Washington, D.C. J. B. Steven's, a local textile company, calls on Ralph's to feed their employees on special occasions. That's sometimes 3,000 people at a time. Ralph used to go to Washington, D.C. and feed the Redskins. Some of the players come down to rockfish (stripped bass) at Lake Gaston and always stop at Ralph's for some of his wonderful 'cue.

The pits have been replaced with stainless steel cookers. Plus, the brunswick stew is no longer made in big black iron pots, but in stainless steel gas kettles. Ralph's cooks

all night and chops in the morning. Kim said that the take-out service does as much business as the dining room. Ralph's also has banquet facilities.

Ralph's sells about 5,000 pounds of cooked pork a week and almost that many pounds of chicken.

They have pulled shoulders on the buffet line and at pig pickin's.

Kim said that Ralph's does not use cryo-packed pork, but get their pork butcher wrapped. She says the flavor is different.

The pulled pork was just like a pig pickin'. It's dark and rich with outside brown that gives this offering a pork flavor that transcends good sex. It's a tiny bit greasy with large specks of red pepper and spices take you where you want to go. It's my favorite offering here.

The sliced pork was fresh, tender and moist with no grease. Some specks of pepper lift this dish out of the slightly sour taste that fresh pork sometimes produces – not this little piggy. With additional sauce at the table, it's a pork lover's dream.

The minced pork was finely chopped with a good peppery taste. Sauced in the kitchen, this offering has enough brown

mixed in to impart a slightly smoky flavor. With sauce, it's hard to tell from wood smoke. The meat was moist, not at all dry, despite the fine chopping.

The crispy fried chicken is moist inside and has just enough fat to be tasty.

The tomato-base brunswick stew is thick with butter beans, corn, potatoes and plenty of meat. It's slow cooked in kettles – 80 gallons cook down to 70 gallons by the time it's ready. There's a nice balance as you can't taste any one thing predominantly. You will want to take some home. It's as thick as you are ever apt to find.

The white slaw is creamy with a good crunch and light mayonnaise. There are no pickles or onions.

The hushpuppies have a golden outside and a cornmeal inside that tastes like sourdough. Have some for dessert.

The sauce is just a good Eastern North Carolina vinegar and pepper sauce that's cooked down until it reaches perfection.

Ralph's Barbecue is located on the north side of Highway 158 in Weldon.

Ralph's Barbecue is open every day from 9 a.m. until 8:30 p.m. Telephone number: (252) 536-2102.

Jordan's Barbecue, West End

Floyd Jordan began barbecuing with the Fletcher brothers in West End about 1960. Later he went into business for himself with Jordan Catering around 1985. Floyd was joined by sons Scott and Ted in about 1991.

Jordan's Barbecue cooks with electricity and gas, and caters over a large portion of North Carolina, South Carolina and Virginia. Sometimes they feed 1,000 to 5,000 people at a sitting.

Jordan's Barbecue cooks hams only and slow roasts their wonderful pork offering for about 12 hours. The sides are the usual red-and-white slaw, potato salad, baked beans and hushpuppies.

The sauce is a hybrid Eastern Carolina/Lexington-style.

Jordan's does not have a restaurant but sells barbecue in bulk to the public (as little as a pound) from their smokehouse behind and beside their home.

To reach Jordan's Barbecue from Highway 220, exit on Highway 211 toward Pinehurst. Proceed approximately 11 miles to West Bend. In West End, turn right on Highway 73 beside the Stanley Furniture factory. Go another half mile and Jordan's is on the left. Look for a brick ranch house with circle drive and lots of white trucks on the right side. Hours are 8 a.m. until 5 p.m., Monday through Saturday. It's closed Sunday. Telephone number: (910) 673-4571.

Joe's Barbecue Kitchen, Whiteville

Joe's Barbecue Kitchen in Whiteville is the home base of Joe's Barbecue. Joe's also has a sister operation at Shallotte. Both serve buffets.

Joe's Barbecue Kitchen slow roasts shoulders and hams over gas fires.

The chopped barbecue is moist, sauced in the kitchen and has a good Eastern North Carolina vinegar taste. Streaks of outside brown give the 'cue a good, rich flavor. The barbecue from the kitchen is hotter and better than the barbecue on the buffet line. The 'cue comes medium chopped and is chewy though not overcooked. It's rich and flavorful.

The pork barbecue ribs are a bit dry for my taste and a tiny bit overcooked. It's good but could be better.

The barbecue chicken is moist and tender. The tomatoey barbecue sauce has a good, mild flavor. It tastes like baked chicken with the sauce applied during or at the end of cooking.

The slaw is finely chopped and has a good fresh cabbage taste. There's only cabbage, vinegar and mayo here. It's just a really fresh white slaw.

The hushpuppies are light and golden. A thin shell houses the moist morsels. They have a good cornmeal taste that's not heavy or greasy.

Joe's Barbecue Kitchen is located on Highway 701 Business South in Whiteville. Joe's Barbecue is open 10 a.m. until 9 p.m., Monday through Saturday. It's closed Sunday. Telephone number: (910) 642-3511.

259

Sutton's Barbecue, Willow Springs

Richard Sutton was one of the first North Carolina Highway Patrolmen in this area. Richard covered three counties. Peggy Walter, his daughter, said when there was trouble people didn't say call the sheriff, call the police, or call the highway patrol, they simply said, "get Sutton." A picture of Richard Sutton and his lovely wife Kitty are the first things you see when you open the door to this quaint restaurant that they started in 1950.

Peggy, who has owned Sutton's Barbecue since 1980, has worked here since 1968. She is very proud of the business her parents started and is determined to carry it on in the best of tradition. Peggy is also pleased to show you pictures of some of her many catering events for the North Carolina Bar Association, the North Carolina Historical Society and various state government offices. She caters throughout the area for small groups and groups of 1,000 or more. If you are in the area, be sure to stop in for a trip down memory lane, some good food and Peggy's wonderful hospitality.

Sutton's Barbecue used to cook with wood on open pits out back but now Peggy cooks with gas. However, Peggy insists on cooking whole hogs and the meat is pulled, not chopped.

The "chopped" barbecue is really large pieces of pulled pork. It is moist, and tender, tender, tender. It's a good whole hog mix of ham, shoulder and tenderloin. The brown and white meat complement each other nicely. It is lightly sauced in the kitchen with a mild Eastern North Carolina vinegar-base sauce. For my taste, it needs a bit of the house hot sauce added at the table. For a sweeter taste, try the house hickory-smoke sauce. This barbecue is chewy and oh so good.

The hot sauce is a brown vinegar sauce with *plenty* of peppers and spices. It's a nice fiery blend and great on the 'cue. The hickory-smoke sauce is a thick, smoky blend with peppers and sugar. It's slightly sweet, but has enough peppers to balance. It tastes like Cattleman's smoky sauce slightly tweaked.

The slaw is white, coarse-chopped cabbage with plenty of mayo and some sugar. It's made fresh daily (hourly if need be) and is a delicious partner to the barbecue.

Hushpuppies are just a good pup; Peggy uses Atkins mix.

Sutton's Barbecue is located on Highway 55, three miles east of Fuquay-Varina at the Wake county line. Going east from Fuquay-Varina on Highway 55, Sutton's is on your right. Going west from Angier, amazingly enough it is on your left.

260

Hours are 9 a.m. until 3 p.m., Monday through Thursday (serving lunch buffet only), and 9 a.m. until 8 p.m., Friday and Saturday. It's open 11 a.m. until 3 p.m. on Sunday. Telephone number: (919) 552-4474.

Stephenson's Barbecue, Willow Springs

Stephenson's Barbecue is one of those rare barbecue stories. There was no family barbecue business for owner Paul Stephenson Jr. to inherit. Paul was a farmer and had hogs. Hog prices were cheap. Paul said one day a man came by and bought 14 of Paul's shoats. Paul asked what he was going to do with the pigs and the man said he was taking them to the BBQ man. Paul continued his farm chores and as he rode his tractor, he pondered how many sandwiches he could get out of a hog. "Who's making the money here?" he wondered.

Deciding he was on the wrong end of the stick, Paul began a barbecue business by raising his own pigs. Although he had never cooked a pig, Paul built a very small building in 1958 to start a barbecue business. So as not to embarrass himself, Paul got behind a tobacco barn, dug a pit and cooked his first pig. A salesman stopped by and asked for directions. He told people at a store up the road that he had met a man back down the road who was cookin' a pig and "burning him up." The salesman exaggerated. Paul's pig turned out fine. In July 1958, Paul opened his little barbecue place. The chopping block that was used to hand chop the pork from July 1958 until December 1986 is displayed in the foyer of the new restaurant. This block is so dished out it looks like a tub. Paul jokingly said he guessed over the years that people had gotten a little cedar fiber along with their pork.

Paul cooks on pits with charcoal. He used to cook exclusively with hickory and oak. Paul said that worked fine until the summertime when his wood supplier would be farming and didn't have time to cut wood. Paul gradually went to charcoal to ensure constant supply.

The wonderful pork offered by Stephenson's Barbecue is cooked over coals for about seven hours. The meat is then turned and slowly cooked for another two hours. Paul then leaves the meat on the pits six or eight hours more to smoke. The pit is three bricks thick. The heat in the bricks and the dying coals cause the meat to drip slowly all night. It is chopped first thing the next morning. This dripping produces smoke for hours and the barbecue has more smoke flavor than any I have ever tasted. It is absolutely wonderful. The outside brown and the fat are separated from the rest of the meat. The outside brown is chopped real fine. Some of the fat is chopped fine as well and blended back with the hand-chopped meat. The cooking methods and the chopping and blending produce an outstanding barbecue product.

In 1999, Paul was joined by Andy, his

262

son. Andy pretty much runs the place now. Paul is senior management. Paul is obviously proud of his son and that Stephenson's Barbecue is in Andy's capable hands. Paul is as equally proud of Lane, his other son, who runs Paul's 50-acre plant nursery.

Paul is also pleased with the wide acceptance of his barbecue product and how people have shipped this wonderful barbecue to California, Florida and as far away as France. One customer even came in and bought barbecue to take on a mule ride through the Grand Canyon.

Willow Springs may not be the hub of the universe but it is worth anyone's time to slip off the highway for a few miles and experience Paul's wonderful barbecue and with luck meet this delightful man.

The chopped barbecue comes in a moderately coarse chunky chop. It is without doubt the smokiest, woodsiest, richest tasting 'cue you will ever eat. It's a good mix of outside brown with inside white and fat, but not greasy. This barbecue is not just good; it is great. Fantastic flavors explode in your mouth. You will pound the table and your toes will crimp. It's that good. The bar-

becue is sauced in the kitchen and you don't need more.

The hushpuppies are golden brown with a crisp outside and light, fluffy and moist inside. These are really good pups.

The slaw is finely chopped cabbage with pickles the right amount of mayonnaise and a hint of sugar. It's a perfect Eastern North Carolina white slaw.

Stephenson's also has barbecue chicken, fried chicken, brunswick stew, six types of sandwiches and desserts that include banana pudding.

Stephenson's Barbecue is located on Highway 50 at McGee's Crossroad, 20 miles south of Raleigh. It is easily accessible from I-40. Take Exit 319 off I-40 and go two miles on Highway 42 West to the intersection of Highway 42 and Highway 50. Take a left on Highway 50, go 4.2 miles south and Stephenson's is on your left. Hours are 10 a.m. until 9 p.m., Monday through Saturday in the summer, and 10 a.m. until 8 p.m., Monday through Saturday in the winter. It's closed Sunday year round. Telephone number: (919) 894-4530.

263

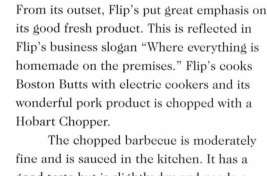

Flip's Bar-B-Que, Wilmington

The day after Bob Church bought Flip's Bar-B-Que in 1986, a local TV channel voted it Best Barbecue in the Coastal Carolinas. Though it was from no effort of his own, the next day the lines were out the door.

Fortunately, the same man that cooked this wonderful 'cue for founder Leonard "Flip" Watts is still cooking for Bob Church. Flip's Bar-B-Que opened in 1950. From its outset, Flip's put great emphasis on its good fresh product. This is reflected in Flip's business slogan "Where everything is homemade on the premises." Flip's cooks Boston Butts with electric cookers and its wonderful pork product is chopped with a Hobart Chopper.

The chopped barbecue is moderately fine and is sauced in the kitchen. It has a good taste but is slightly dry and needs a few drops of sauce at the table. The sauce is a vinegar base with traditional spices and a hint of mustard. It is fairly hot without meat but tones down a bit with the meat.

The sliced barbecue is very moist and tender, and, again, comes sauced from the kitchen. It's much more flavorful than any sliced barbecue you are accustomed to enjoying. It is a very warm, tasty treat. Try some.

The slaw is a yellow and white coleslaw that's very crunchy. The hushpuppies are golden with a good outside crunch and cornbread taste.

The barbecue chicken is golden roasted but is slightly dry and needs a little sauce at the table.

I asked a half dozen people in and around Wilmington where they would go to eat barbecue in their area. All answered Flip's.

To reach Flip's, take I-40 East into Wilmington where it becomes College Street. At the intersection of College Street and Oleander Drive, proceed north on Oleander Drive for two and a half miles. Flip's is on the right at 5818 Oleander Dr. Hours are 11 a.m. to 9 p.m., Monday through Saturday. It's closed Sunday. Telephone number: (910) 799-6350.

Bill Ellis Barbecue, Wilson

Bill Ellis Barbecue in Wilson, owned and managed by Bill Ellis, is the Microsoft of barbecue in North Carolina. Nearly 40 large trucks, many of them 18-wheelers, carry Bill Ellis' famous pork barbecue all over the country. Bill has catered as far away as Palm Springs, CA. It is also a barbecue hub for the locals and that's saying something in a town that has several major players in the barbecue game.

Bill Ellis is the ultimate survivor. Bill had built a barbecue empire and one dark night in September 1999, Hurricane Floyd dealt him a bad hand and before the game was over, he lost over $3.5 million. This was not the only loss Bill has suffered in the last number of years. In a period of two years, Bill lost five family members, including his father, wife, son and brother. For most, experiencing only a portion of Bill's losses would have caused total meltdown. Not Bill whose philosophy is "God will not put more on you than you can tote." He hitched up his trousers, Arnold Palmer style, put that creative entrepreneurial mind of his to work and in two years is back bigger and better than ever.

Despite not having on one item of Western clothing, Bill looks like a cowboy. This lean and tan man with a full head of white hair and piercing blue eyes has an easy gait, a disarming smile and a firm handshake that makes you like him from the start.

It was with a great deal of pride that Bill took me on a personally guided tour of all of his new creations. Having formerly been in the stock car racing game before his son's death, Bill has the garage and equipment to repair his own fleet as well as his portable cookers. Everything about his new buildings, cooking operation, buffet line and carry-out service incorporate all of the knowledge that he has gained in his years of barbecuing experience. This place literally hums with activity. I have never seen so much product go out the door in so many different ways.

Bill grows his own hogs on his farm. He said he had 450 to 500 sows being serviced by 26 boars. Thus, he is able to control the quality of his meat and ensure the best pork product that anyone can serve.

Bill cooks whole hogs over hickory coals with gas heat from above on specially designed cookers that Bill designed and had custom built. Some 15 of these large cookers can easily produce more than 100 cooked hogs on a given day as needed for Bill's catering operation.

The chopped barbecue was good, hand-chopped 'cue with a rich, nutty brown flavor that only comes from the right amount of slow roasting over wood. The chopped barbecue was sauced in the kitchen with Bill's special sauce. I watched him make it from premium vinegar, crushed red pepper, black pepper and salt. The vinegar was cooked down before the peppers and salt were added. Pitchers of sauce are poured over the barbecue in large stainless steel trays. Then, gloved hands worked the sauce into the 'cue. The barbecue comes from the kitchen sauced with this tangy, Eastern North Carolina-style sauce. Bright eyes of red pepper wink from behind coarse-chopped pork and whisper "you're in for a treat." Add a couple of drops of the hot sauce at the table and you've got a winner.

The pulled pork is as tender as a mother's love. Add the spicy, thick red sauce at the table and create magic.

While we were in the kitchen, Bill pulled some outside brown off a hog that was only moments off the pit. It was ecstasy.

The slaw is yellow and has a mustard taste, which is different from most Eastern North Carolina coleslaws. It makes a nice combination with the barbecue though. The mustard complements the acidity of the vinegar-base sauce.

The collards are absolutely delicious. They are clean, gritless and medium chopped with just enough drippings and spices to make you want to order seconds and skip dessert. Don't. The banana pudding is spectacular.

The chopped barbecue with the thick red sauce is different. It tastes much richer. I like it.

The golden cornsticks are crisp with a soft center and a good cornbread taste. The hushpuppies are light, have a good coat and a soft center with a lightness betrayed by the color. It's not at all greasy.

The brunswick stew tastes fairly bland for stew. It's more like a very, very thick vegetable soup. I didn't see or taste potatoes but there were tomatoes, lima beans, kernel corn, green beans and lots of chicken.

Traveling east on Alternate Hwy 264, turn right on Forest Hills Road, continue 2.2 miles, restaurant is on left. From 301 South, pass the Parkers. At the first stoplight (Forest Hills Road) turn right. Hours are from 11 a.m. until 8:30 p.m., Tuesday through Saturday, and 11 a.m. until 8 p.m., Sunday. It's closed Mondays. Telephone number: (252) 237-4372.

Cherry's Barbecue, Wilson

As you proceed east on Highway 42 out of Wilson, you're immediately impressed that you are in the country. I do mean the country, not the suburbs. As one continues eastward on Highway 42, you get further and further out in the country. As you continue east on Highway 42 about five miles from the Highway 301 bridge, you see a sign that reads, "End of Earth 4 miles, Cherry's Barbecue, 6 miles."

When I reached Cherry's Barbecue, I had the distinct feeling that I was in the Kevin Costner movie *Field of Dreams*, and that ghosts of barbecue greats were going to come out of the 10-foot high corn fields that enclose this Eastern North Carolina treasure. "Enclose" is the operative word here. There is just enough room to get a few cars off the road. As Kevin Costner said in the movie, "If you build it, they will come." Well, they built it and they did come. Barbecue lovers from all over trek though the countryside and meander through the cornfields to this Holy Grail of barbecue.

Cherry's Barbecue cooks whole hogs with gas flame. The hog is chopped and mixed to create what is Cherry's wonderful gift to the barbecue lovers of the world.

The chopped barbecue is moderately coarse and comes sauced from the kitchen. The fiery, peppery flavor has vinegar over-tones on the rich, dark brown, woodsy-tasting 'cue. Good hunks of chewy outside brown mix with white meat to give this barbecue many shades of color. The outside brown especially kicks in the flavor. This barbecue tastes like it was roasted on a spit over an open fire. The accompanying sauce is just the trick to tickle your barbecue fancy. It's absolutely delicious!

The white slaw is finely chopped cabbage with celery seed, mayo and mustard that gives this Eastern North Carolina classic the right spirit. It's very fresh tasting with a nice crunch. It's a perfect mate for the 'cue.

Cherry's large hushpuppies are ever so golden, thin and light. A crisp shell hides a cake-like interior that's simply scrumptious. They are cooked to perfection with a slightly sweet, wonderful corn taste. These pups are as light as cotton candy; they actually compress and expand as you bite. This is food for the gods. Have some for breakfast, lunch and dinner. Give it to friends as Christmas, birthday and wedding presents.

The brunswick stew was really good and thick with tomatoes, corn, butter beans, lots of meat and just the right amount of seasoning. This is not vegetable soup – this is the real thing.

Cherry serves barbecue pork, barbecue chicken, fried chicken, brunswick stew and 10 sides. Everything looks wonderful. The desserts are cakes and banana pudding.

To reach Cherry's, proceed on Highway 42 east out of Wilson. Approximately five miles from crossing the Highway 301 bridge, you will see a Cherry's sign on your left. Turn right on Webb Lake Road and proceed a mile and a half. Cherry's is on the left at 5139 Webb Lake Road in Wilson. Hours are 11 a.m. until 8 p.m., Wednesday; 11 a.m. until 8:30 p.m., Thursday, Friday and Saturday; and 11 a.m. until 7 p.m., Sunday. It's closed Monday and Tuesday. Telephone number: (252) 237-2070.

Mitchell's Barbecue, Wilson

Mitchell's is a restaurant/barbecue place. Mitchell's serves about everything a hog produces but the squeal. They have country ham, ham hocks, backbone, spare ribs, chitlins, etc. along with fried chicken and meatloaf. This is accompanied by a host of country vegetables and desserts that run to the sublime including various kinds of homemade pies, banana pudding and, my favorite, homemade fried apple pies like my mother used to make.

Owner Edward Roy Mitchell was very proud to show me his pits and cooking operation. He burns his wood outside in a firebox connected to the pit room. Thus, one goes outside to feed the firebox. The wood is burned down to coals. From the inside, one can pull a lever and drop coals into a bricked pit. The coals are then shoveled into the fireplaces under the cooking pits. Eddie has designed dual exhaust systems. There is a hood over the cooking area to take the smoke out. There is a fan to bring in fresh air. Then he designed two jet streams, as he calls them, which consist of fans in the peaks of the roof over the pit room on opposite sides that are thermostatically controlled. They remove any soot, dust and heat that gravitates to the ceiling of the cooking area. He has built two observation windows, one on each floor in the new brick restaurant building being constructed to adjoin the pit room and the old building. He said everything was built of brick and stainless steel and it is all fire proof.

Before cooking his hogs, Eddie bastes them down with his pepper, sugar, vinegar and cayenne pepper sauce. He also rubs the skin with salt before cooking. He puts the pig on flesh down for six or seven hours and then turns it, sauces it and cooks it for an additional hour.

Eddie was named after his grandfather, Eddie's father told him, because the elder Edward Roy Mitchell liked to watch Roy Rogers. His brothers do not have middle names. While the younger Edward Roy Mitchell is called Eddie, he also answers to Edward, Mitch and Roy.

Eddie's parents ran a grocery store for many years. They used to open the store at 5 a.m. and sell cookies and penny candy to the children waiting for the school bus. His folks worked hard until about 7 p.m. every night. Eddie, who was working in Raleigh with the state department when his dad died in 1990, came by to visit his mom later that year at the grocery store. On that particular day, Eddie's mom had put on a pot of turnip greens. She seemed a bit down and Eddie wanted to cheer her up. He knew how much she liked barbecue, so he bought a

269

34-pound pig and $5 worth of wood and cooked the pig. He and his mom were having a late lunch. Eddie said he was stoking down turnip greens, barbecue and potato salad when a woman came by to buy a hot dog. She smelled the barbecue and wanted to know if they had any for sale. Eddie said his mom kind of hesitated and said; "well, I don't know." Eddie punched his mom and she said, "sure we do." They sold the woman some barbecue. In a matter of hours they sold the entire pig. This was the start of his barbecue career.

Eddie said that until 1990 his exposure to cooking barbecue was watching his dad and other family members cook a hog as part of a celebration that was the custom in Eastern North Carolina. He said that he knew he needed to know more about cooking barbecue if he was going to do it on a commercial scale. He researched it and was given the names Sam Morgan, Bud Jenkins and James Kirby as men who knew barbecue and could teach him the trade. Eddie was lucky enough to get James Kirby as his tutor. Mr. Kirby was in his 80s.

Eddie told Mr. Kirby that he was going to buy an electric cooker from a Mr. Woodard. Mr. Kirby shook his head and asked Eddie "Do you really want to get into the barbecue business?" Eddie nodded. Mr. Kirby said "I will put you in the water, then its up to you to swim."

Mr. Kirby said, "Go buy a 100-pound pig and cut yourself a drum cooker. Meet me at 7 o'clock tonight and we'll cook a pig." Eddie did as he was told. That night, Eddie took his pig and cooker and bid his wife goodnight. He told her he would see her in the morning. He met Mr. Kirby at the appointed place. Mr. Kirby imparted to him the banking technique for cooking a pig. Mr. Kirby built his wood fire around the edges of the cooker. When the wood had sufficiently cooked down, Mr. Kirby put the pig on, shut the top, closed the dampers and said "lets go home." In amazement, Eddie said, "don't we got to watch the pig?" Mr. Kirby replied, "You can stay here and watch all night if you like, but I'm going home and go to bed." Eddie said that he told Mr. Kirby he thought that a hog being barbecued had to be attended all night long. Mr. Kirby said that the custom was developed by men to get away from their wives and have a place to go take a snort of homemade moonshine. He said, "you don't need to tend the hog, the hog will be fine." Mr. Kirby told Eddie to meet him at the cooker at 4 a.m. the next morning.

Eddie said he didn't want to be late and got there at 3:30. At 4 a.m., Mr. Kirby arrived and lifted the lid. Eddie said that he saw the prettiest pig that one could ever hope to cook. He said it was perfectly golden with no scorches or brown spots and

270

done to perfection. Mr. Kirby worked for Eddie for four years. He helped Eddie perfect his cooking techniques and Eddie has never departed from banking his fires and following the methods employed by James Kirby.

Eddie has never advertised. His business comes from word of mouth. However, Eddie's young son wants dad to construct a Web site.

His barbecue is great. It has a good vinegar, pepper taste but it's not too spicy. It has a good finish, but it's not too hot. Like the baby bear's porridge, it was "just right." It's moist and hand chopped. The old-fashioned way is alive and well at Mitchell's.

Mitchell's Barbecue is located on the west side of U.S. 301 (Ward Boulevard), several blocks north of U.S. 264. Hours are 10 a.m. until 5 p.m., Monday through Saturday, and 10 a.m. until 6 p.m., Sunday. Telephone number: (252) 291-9189.

(The Original) Parker's Barbecue, Wilson

Founded by brothers Graham and Ralph Parker and a cousin, Henry Parker Brewer, Parker's Barbecue has for years been one of the best-known names serving Eastern North Carolina style barbecue. One of the reasons for this is that Parker's originated in a town with tobacco markets. The tobacco company buyers, as they moved about their circuit, helped spread the word about the good barbecue they had encountered. Parker's name and stories about their good barbecue soon spread about the coastal plain.

Another reason for Parker's popularity is its business site. Ask realtors what is important and they will say "location, location, location." Well, Parker's has been in the right location since 1946. Parker's opened its business on U.S. Highway 301, which was a major north-south artery through Eastern North Carolina. Today, most people traveling north and south across the state use I-95 which is about seven miles to the west of U.S. 301 as it passes Wilson. But the most important factor in Parker's widespread fame is they have always served good barbecue.

Despite a changing of the guard about 14 years ago (brothers Ralph and Graham retired and cousin Henry died), nothing much has changed about the Parker operation in the last 55 years. In 1987, the original owners sold the restaurant to Bobby Woodard and Donald Williams, two long-time Parker employees. Bobby Woodard died in 1996 and Donald Williams became the sole owner. And the fires kept burning. Parker's used to cook its barbecue on pits with oak wood. However, as with most barbecue places in the east, the cooking method has been modified a bit. For the last number of years, Parker's has still cooked its whole hogs on pits but have added gas hoods over the pits to brown the pig so they do not have to be turned. Hardwood charcoal has replaced the oak wood to produce the coals in the pits. I did not find that this has taken anything away from the delicious flavor of Parker's Barbecue.

Most large barbecuing operations, such as Parker's, have gone to electric cookers exclusively. Only a few barbecue places in the east, large or small, are using hardwood charcoal or wood. I cannot ascertain any appreciable difference in the flavor of Parker's Barbecue today from the time I first experienced this delightful 'cue as a young adult. Like the other major player in the barbecue game in Wilson, Parker's raises it's own hogs and has been doing so since the early 1970s. Owner Donald Williams

believes that raising their own hogs gives them better control over the quality of the meat that goes on their pits.

In the course of a number of visits to Parker's in Wilson, I observed that most people generally order the combination plate which consists of chopped barbecue, fried chicken, brunswick stew, coleslaw, boiled potatoes and cornsticks. A number of the patrons shared with me that they had been eating at Parker's for 40-50 years. Some had been eating there since it opened the doors. Some eat there several times a day, some several times a week and most shared they didn't let a week pass (unless they were on vacation) that they didn't stop by to partake of Parker's good food. Bowing to the wisdom of my elders, I followed suit.

I found the chopped barbecue to be a bit dry for my taste. It is finely chopped by machine and seasoned in the kitchen with an Eastern North Carolina vinegar-base sauce. My preference is pulled barbecue that is more moist and in coarser pieces. However, Parker's knows and understands its customers and gives them exactly what they want. And the faithful like it finely chopped or shredded, drier, leaner and lightly sauced. Parker's cooks whole hogs. The mixture of the drier hams with the shoulders along with being finely shredded, contributes to the texture of Parker's 'cue. If you prefer, more moisture can be added

with the house sauce at the table. Be careful here. It doesn't take much additional house sauce to light up the 'cue, and you as well.

The slaw is yellow with lingering hints of mustard but is slightly sweet. This crisp coleslaw has a good, fresh taste and a prominent cabbage flavor.

The brunswick stew tastes more like a good, rich vegetable soup. It is flavorful but a bit thin, which I am told is the way the locals like it. It has green beans which, like peas, carrots and onions, I have never considered to be part of an Eastern North Carolina Brunswick stew. Many in the Piedmont add these ingredients, but in the east they generally do not.

Parker's cornsticks are baked and then deep-fried. I found them delightful. They are golden in color, have a nice crisp outer shell, a moist center and a wonderfully satisfying cornbread taste.

Parker's fried chicken will rival any at a family reunion. This is good ol' country fried chicken at its best. It has a crisp outer skin and is moist and tender. Simply, it's cooked to perfection. I would rather have a second drumstick than most any dessert Parker's or any other restaurant has to offer.

There is a second Parker's location in Greenville which is owned and operated by Graham and Ralph's brother and nephew. This is a separate business entity. However, I found the food, décor and ambiance to be

273

much the same as Parker's in Wilson.

Parker's in Wilson is located on U.S. Highway 301, just south of the intersection of 301 and U.S. 64. Hours are 9 a.m. until 9 p.m., seven days a week. Parker's is closed on Thanksgiving, two days for Christmas, and one week during the summer for vacation. Telephone number: (252) 237-0972.

Notes

Notes

SECTION IV

Coastal

Location

Skylight Inn, Ayden **1**

Piggybacks BBQ, Creswell **2**

Lane's Family Barbecue and Seafood, Edenton **3**

Tuck's Restaurant, Elizabeth City **4**

Bubba's Bar-B-Que, Frisco **5**

B's Barbecue, Greenville **6**

Captain Bob's BBQ and Seafood Restaurant, Hertford **7**

Fisherman's Wharf, Jacksonville **8**

King's Restaurant, Kinston **9**

F.B. Duncan's Bar-B-Que, Manteo **10**

Whitley's Barbecue, Murfreesboro **11**

Moore's Bar-B-Que, New Bern **12**

Simp's Barbecue, Roper **13**

Joe's Barbecue Kitchen, Shallotte **14**

Abrams Barbecue, Tarboro **15**

Boss Hog Backyard Bar-B-Que, Washington **16**

Hog Heaven, Washington **17**

Shaw's Barbecue House, Williamston **18**

Bunn's BBQ, Windsor **19**

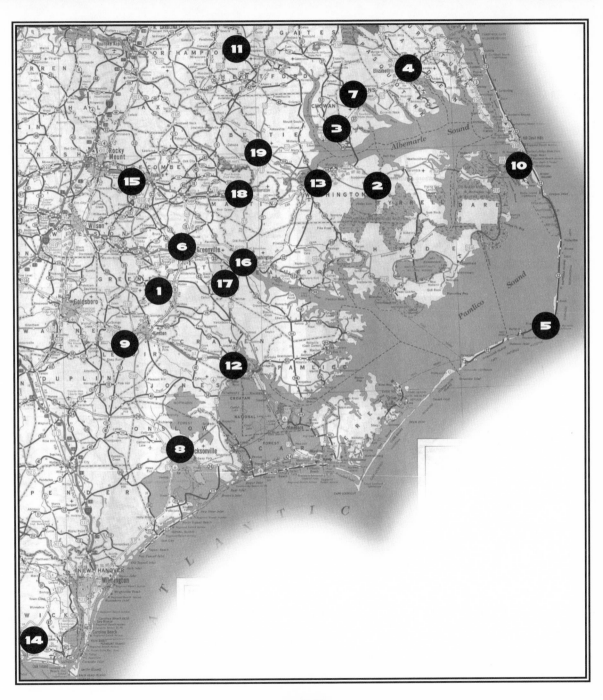

281

Skylight Inn, Ayden

Who cooks the best barbecue in the world? With more than a little sense of pride, Pete Jones, owner of the Skylight Inn, will tell you that he does. He will quickly add he believes this to be so because *National Geographic* magazine told him just that in 1979. He says that every year or so since, *National Geographic* sends him a letter and tells him that, in all of their travels, they have still found none better.

Pete's barbecue roots run deep. His great-great-grandfather, Skilten Dennis, was

born in 1811 and started selling barbecue out of an old mule-drawn wagon at age 19. He sold his barbecue with bread he made. Pete Jones still makes the bread today with the same recipe. Friends told Skilten that he ought to set up a place in town to sell his barbecue, and let people come to him.

In 1842, Skilten's wife gave birth to Skilten's heir, Skilten M. Dennis. Following in his daddy's footsteps, and heeding the advice of friends, young Skilten set up a barbecue stand in Ayden. This may have been the first commercial barbecue place in North Carolina. At that time, Ayden was called Otter Town and was known by this name until the railroad came through in 1890.

Bill, Skilten M. Dennis' son, took over the business and moved it to Second Street in Ayden. Bill had four sons and two daughters. Two of Bill's sons, Emmit and John, worked with Bill until his death in 1924. Then, both Emmit and John opened barbecue places. John's place seemed to have thrived a little better than Emmit's did. This may have been due to better business skills more than having a better pork product.

Josie, Pete Jones' mother, was Emmit's sister. At the tender age of 7, Pete went to work with his Uncle Emmit. Pete said that on the first day of working in barbecue, he came home and told his Aunt Gracie that he loved it and that he would work at it until he was the best. Pete continued to work for Emmit from July 1935 until July 1947. On July 8, 1947, Pete opened a curb-service diner in Ayden next to the airport and called it Skylight. Pete's Uncle Emmit died in 1970 and his Uncle John sold his barbecue place to Bum Dennis. Bum, who had worked with Pete, initially cooked over pits with wood the way Pete has always done. One day Pete heard news that saddened him greatly. Bum's got gas. No, not indigestion; he had broken the code among old-time barbecuers and switched to gas to cook his pigs.

Cooking pigs over live coals is long, tedious, hot and often unappreciated work. Pete says he gets up at 3 a.m. and cooks to serve lunch at 11. He still does it the old-fashioned way: whole hog, cooked over oak and hickory wood and then hand chopped. Pete says that "if it's not whole hog and cooked over wood, it ain't barbecue." Pete says you have to cook the whole pig because the pigs nose is the "bob" and the curly tail is the "Q." Pete's rule of thumb is to cook an hour per 10 pounds.

Pete said that when he worked with his Uncle Emmit, Emmit's hogs were fed a special diet of corn and peanuts soaked in water in 55-gallon drums. They would add two or three tablespoons of Red Devil lye to a 55-gallon drum to worm the hogs since there were no commercial wormers at that time. This kept the hogs clean from parasites and removed any blots they may have had on the liver. Emmit also fed the hogs oak ash from the barbecue fires. This served to further clean the hogs before slaughter. Emmit's hogs at age 6 months weighed about 65 pounds.

Pete stated that today you can get a 5-month-old hog from the slaughterhouse that weighs 200 pounds. He said this is due to the pigs being on a program to create rapid growth and get the weight gain the growers want to move the pigs to market. Pigs are sold by the pound, not by the pig. In Pete's opinion, this rapid weight gain does not produce the quality meat that Pete was accustomed to when he raised pigs with his Uncle Emmit. Pete said there is also a lot of water gain in the hogs today and when cooked the hog doesn't produce nearly as good a yield as Emmit's pigs.

The first time I ever met with Pete was on his 73rd birthday and I asked him if there were any defining moments in his career. "No not really," he said, "All I've ever done is cook barbecue all my life." He said that sometimes he gets a special pig that turns out really well, much better than all the others and this pleases him. He said that he used to get four or five special pigs in the course of a year, but now he is lucky to get one or two. I asked if there were any identifiers that enabled him to pick a special pig. "It's hard to explain," he said, "but if you have been barbecuing pork for 66 years, you just kinda know."

Thousands and thousands of people have enjoyed Pete's barbecue over the years. Pete has a wall encasing pictures of notables who have eaten and enjoyed his barbecue and took the time to acknowledge the admiration they have for Pete and his wonderful barbecue. These notables include former presidents Jimmy Carter, Ronald Reagan, George W. Bush Sr., Richard Nixon and

Gerald Ford as well as former governors Jim Martin and Jim Hunt. In addition to other politicians such as Jesse Helms and Strom Thurman, there are pictures of starlets, beauty queens, musical groups, athletes and judges. Pete's fame in the barbecue world is well known and he has won many awards.

In addition to his passion for making the best possible barbecue, Pete loves harness racing and keeps his horses next door. He also likes bird hunting. I knew from the moment I met him, I would like this man. How can you not like a man that loves barbecue, horses and bird hunting?

Pete's barbecue without sauce has almost a sweet taste with rich, smoky overtones. The barbecue with Pete's sauce which is a special blend of vinegars, peppers and seasoning, has a slightly wood-smoked flavor. It's as tender as veal. Dark and white meat with tiny pieces of pork skin mixed in with the barbecue. These tiny morsels, smaller than Rice Krispies, add a unique new flavor when crunched along with the barbecue pork. I found this delightful!

The slaw (something Pete says he just "whipped up") was firm, chopped slightly and pleasantly sweet.

Emmy Lou Jones, Pete's wife, makes the cornbread from Skilten Dennis' 1830 recipe. The hard-crusted bread is flat but soft inside. It is made from a batter of cornmeal, water, salt and drippings from barbecued pigs. The batter is poured into big flat pans and baked for about an hour. It has kind of a sourdough/flat bread texture and is the perfect accompaniment for Pete's barbecue and slaw.

Barbecue, slaw, bread and sweet tea or soft drinks are all that Pete sells. Who needs more?

Does Pete Jones of the Skylight Inn serve the best barbecue in the world? Well, *National Geographic* said he does and who am I to argue with *National Geographic*?

The Skylight Inn is located in Ayden on Highway 11, about 10 miles south of Greenville toward Kinston. Traveling south from Greenville, turn left at the stoplight on Highway 11 and proceed into downtown Ayden until reaching Lee Street. Turn right onto Lee Street and proceed for another mile. The Skylight Inn is on the right. You can't miss it.

The Skylight Inn is a rectangular, one-story brick building with a Capitol-type dome atop it, proudly flying the American flag. There is also a large billboard which depicts owner Pete Jones. If you are there at lunch, there will be cars scattered all over the lot. Adjacent to the west of the Skylight Inn are the racing stables of Walter B. (Pete) Jones.

Hours are 9:30 a.m. to 7 p.m., Monday through Saturday. Telephone number: (252) 746-4113.

Piggybacks BBQ, Creswell

Tim Spear is serious about cooking hogs. Tim says he's been doing this all his life. Three years ago, he decided to go into the restaurant business so he opened a little hog heaven along side Highway 64 outside of Creswell and named it Piggybacks.

Tim designed the cooker used by Piggybacks. The firebox is outside the smokehouse and looks like an old Ben Franklin warm morning stove. Tim burns cherry and hickory wood. Tim is the only one I know that uses cherry wood. The meat is on a cooker inside the smokehouse. It is cooked in a convection-type manner with the smoke and heat from the firebox outside being drawn over the meat and up through a chimney inside the smokehouse. The meat is never exposed to direct fire. Tim said he can control the heat from 100 to 400 degrees and he has less than a 5-percent heat loss. This means that he can use less wood and obtain the same good results as a less-efficient cooker. It also makes for a very, very tender product.

The sliced barbecue produced by Piggybacks is pink throughout from good smoke penetration. The barbecue is moist and oh so tender. It's sauced in the kitchen. With the vinegar sauce, it titillates your sensibilities. It has a slow-smoked woodsy taste that is really good.

Piggybacks chopped barbecue (minced) has a good, rich, nutty taste and has a little different smoked flavor due to the cherry wood. The chopped 'cue is very moist, sauced in the kitchen with an Eastern North Carolina vinegar-base sauce, and is an absolute delight on your palette.

Tim's slaw is finely chopped white cabbage and has a hint of vinegar and a really fresh clean taste. Coupled with the 'cue, the slaw is a delicious contrast.

Tim also makes brunswick stew. I found his stew to be very good, thick with the right taste despite having June peas. This is not your mamma's vegetable soup.

Tim is an affable fellow. With his mustache, jeans and cowboy boots, he looks like he would be more at home on a cutting horse than at a barbecue pit. I don't know how much he knows about cows but he sure knows barbecue.

Piggybacks BBQ is located on the north side of Highway 64 just east of Creswell.

Hours are 11 a.m. until 8 p.m., Tuesday and Wednesday; 11 a.m. until 9 p.m., Thursday and Friday; 11 a.m. until 8 p.m., Saturday; and 11 a.m. until 3 p.m., Sunday. It's closed Monday. Telephone number: (252) 797-7607.

Lane's Family Barbecue and Seafood, Edenton

Owned by Ima Jean Lane, Lane's Barbecue used to be an old gas station. Bobby, Ima Jean's son, turned the station into a restaurant. Bobby ran the place for a while before Ima Jean bought it from Bobby in the late 1980s. That's when he moved on to Hertford and opened Captain Bob's Barbecue and Seafood.

The pork barbecue is cooked over charcoal in a great iron pit out back. It looks like a small train car. Lane's cooks shoulders only and the meat is chopped with a Hobart chopper.

The chopped barbecue is actually minced. It is a finely chopped product and comes sauced from the kitchen with an Eastern North Carolina vinegar-base sauce. It comes to the table mildly hot, medium tangy with a strong vinegar presence that has enough pepper to keep it from having too much acidity or tartness. The 'cue has a good rich pork flavor, is moist and has a rich taste with overtones of vinegar and pepper. It's a floral bouquet of flavor on your palate. Nice 'cue. Enjoy.

The sliced barbecue pork is sliced ham. It has a good roasted-pork taste, and tastes almost like roast beef. It's a bit grainy and a little dry for my taste. It is good but needed sauce at the table.

The slaw is yellow and is a nice change from most Eastern Carolina white slaws. It has cabbage, pickles, mayo and mustard.

The vinegar-base sauce has cracked red pepper, seeds, spices and salt. Fiery by itself, it's hot with peppers and nice on the 'cue.

The hushpuppies are made with Abbott's Meal from Williamson. Lane's adds a bit of onion and produces a hushpuppy that is brown and crunchy with a slightly dry center. My pups were ever so slightly greasy, but good nonetheless. A little less cooking would make these pups not quite so crunchy, a little more moist, and a little less greasy.

Lane's is located in downtown Edenton on East Church Street, three blocks off of Highway 17 Business. It's open daily from 11 a.m. until 8 p.m. Telephone number: (252) 482-4008.

287

HAVE BEEN INFORMED THAT RESTAURANT
HAS CLOSED SINCE FIRST PRINTING OF BOOK

Tuck's Restaurant, Elizabeth City

Built by Tuck Webb in 1955, Tuck's Restaurant has been a fixture for good food in Elizabeth City ever since. Its present owner, Bobby Jones, came onboard in 1970 and remodeled it in 1978. Tuck built the restaurant as a barbecue-only place, but because of its close proximity to water later added seafood.

Bobby was fortunate enough to have a number of the older employees from Tuck's remain with him. One such fella was "Hamp" who cooked for Tuck's. Hamp cooked for Bobby for a few years, even though he was 65 when Bobby bought the restaurant. At that time, Bobby cooked with open pits and wood. The coals were freshened every 30 to 45 minutes; thus, it was a continual, as Bobby put it, "waxing and waning," coals dying, fresh coals added.

Bobby said that when he bought the business they were using New York shoulders. When he couldn't get picnics and Boston butts (the bottom and top half of the shoulder) to cook the way he wanted, he went to whole hogs. Bobby was particularly pleased at the way pork producers have been able, through diet, to get pork as lean as the pigs he receives today. He said that years ago when he cooked two hogs they would render 50-60 pounds of lard. He said two hogs cooked today will give you less than 10 pounds of lard. This is a much healthier product than any pork we have ever known.

Tuck's barbecue is cooked today on electric cookers. The whole hogs are hand chopped.

The chopped barbecue has a good coarse chop. It is chewy, moist, tender and sauced in the kitchen with an Eastern North Carolina vinegar-base sauce. It has nice pieces of brown outside mixed with the white part of the shoulder that gives the 'cue great texture and flavor. The chopped 'cue with the sauce is slightly hot with peppers but not fiery. There is just enough zip to make it interesting. It complements the flavor of the pork. This barbecue starts easy and finishes strong.

Tuck's has a red barbecue sauce for its chicken. It is bright, hot and some use it on the pork. I prefer the vinegar-base sauce from the kitchen. I would not add sauce at the table.

The fried chicken is crisp and crunchy with brown skin outside and moist meat beading with droplets of juice inside. It's very tender, very tasty and just greasy enough to be delicious.

The white slaw is Eastern North Carolina style. The fine chop has flakes of carrot, celery seeds, medium mayo, sugar and juice. It's good coleslaw.

288

The hushpuppies look and taste like small doughnuts. They are light brown and have a thin shell with a cake-like center. Some sugar added makes a tasty treat that balances well with the tangy 'cue and the bright slaw.

Tuck's has an extensive buffet as well as food that can be ordered by the plate. Tuck's serves minced barbecue pork, fried and barbecue chicken, 10 seafood items, a Delmonico steak and six sandwiches.

Tuck's is located on Highway 17 Bypass as you enter Elizabeth City on Hughes Boulevard. The address is 404 South Hughes Blvd. Tuck's is open daily from 11:30 a.m. until 8:30 p.m. Telephone number: (252) 335-1509 or (252) 335-1011.

Bubba's Bar-B-Que, Frisco

Larry Schauer, known as "Bubba" and wife Julie originated Bubba's Bar-B-Que at Frisco on Hatteras Island on the Outer Banks in 1984. Bubba continued to run the barbecue establishment until his death in 1998. Wayne Lehman bought Bubba's Bar-B-Que and says that he has made no changes to the menu or the sauce.

Wayne says he still cooks just the hams, not the whole hog. The sauce is the same that Bubba originated. The sides are the same. The only difference is they don't cook on open pits anymore. They cook with electricity.

Bubba used to cook with wood over an open pit in the back of the restaurant. Bubba later built another pit in the front part of the restaurant that customers could see. He used both. Bubba needed more cooking capacity so he replaced the open pit in the back with electric cookers made by Nunnery Freeman, which is located in Henderson. He would cook the meat in the electric cookers in the back and then bring the meat to the front to smoke on the open pit where people could see it. Bubba only used hickory, no oak.

Wayne said that his theory is "if it ain't broke, don't fix it." He continued the cooking methods that Bubba used. He had the good fortune to have both of the older managers stay onboard. Wayne uses hickory wood splits in the electric cookers just as Bubba did. These hickory splits inserted into the wood shaft impart a hickory-smoked flavor to the meat as it is cooked over electrical coils. Wayne says he uses about a cord of wood a year.

Mack Ericksen, who runs the cooking operation, said that their ribs are the standard three-and-a-half-down pork ribs. They cook peeled beef knuckles and add sauce.  They also cook BRT bone-rolled and tied fresh ham. He said that, in season, they cook 800 pounds of meat per night. He said they cook at a 50 percent power setting. The internal temperature of the smoker is 550 degrees. The hogs cook for approximately 12 hours. The internal temperature of the pork when cooked is 180 degrees. The chopped pork is cooked at 200 degrees internal temp while the sliced is cooked to 160 degrees. He said they cook the beef knuckles rare to 130 degrees internal temperature because they reheat them. He said the following day you can reheat them and still have a good product.

Bubba's has two locations, one at Frisco and one at Avon at the Hatteras Plaza shopping center. All the food is cooked at Frisco and the food served at Avon is taken there. Wayne said that one week he ran into the same man 10 times at the two locations. Apparently, this man had all of his meals at Bubba's while on vacation. He said that some people say they have to come to Bubba's before they even unpack. He has customers from California to the East Coast. He said that one day some men from Pennsylvania ate and were so taken they wanted to stick around and help him unload his trucks.

Wayne said he gets his meats from vendors at the best prices he can find for the best meat available. Wayne states that he will not sacrifice the quality of the meat for better price. The meat is very lean. He said people are more fat-gram conscious then ever before. The roll butt that he cooks is the Sterling Silver brand. He said it holds up well and has very little shrinkage. Pork is ordered as pork leg, fresh ham, boneless-butt end, boneless short shank, trim-shank, end-rolled and netted.

Bubba serves ribs, barbecue and chicken. All are served with Bubba's original sauce. It is not the Eastern North Carolina sauce. This sauce contains water, vinegar, brown sugar, chili powder, paprika, garlic powder, turmeric, soybeans and vegetable oil. It is brown, peppery and slightly hot. You can taste the spices, but not one spice in particular. It has a good strong finish, but no heavy aftertaste.

Bubba was a big Redskins football fan. In 2000, Wayne went to Manassas, VA and did a meal for the Hogettes at a fundraiser. You may have seen the Hogettes on television during a game or in commercials. These large men dress up as female hogs as a tribute to the Redskins' offensive linemen who were dubbed, "the Hogs." This trip provided him immense pleasure.

He also does catering at the local schools. Wayne said one day a busload of kids from Charleston, WV came in. He talked to the kids and served 70 eighth graders in less than an hour. Each ordered separately. He seemed pretty pleased with this accomplishment.

Hours are 11 a.m. until 8:30 p.m., Tuesday through Sunday. It's closed Monday. Telephone number: (252) 995-5421.

B's Barbecue, Greenville

William and Peggy McLawhorn started B's Barbecue in the late 1970s. Initially, William, Peggy, their youngest daughter Tammy and their middle daughter Judy worked in the business. Donna, the oldest daughter, was away at school. Now, William has retired, Peggy works part-time and their three daughters run the business.

Dexter Sherrod, who has worked with the family cooking the pigs and chopping the barbecue since the business opened, ably assists the girls. Dallas Moore cooks the chicken. Dexter says he cooks about 40 whole pigs per week. They had a fire in June 2000, which cut the size of their cooking facilities approximately in half. Before the fire, they could cook approximately 12-14 pigs a day. Now they can cook only eight pigs per day.

Dexter Sherrod

As with any good barbecue place, the way the pigs are cooked, the chopping by hand and the sauce make the product. I watched Dexter cook. He cooks his pigs over charcoal. Half pigs are brought from the elevated pit to the kitchen for chopping. Dexter chops at a big chopping board with two cleavers that beat out a rhythmic staccato as hunks of meat are cut into just right bite-size pieces. There is a large garbage can to Dexter's left that he deftly flicks pieces of the cooked pig that he does not wish to be part of his barbecue. Watching him chop, I was shocked to see some of the meat Dexter was throwing into the garbage. I would gladly have eaten most of it. Dexter explained that they do not permit any grissle, veins or seared meat to go into their product. All the meat is clean, fresh, tender and the very best of the cooked pig. You only have to watch Dexter at work and look into the trash barrel to realize why B's Barbecue is as good as it is.

William said that their sauce consists of select vinegars, red peppers, black pepper, salt, and a dab of white sugar. Just as you do not ask a rancher how many acres he has, you never ask a barbecue man for his sauce recipe.

I asked William if, after looking back over his long career, there were anything he would have changed about his cooking methods, sauce or facilities. He said that he would not change anything but the arrangement of the customers eating space. He said it just kind of grew and is not as well planned as he would like. It seems to get the job done. Otherwise, he said he would not change anything about his cooking technique, sauce, or his product. He said that people seem to like it pretty well and they keep coming back so he figures he must be doing something right.

William said he does not get the kind of pigs today that he cooked when he and his father raised pigs. He said that when he and his father raised hogs, they placed them in a floored pen for two weeks before slaughter. This allowed the droppings to fall through so that the pigs ate nothing but what he and his father wanted them to. They were fed a special diet and this enhanced the flavor of the meat. I asked him if there were any identifiers of a "good pig" when you received hogs from the slaughterhouse? He said there were, but they were apparent only to a trained eye of someone who had raised, slaughtered and cooked hogs for many years. He said a "good pig" could be identified by the grain of the meat. He said you look for a medium grain meat, not too much fat and a pig in the 92-to 125-pound range. He said below 65 pounds, the meat is soft and fluffy. He

said on a large pig, the meat tended to be a coarse grain. He figures a 100-pound uncooked hog will yield more than 12 pounds of barbecue. If you get 30 pounds of good barbecue from a 100-pound hog, you have done great. He said he used to go to Rocky Mount and go in the cooler and pick the hogs himself. Now the slaughterhouse sends him his hogs and he looks them over. He keeps most but sends some back that are not to his standards. In his opinion, the hogs that he gets today are not as flavorful as the hogs he used to have, but are more uniform in flavor. This is because large hog farms raise the hogs. All of them are fed the same diet, and all of them are shipped to market at about the same size/time. Thus, most of the pigs he gets may be average in flavor but are uniformly average. He said that when you bought hogs from farmers who only had a few pigs in a pen in the backyard, you never knew what they had been fed. Some farmers may feed the pigs a good diet as William and his father did. Others may feed the pigs slop, fishmeal, whatever. All of these things factor into the flavor of the meat.

William said that if you stood a hog up on a floor pen for two weeks and fed the hog good grain, you could change the flavor of the meat from an average-tasting pig to a good-tasting pig.

Every time I have visited B's

293

Barbecue, the McLawhorn girls have been crankin' it at a 110 mph serving B's good food to a hungry luncheon crowd. I generally eat the barbecue plate. The barbecue is lightly seasoned and has a hint of wood smoke from the cooking method (open pit with charcoal). The sauce is on the table in whiskey decanters. You don't need much. The sauce is a vinegar and peppers Eastern North Carolina sauce and it has good flavor. The white slaw, potatoes and green beans were good but not special. The chicken was very, very good. It's not overdone and comes lightly sauced.

I have eaten inside at B's and, weather permitting, outside. If you eat outside at the picnic tables, be prepared to be the envy of your office when you return and the object of attention for neighborhood dogs when you go home. The smoke from the smokehouse always seems to waft over the picnic tables while you dine. If you don't want your clothes to smell like you spent the last week with Jeremiah Johnson, I suggest you eat inside or in your car.

Another bit of information: with East Carolina University Medical Center only blocks away, B's is a very busy place at lunch. From about 11 a.m. to about 2 p.m., or earlier if the food runs out, there are cars

and trucks sprawled all over B's lot and vehicles parked on the shoulders up and down the road. If you want to be assured of partaking of B's good food, I 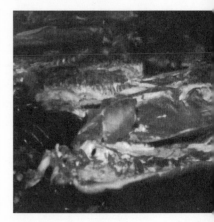 suggest you arrive close to the noon hour. When B's runs out of food each day they close the place. Since B's does not have a telephone, your only notice of this would be sign on the door and an absence of cars on the lot.

Hours are 11 a.m. until the food runs out, Monday through Saturday. Telephone number: No phone.

Captain Bob's BBQ and Seafood Restaurant, Hertford

Captain Bob's slogan is, "Only two places to eat... home and Captain Bob's."

Captain Bob's history is that of a restaurant originally started as Chub's by Chub Goodman in Hertford. Chub's later became White's Barbecue, which Bobby Lane bought in 1987. Bobby moved Captain Bob's to its present site in 1993.

Owners Bobby and wife Sharon have two children, Ashley and Keith, who are too young to work in the business. Bobby continues, with the assistance of manager Earl Ward, to produce good Eastern North Carolina Barbecue, prepared in the old traditional manner.

Captain Bob's has one of the slickest catering outfits I have seen. It is a shiny black four-door long bed Chevrolet Dooley with a matching black trailer that's longer than July and August. Earl Ward said it was custom made and has a complete stainless steel kitchen with more cooking power than the restaurant. I like this rig.

Captain Bob's BBQ and Seafood Restaurant cooks shoulders and hams over charcoal. The shoulders are used for the chopped barbecue and the hams are used for the sliced barbecue. Captain Bob's cooks approximately 650 pounds of pork three times a week. The chopped barbecue

is ground with a Hobart chopper. The meat is run through three times. They call it minced. I personally prefer barbecue not chopped this fine. I prefer the coarse chopped or pulled pig, like pig pickin' meat. Earl, who has been Captain Bob's manager since 1993, said that is his preference also. However, most people in this area, for whatever reason, seem to like "minced" barbecue. The chopped barbecue still had a good flavor and, sauced in the kitchen, was a very flavorful pork product.

The sauce is vinegar base with salt and pepper (red crushed, red grain) and several

other spices. It is light, thin, reddish and quite fiery by itself. On the chopped barbecue, it brings back some of the flavor that to me mincing removes.

The moderately thick brunswick stew has tomatoes, diced potatoes, corn, butter beans, onions and chicken. It is one of the better stews I ran across. It has the right balance of ingredients, including spices, and is not too tomatoey.

In addition to barbecue, seafood and brunswick stew, Captain Bob's serves 16 sandwiches, salads, the usual beverages,

homemade cakes, pies, cobblers and ice cream.

Captain Bob's is located in Hertford on Highway 17 South. Hours are 4 a.m. to 9 p.m., Monday through Saturday, and 11 a.m. to 9 p.m., Sunday. Telephone number: (252) 426-1811.

Fisherman's Wharf, Jacksonville

The dining rooms at Fisherman's Wharf in Jacksonville are built out over the river and provide a wonderful view and a very peaceful and tranquil setting which adds to the enjoyment of the meal.

Owner Edward Bynum opened Fisherman's Wharf on this site on Dec. 7, 1972. My server, Edna Noblot, had been here all but three weeks of that time. Edward Bynum has enjoyed many successes in the food business, particularly barbecue for the past 60 years. Today, Mike Bynum, son of Edward Bynum, cooks the 'cue. Mike said that he cooks his wonderful pork offerings with a gas cooker and cooks only whole hogs. The pigs take about 12 hours for each cooking. It is Mike's opinion that the way one cooks a pig and the sauce are more determinative of the end product than the method one uses to cook a pig.

Mike remembers burning palates of hickory wood down for cooking coals and cooking pigs all night, and chopping the cooked pig. It took 16 hours to produce good 'cue. Mike said that today, by careful monitoring and technique, he can cook about as good a product with gas. He, like many, believes that cooking the whole hog produces better barbecue. He gets different textures and moisture from different parts

of the hog which, when mixed together, form a barbecue bouquet that can not be achieved by serving any one part of the pig. I whole-heartedly concur.

In addition to good barbecue, slaw and hushpuppies, Fisherman's Wharf serves great seafood, prime rib and steaks. The low-country clam chowder is delicious. It's all really good food served by friendly people in a picture-book setting.

The chopped barbecue pork is moderately coarse chopped and is sauced in the kitchen. This is a really good Eastern North Carolina-style 'cue. The roasted pork is accented with a vinegar-base sauce. The outside brown mixes with white to give it a nice texture. This flavorful pork comes in chopped meaty pieces. It's not minced like many of the places in this area. The outside brown is chewy and good. The 'cue needs a few drops of sauce at the table for me but it's classic Eastern North Carolina Barbecue.

The crisp, white cabbage slaw is juicy with chips of carrot and light mayo. It's slightly sweet and has a fresh garden taste. With the 'cue, the slaw makes a great combo and a great sandwich.

The hushpuppies are caramel brown with a perfectly crisp shell and a moist center with a really good cornmeal taste.

297

Served hot, this very tender pup has a hint of sugar making it a favorite with barbecue or seafood.

The Eastern Carolina vinegar-base sauce with red peppers and spices is not unduly hot by itself. It's very good on the barbecue.

Fisherman's Wharf is located on the New River just east of the junction of Highway 17 and Highway 258 in Jacksonville. It's just before you cross the bridge over the New River. It is a charcoal gray, board and baton building with a large red sign across the front that reads: "World's Famous Fisherman's Wharf."

The Wharf is open daily from 11:30 a.m. until 10 p.m. Telephone number: (910) 455-5200.

King's Restaurant, Kinston

In 1936, Frank King Sr. moved his family to a small one-horse farm in Lenoir County, the present site of King's Restaurant. Frank attempted to supplement his income by building a country store on the highway in front of his farm. The store was built in 1937 by two local carpenters, a Mr. Byrd and a Mr. Dorman. Wilbur King and Stanley Robertson Sr. spread soil for the parking lot while the building was under construction. Upon Frank's death in 1938, his son Wilbur took over the operation of the store. A poolroom was added on the back of the store and it became the first King's Restaurant.

Canned foods from the store were heated on a pot-bellied stove for the pool players. A hot dog pan was installed and the food operation was born. Wilbur left for the military service and was overseas until 1946. Upon his return to Kinston, he continued in the store business and soon added a grill in the poolroom area. In 1947, Wilber's brother Victor came to work for him at the grill.

Soon thereafter, the King brothers expanded their menu to include "bar-b-que" pork, cooking only half a pig at a time.

During the '50s, as the small café grew, it became a popular gathering place for teenagers. Many people have fond mem-

ories of treating their best girl to a delicious King's hot dog and milk-shake while listening as the jukebox belted out Frankie Lane's famous "Mule Train." At one time the back parking lot was the most famous "Lovers' Lane" in Eastern North Carolina.

During the '60s, the King brothers remodeled several times and brought the seating capacity up to 275, but they still used the grill-and-counter concept. The business continued to grow and became famous for its varied menu, family atmosphere and down-home "folksy" service. Millions of travelers going to and from the beaches stopped at King's for a welcome break in their drive. The business name became King's Bar-B-Que and Restaurant.

In the early '70s, the King brothers decided it was time for a major move. In 1971, groundbreaking began for what would be one of the South's largest restaurants.

Today, King's seats more than 800 and caters to thousands of North Carolinians and travelers from across the U.S. King's prepares more than 8,000 pounds of their "bar-b-que" pork, 6,000 pounds of chicken and 1,500 pounds of collard greens per week. King's is now serving third and fourth generations of travelers to North Carolina's crystal coast. The structures and equipment are modern but the family atmosphere, good service and down-home country cooking have remained the same.

King's barbecue is cooked electrically on a Barbecue Slave and is mixed with barbecue that is smoked. All of it is hand chopped.

The chopped barbecue is a medium chop and comes sauced from the kitchen. It has that good ol' Eastern North Carolina vinegar-base taste. It's slightly spicy with peppers standing up front. The vinegar taste is tart, not hot, and has enough spices to keep things interesting.

The thick brunswick stew has toma-

toes, corn, June peas and lots of meat (pork and chicken). It's not sweet, not spicy and definitely is not a vegetable soup.

The hushpuppies have a nice golden-brown outside that is crisp. The center is moist and has good flavor. Lakeside Mills produces the cornmeal used for King's hushpuppies.

Hours are 10:30 a.m. until 9 p.m., Monday through Friday, and 7 a.m. until 9 p.m., Saturday and Sunday. Telephone number: (252) 527-2101 or 1-800-332-OINK (6465). King's Web site is www.kingsbbq.com

F. B. Duncan's Bar-B-Que, Manteo

Good barbecue is a rarity when you can smell salt air. Generally you have to be much further inland. Such is not the case with F.B. Duncan's Bar-B-Que. Duncan's is formerly Saul's Barbecue which was operated by Doug Saul for nearly a decade. Freddy and Betty Duncan worked for Doug for many years and, in 1999, took over ownership and operation of the restaurant.

Duncan's serves a buffet of barbecue and seafood with lots of sides. Betty said they feed mostly the locals along with tourists in season.

Freddy does the slow roasting of whole hog splits on a Nunnery-Freeman Kook Rite Kooker. Freddy said he grinds about 10 percent of the pork and hand shreds the rest. He said it takes him about an hour to hand shred half a pig. He said the 10 percent ground is mixed with the hand shredded to give the pork enough consistency to hold together in a sandwich.

Duncan's chopped barbecue pork is a typically good Eastern Carolina-style 'cue. The barbecue is moderately chopped, sauced in the kitchen, and has a good prominent vinegar taste with little seeds of red pepper. It was sauced just right for me. I would not require more at the table.

The finely chopped, crisp white cabbage coleslaw has a little mayo and sugar and makes for a good combination with the barbecue.

The hushpuppies are thin crisp rings of cornbread with a light brown shell. It has a moist center and a hint of sugar. Duncan's uses Abbott's mix, which does have a little sugar in it.

F.B. Duncan's Bar-B-Que is located on your right on Highway 64, approximately two miles after entering the island. It is tucked back from the street and the building preceding it, when you are traveling east, totally blocks the view. In all probability, you will have to turn around. It's worth it. Look for a Tymco service station on your right. When you reach the Tymco service station, you have passed it. It was two buildings back.

Hours are 11 a.m. until 8 p.m. Tuesday through Saturday. It's closed Sunday and Monday. Telephone number: (252) 473-6464.

Whitley's Barbecue, Murfreesboro

Whitley's Barbecue is a picturesque white Eastern North Carolina-looking building with manicured grounds. From the exterior, it looks more like a country club than a barbecue place. The deck for outside eating overlooks a landscape of lush greenery, peanut fields, bean fields and a lake nestled in a vail surrounded by Eastern North Carolina Long Leaf Pines. Interspersed in this lovely scene are about 100 white geese picking their way about the premises. This tranquil setting was and still is a part of the farm owned by Eldridge Washington Whitley many years ago. E.W. Whitley left the farm to his son Robert Eldridge Whitley. It is now owned and operated by Robert's daughter, Ruth Whitley.

Even if Whitley's Barbecue did not offer outstanding food products in the most picturesque setting of any barbecue place I've ever seen, it is worth the trip to Murfreesboro to meet Ruth Whitley. Ruth is the epitome of all that is gracious and good about Eastern North Carolina hospitality. A graduate of UNC-Chapel Hill, Ruth has traveled extensively about the planet and I am sure has charmed all she has met. When this lovely lady of the Manor smiles, you feel like a deer caught in headlights.

Ruth worked at her father's side for seven years and after his death in the late '80s, took over full management of Whitley's Barbecue. Like most children growing up in a barbecue business, Ruth can do everything required to produce Whitley's famous barbecue and brunswick stew. To make her task easier, she is ably assisted by a number of exceptional employees who have been with her for many years. Bernice Jenkins was with Whitley's from 1974 until her recent death. Dorothy Johnson has been with Whitley's since 1989. Herbert Wood has been with Whitley's since 1984 and Marie Faison was with Whitley's from 1987 through 2000.

Whitley's is located on what used to be a dirt path on the family farm. Robert and Mildred Whitley established the business in 1963. A few years later, Highway 11 split the farm and put the business on a paved road. In 1973, the original building was enlarged with the addition of an east dining room and later a deck overlooking a lake.

In the early days, cooking was an all-night affair for two men who kept wood fires burning in the pits behind the original restaurant. Today, the pork is slow cooked all night in Nunnery-Freeman electric stainless steel cookers.

The chopped barbecue is medium chopped and comes sauced from the kitchen with flecks of red pepper. This com-

302

bined with the brown pork is eye candy for any barbecue enthusiast. It has a fresh, rich taste as the dark and white meat create a medley of ham and shoulder flavors that dance with the sauces like Fred and Ginger – tastefully done, lots of fun.

The vinegar-base sauce is very tart and has just the right amount of crushed pepper to add zest. It's Eastern North Carolina sauce at its best.

The slaw is coarse chopped, crisp and has the freshest, greenest taste ever.

The golden cornsticks are crisp outside with a good cornmeal taste inside. It's not greasy and has a very rich flavor.

The sweet and sour sauce is just that. It's tangy but has good balance.

The delicious fried chicken has a crispy caramel brown and gold skin. It is in no way greasy. The breast I enjoyed was moist. It tasted like everything you dream good fried chicken could be.

In addition to Bernice's Milky Way

Cake (11 Milky Way bars in every cake), cheesecake and hot fudge cake, there are five different homemade pies. All reach the level of grandma's best. However, the homemade churned ice cream (I had banana) made from Whitley's own carefully cooked custard added to un-whipped cream, was so rich, so decadent and so good I did not want to swallow. It is worth a 100-mile trip out of the way to visit Whitley's Barbecue for its good food. When you add the hospitality of and graciousness of Ruth Whitley, you will feel you have discovered a treasure.

Whitley's is located on Route 11 South in Murfreesboro. From Highway 158, go to the intersection of Highway 11 (Murfreesboro/Ahoskie) and turn north on Highway 11. Whitley's Barbecue is one mile on the right. Hours are 11 a.m. to 9 p.m., Tuesday through Sunday. It's closed Monday. Telephone Number: (252) 398-4884.

Moore's Bar-B-Que, New Bern

Located on Highway 17 South, just out of New Bern, the present Moore's Bar-B-Que is the seventh location of this restaurant in this area in the past 50 years.

Moore's Bar-B-Que almost never got off the launching pad. Its founder, John Moore, borrowed $35 and a cooker and bought himself a live pig. When John got back home with the pig, the pig got away. After an extended one-contestant pig rodeo, John finally corralled the pig. After much persuasion, the pig graciously made the ultimate sacrifice and Moore's Bar-B-Que began.

John Moore started Moore's Bar-B-Que in 1945 in James City, just across the river. Moore's grew, changed and moved. It's been at the same location now since 1973. In 2001, they expanded another 25 percent.

John Moore died in 1989 and Dot, his wife, died in 1995. Tommy Moore, John and Dot's son, carried on the business with help from his wife. Bryan Moore and D.J. Moran manage Moore's Bar-B-Que. Tommy Moore still comes by a couple of days per week to be sure that young Bryan is doing things in Moore's time-honored tradition. He is. Moore's motto is: "Moore's does it the Olde Tyme way." Despite his youth, Bryan has learned at the feet of the masters and does

it the "olde tyme way."

Bolt the door, this is the place. The chopped pork is tender and moist with just the right amount of twang without additional sauce. The good, strong vinegar presence is accompanied by crushed red pepper and a blend of spices that make your mouth water.

Moore's cooks on pits with charcoal and wood at least three times a week. They cook the whole hog in split halves. It is cooked 50 percent electric and 50 percent wood.

The ribs are good, meaty pork ribs with a Kansas City-sauce that takes me home. The barbecue chicken was outrageously tender with a reddish sauce just made for this bird.

The golden-brown hushpuppies have a nice crunch and a moist center that is very, very tasty.

The crispy Eastern North Carolina-style white slaw is long on cabbage with crisp tiny chips of carrot. It's juicy but not watery at all.

The sauce for chicken is a reddish-brown, Kansas City-type sauce that's moderately thick and spicy.

The sauce for the pork is a thin vinegar-base sauce with lots of pepper. It looks like potpourri in vinegar in the bottle. It will light your fire, make you moist under the

304

eyes and have you reaching for water. On the meat, it is more gentlemanly. You don't need much, if any.

Seafood entrees round out the menu. Moore's has shrimp, flounder, trout and soft-shell crabs in season.

Moore's serves fountain drinks and tea. The desserts are apple, pecan and lemon pies.

On Saturday nights, Moore's serves St. Louis ribs, Kansas City style. Plan your trip accordingly. Barbecue, slaw and the hot sauce are a triple threat.

Moore's Bar-B-Que is located on the east side of Highway 17 South, just outside New Bern. Hours are 10 a.m. until 8 p.m., Monday through Thursday, and 10 a.m. until 8:30 p.m., Friday and Saturday. It's closed Sunday. Telephone number: (252) 638-3937.

Simp's Barbecue, Roper

Officially named Simpson's Barbecue, Inc., the locals have shortened the handle to "Simp's."

Dan and Ruth Simpson and their son Red cooked their first pig at Simpson's in 1957. Now Red and his wife Rachel, run Simp's with the able assistance of Carol and Vicki, their daughters.

Some 45 years later, Red is still firing the pits to prepare more than 500 pounds of

pork shoulders and hams per week. "Shoulders and hams are the leanest parts of the pig and that's what we want

to serve," Red says.

Red uses only the most expensive brand of charcoal to fire his pits. This produces the delicate smoke that flavors the pork that is the hallmark of Simp's Barbecue. Red switched to charcoal from oak wood in 1965 because of the difficulty of getting good wood in his area.

Despite opening at 7 a.m., the local farmers gather at Simp's at 5 a.m. for their morning coffee. Of course the owners are preparing for the day's business and have

always let the farmers in the back door so they can have their coffee and talk farm news and "guy stuff" until the business opens some two hours later.

Simp's Barbecue has been enjoyed by many people the world over who have made their way to the Outer Banks along Highway 64. Neighbors have shipped this wonderful product as far away as Alaska.

Formerly an old Phillip's 66 gas station, Simp's still has that look outside. Rachel has added tomato plants out front where the pumps used to be to ensure that Simp's has the freshest tomatoes. It still looks like a filling station. Inside it looks part country store and part barbecue place. There is the usual door in the middle and windows with bars on either side. Parking is limited.

Talking with Red back in the kitchen while he cooked hushpuppies and french fries, Red said that a lot of the people that stop are more fat-gram conscience than people used to be. He says they cook only the leanest, best parts of the pig to ensure that their barbecue is the freshest, leanest and the best that he or anyone else is able to produce.

One of Red's delicious barbecue sandwiches in one hand and a little glass bottle Coke (retro 1940s) with a candy stripe

306

straw is not only the right balance, but the perfect combination of good food and drink.

I found the chopped barbecue to be rich, nutty, smoky and tangy with a combination smoky/vinegary flavor. Peppers are prominent. Check out the tiny black specks. The outside brown mixed in with the white makes this a toothsome treat.

The hushpuppies are the size of walnuts with an almost flaky pastry shell. It's golden tan outside and moist yellow inside. It's not at all greasy and has a cake-like texture.

The slaw is white minced with spices, mayo and mustard. It's not sweet but it is ever so slightly tart.

With a little bottle of Coke that has just the right heft in one hand and the other hand guardingly holding one of the best barbecue sandwiches you ever popped a bill on,

you have attained what most people are still searching for – good barbecue and good balance.

I don't think the small six-ounce Coke has quite as much effervescence as I remember as a child, but thank goodness Simp's hasn't changed a thing. Happy 45th! Keep the fires burning. By the way, my bottle was made in Roswell, New Mexico. Wanna travel?

Simp's is a light mustard-colored building on the north side of Highway 64, east of Roper. There is little to distinguish it, including signage. Parking is limited. From Roper, look carefully to your left. From Columbia, look carefully to your right. Hours are 7 a.m. until 7 p.m., Tuesday through Saturday. It's closed Sunday and Monday. Telephone number: (252) 793-2701.

Joe's Barbecue Kitchen, Shallotte

Joe's slogan is "As good as the best, better than the rest and just a little bit habit forming." This apparently is the case. One of the members of the waitstaff proudly told me that in 2000 Joe's was voted the best barbecue on the East Coast by a local television station.

Joe's is a favorite eating place for the beach crowd and locals in the Shallotte area. I was there on a Saturday night and the place, which seats more than 200, was filled. The line was out the door and into the parking lot.

Joe's serves barbecue pork, spareribs, chicken (fried and barbecued), brunswick stew, shrimp, fish, crab and catfish. There are lots of side dishes. One of their famous desserts is peach cobbler.

The food is served buffet style and the volume was so great that nothing seemed to stay in the trays on the steam table more than a couple of minutes.

The chopped barbecue is a moist, medium chop with pieces of brown skin mixed in. It had a rich pork flavor, slight smoke flavor and came slightly sauced from the kitchen. It tasted good to me without adding any sauce. When I added a few drops at the table, it tasted even better.

The sauce is a reddish-brown vinegar base Eastern North Carolina sauce with pep-pers shining through. Pretty spicy by itself, it is much better on the meat. It's hot but has no aftertaste. You only enjoy it when you eat, it does not take equal time later.

The pork ribs are nice and meaty with good flavor. It's the same sauce as the chopped barbecue but it's not heavy with ribs.

The golden hushpuppies are better than average. They are not too crispy and have a moderately moist center.

The barbecue chicken is tender, moist and not overcooked. Saucing at the table adds to the flavor of this dish.

The brunswick stew is made up of corn, butter beans, chicken and lots of tomatoes. The tomato taste is predominant here. To my taste it is really more like thick vegetable soup than a stew. It has a mild taste and is fairly thin in texture.

The slaw is good Eastern North Carolina slaw that's not spicy but is a bit juicy. The slaw with chopped barbecue and added sauce makes a good taste treat.

Joe's Barbecue is located on Business Highway 17 North in Shallotte. Hours are 10 a.m. until 8:30 p.m., Monday, Tuesday and Thursday, and 10 a.m. until 9 p.m., Wednesday, Friday and Saturday (buffet nights). It's closed Sunday. Telephone number: (910) 754-8876. Joe's replica location is located on Business Highway 701 South

in Whiteville. Telephone number: (910) 642-3511.

Abrams Barbecue, Tarboro

When the telephone company left Tarboro, a large number of Abrams customers had to move from the area. It seemed to Gerald Abram, the owner of Abrams Barbecue, that Rocky Mount and Greenville were growing at a greater rate than Tarboro. Gerald decided he needed to go into the catering business to have the expansion for the company that he desired. Catering proved to be the right move. The catering side of Abrams Barbecue now constitutes about 80 percent or more of its gross business.

At one time, Abram had a barbecue place in Pinetops, Gerald's hometown. Now, in addition to the Abrams Barbecue in Tarboro, Abram has a place in Wilson, but it serves primarily breakfast. The Abrams Barbecue in Tarboro has been in business at its present site since 1974.

Though barbecue is the name, barbecue is only part of the game. Abrams is an event provider. In fact, Abrams is one of the biggest event providers on the Eastern seaboard. Abrams can not only provide wonderful food, but it can also provide the games and rides for corporate outings. The weekend before my visit, Abrams fed 10,000 people at one event. This is barbecuing in a big way.

The pit boss said that he cooks 1,600 to 2,800 pounds of meat per week. Some weeks he cooks 7,000 to 8,000 pounds. On weeks with large catering parties, Abrams sometimes cooks as much as 21,000 pounds of pork. The pit boss said that he normally cooks a 100-pound hog for about six hours. They cook with electricity. All the sauces used with Abrams Barbecue are their own special-made sauces.

Abrams has a number of employees that have worked for the company for many years. Mangraum Whitaker has worked at Abrams since it opened. Mangraum is in his 90s. He can still throw a pig up over his shoulder and walk away with it. Jerry Abram, the owner's son, said that Mangraum checks in with Abrams about everyday to make sure they are still doing things right. Rest easy Mangraum, they are.

Abrams won first place in the North Carolina Barbecue Festival at Raleigh four years ago. Their delightful pork products have been enjoyed not only by the natives of North Carolina but, because of extensive catering, those people in other states as well

I have bird hunted in the Tarboro area for more than 20 years. After a good day, afield with good dogs and good friends, coming to Abrams for one of their scrumptious barbecue dinners is a perfect end to a perfect day.

In September 1999, I got to sample Abrams good pork products when I waded the swamps with the North Carolina/Tennessee Army National Guard Dmort team during the flooding after Hurricane Floyd. Having some of Abrams good 'cue after a day like we experienced proved to be a comfort zone in a world suddenly turned upside down. Abrams Barbecue and many of its neighbors are to be commended for their efforts during those heart-rending times.

I like Abrams Barbecue. It is moist with a spicy, tart, vinegary and peppery taste. It has a strong finish yet it is not too heavy. There's not too much fat. It's just perfect. The outside brown and the inside white create a good balance of flavors. The way it comes sauced from the kitchen with the Eastern North Carolina vinegar-base sauce is just right for me, I would add nothing. Abrams Barbecue: the cooking methods, the chopping methods and Abrams special sauce make for a great combination. Enjoy.

The white slaw and hushpuppies are yummy and complement the 'cue, but it is the barbecue that brings them in and the barbecue that brings them back.

Hours are 6 a.m. until 8 p.m., Monday through Saturday, and 7 a.m. until 4 p.m., Sunday. Telephone number: (252) 823-4522.

Boss Hog Backyard Bar-B-Que, Washington

Do not look for a short, fat white man in a white suit and vest with a white Stetson. The owner of Boss Hog looks more like an older man on a daytime soap opera or a retired athlete. Owner Charlie Baker retired as a golf pro from a local country club and decided to open a barbecue place. Boss Hog opened Sept. 1, 2000 at its present site.

The wonderful pork products that Charlie produces are cooked on pits with charcoal. Boss Hog cooks whole hogs. Charlie said sometimes when there is a large catering job, he will cook the hogs three to four hours on a Nunnery-Freeman Kook Rite Kooker and four hours over charcoal. Whatever he's doing, he's doing it right.

Boss Hog's chopped barbecue pork is moist, tender and moderately coarse with a good, rich roasted-pork flavor. With strong smoky overtones, the outside brown mixes nicely with the white meat to add texture and flavor. This tasty offering is lightly sauced in the kitchen with a classic Eastern Carolina vinegar-base sauce. I suggest adding a few drops at the table to bring the flavor up a click or two, as the sauce in the kitchen is very mild. This 'cue is absolutely delicious.

Boss Hog's succulent pork is part of a scrumptious buffet. I only sampled the pork, slaw, hushpuppies and laced cornbread. The slaw is a crisp, crunchy white cabbage Eastern North Carolina-type slaw with light mayo and a prominent fresh cabbage taste. The slaw goes well with the 'cue and makes a great sandwich. The hushpuppies are light brown and have a crisp outer shell and a moist center. When you say good pup, you've said it all.

The lace cornbread is a very thin, wispy cornbread that is about the size of a saucer. Charlie makes these delectable treats by placing ice cream scoops of hushpuppy mix between sheets of wax paper in the parking lot and having a friend back over them with an 18-wheeler. The smooshed pups are then gently lifted with a spatula from the asphalt and placed in layers in a wheel-barrow separated by more wax paper. The lacey treats are then transferred by specially designed aluminum spatulas with a convection air flow handle into a slightly boiling oil of macadamia nuts and butterfly tears (if you've bought it this far, I have some land in Florida I'd like to tell you about). The laced cornbread is actually cooked much like a funnel cake. It has a crisp outer edge, moist center and has great flavor. Eat it hot, don't let this one cool. Have a couple of hot pieces for dessert.

Boss Hog is off of Highway 17 north out of Washington, two blocks east from the intersection of Highway 17/15. Boss Hog is located in Washington Plaza. Hours are 10:30 a.m. until 8:30 p.m., Monday through Saturday. It's closed Sunday. Telephone number: (252) 946-5251.

Hog Heaven, Washington

Hog Heaven has been at its present site since the early '90s. The owner for the entire time has been Manfred Alligood, who has more than just good barbecue going for him at Hog Heaven. His lovely daughters – Stephanie Bowen, Amanda Alligood and Denise Hednell – manage the place. These charming ladies could sell a snowball to an Eskimo who is standing knee deep in the stuff.

Hog Heaven's chopped barbecue pork is sauced in the kitchen with an Eastern Carolina vinegar-base sauce. The 'cue comes to the table in a moderately chopped form with a vinegar prominence. The barbecue is not hot with the sauce and has a good lean rich flavor. It has the wonderful flavor that only whole hog chopped produces with a good mix of outside brown and inside white, shoulder, midlin and ham. A little additional sauce at the table cranks the barbecue up to the right place.

The slaw was very fresh, crisp and tart with a good white cabbage flavor and tiny carrot chips, celery seed and light mayo. The hushpuppies are golden and have a crisp outside shell and a fairly moist center. The pups have a good cornbread taste.

The brownish sauce is a vinegar-base Eastern North Carolina sauce that is tart with mostly vinegar, though it has some peppers and spices. Vinegar is the strongest flavor here.

The slaw and 'cue together have a slightly salty taste to my palette.

Going east on Highway 264, Hog Heaven is on the right just before you cross the little bridge into Washington at the city limits. Traveling west on Highway 264, Hog Heaven is two miles west of Highway 264/17 intersection on the left.

Hours are 10:30 a.m. until 8:30 p.m., Tuesday through Sunday. It's closed Monday. Telephone number: (252) 975-5829.

Shaw's Barbecue House, Williamston

The end of World War II brought our troops home from foreign shores and brought a new economic boom for our country. It also brought Shaw's Barbecue House to Williamston. Ricky Roberson, the owner of Shaw's Barbecue House since 1975, said that his maternal grandfather started his little barbecue operation right after WWII. It was started behind his house. Initially he raised his own hogs. Later he bought from a packing company.

Ricky said that his grandfather ran the business for many years and then it went to his mother, Lucille Shaw Roberson. She ran the business for 10-12 years after her father retired. Lucille still plays a limited role in the business and comes by almost daily.

Shaw's cooks hams and shoulders. Ricky said that hogs today have less fat than hogs he purchased 10 years ago. He said that the pigs he gets today from the packinghouse consistently have good quality and that's important in his business. Like most barbecue places, Shaw's originally cooked with wood. In the late '60s, Shaw's began cooking with electricity using the Nunnery Freeman Cookers made in Henderson. They cook about 4,000 pounds of fresh meat per week.

The sauce is vinegar, water, ketchup, sugar, salt, pepper and spices that he of course would not divulge. When asked what sets his barbecue apart, Ricky said that they have continually tried to use the same brands that his grandfather used to make their sauce. He said that hasn't changed, nor have the recipes.

He felt that the business being a family business with hands-on attention everyday gave the business more continuity.

Tammy Cratt

Ricky said that one time they tried to change the vinegar and use a cheaper brand. It didn't work. He said he wasn't sure the customers noticed but he did. They immediately went back to the old brands and they have stayed with them ever since.

Williamston is on the route for Raleigh traffic going to the Outer Banks, as well as Virginia traffic doing the same. Also a lot of Virginia to Wilmington traffic passes

315

through Williamston. Ricky said that in the more than 25 years he has run the place, he has seen families come in vacation after vacation. He's watched children grow up into young adults. This continued business and loyalty pleases Ricky. It also makes the customers seem like family for them to have eaten at Shaw's for such a long period of time.

In addition to Shaw's barbecue products (pork and chicken), Shaw's serves fried chicken and the usual sides of slaw, green beans and potatoes. Shaw's also sells sliced barbecue ham and souse meat. Shaw's used to make it's own sausage. Now Shaw's sausage is made for them. Shaw's bottles its own sauce on premises and has it for sell to the public.

Shaw's has pulled meat from the ham like a pig pickin'. It comes with a vinegary pepper sauce that is slightly tangy but no smoky flavor. The pulled pig pickers are not as saucy as the chopped.

The chopped barbecue is tender, moist and comes already sauced from the kitchen. The peppery taste leaps to the forefront. It also has a good vinegar taste, but it's not overpowering. The sauce is not heavy as it has red and black peppers, vinegar and salt. There's no smoke flavor to this barbecue.

The slaw has a vinegar and mustard taste that is fresh and makes for a good complement to the barbecue. The cabbage is crisp and crunchy.

The brunswick stew has lots of lima beans, corn, June peas and tomatoes. It has meat but so little I could not tell what. You can't taste the meat and there are no potatoes. It tastes as if were made to be a side, not a main dish. It has a veggie, succotash taste. It's rather bland and not spicy at all.

Hours are 6 a.m. until 8 p.m., Monday through Saturday. It's closed Sunday. Telephone number: (252) 792-5339.

316

Bunn's BBQ, Windsor

When you enter Bunn's BBQ, you immediately expect to hear the Andrew Sisters singing the "Boogie Woogie Bugle Boy" or Glenn Miller's orchestra belting out "In the Mood" or Artie Shaw's clarinet swinging with "Summit Ridge Drive." It is a time-warp experience. The building dates back to the mid-1800s. It was originally a doctor's office and later became a Texaco filling station from 1900 to 1920. In

1938, it became the home of Bunn's BBQ.

Only two families have owned Bunn's BBQ since its inception. The Russell family has run it since 1969. Brothers Randy Russell and Russ Russell, the present owners, are ably assisted by their mom, Grace Russell. Bunn's BBQ is everything that you expect a good ol' Eastern North Carolina barbecue place to be.

Bunn's BBQ has maintained the same country filling station configuration inside, but they have added a door on both sides and two small wings for customer seating. The prime seating is at the back where the cooking is done. Seating takes the form of a small L-shaped counter with a permanent bench. You climb over the bench and take your place. I love the feeling of this barbecue place.

Despite its retro appearance, the Russell boys cook 21st century. Bunn's cooks Boston Butts and shoulders on a Nunnery-Freeman Kook Rite Kooker. The wonderful slowly cooked roast pork that Bunn's produces is minced (fine chopped) and sauced in the kitchen with an Eastern North Carolina vinegar-base sauce. There is plenty of good outside brown mixed with the inside white. The 'cue has a nice, rich slowly roasted pork flavor. It's moist and so good that you'll slap the tabletop. It needs a few drops of additional house sauce at the table for my taste. If you want it even hotter, Texas Pete is provided.

Bunn's fine 'cue is accompanied with cornbread squares and slaw. The cornbread squares are thin, less than a half-inch thick, and have a crisp outside and a moist inside.

It's almost like a sourdough bread. It's very good.

The slaw is coarse shredded coleslaw that has a good fresh cabbage taste with tart, vinegary overtones. This is really good with the barbecue.

Bunn's sauce is a red vinegar-base Eastern North Carolina sauce with lots of peppers and spices. It's a tart, pungent Eastern sauce that steps up to be counted.

Bunn's also serves really good brunswick stew that has a special, rich flavor that a good stew should have. It is unique and you can't taste any one ingredient. That's the mark of a good Long Island Ice Tea as well as the mark for all good brunswick stews.

Bunn's BBQ is located in downtown Windsor. As you come into Windsor on Highway 17 North, the highway will T at a stop sign. Go to the right and you turn left off of Highway 17. Follow this street into downtown Windsor. Bunn's BBQ is located on the right, across the street from the post office. You can't miss this delightful, old, classic Eastern North Carolina barbecue place.

Janice Riddeck

Hours are 9 a.m. until 5 p.m., Monday through Saturday. It's closed Sunday. Telephone number: (252) 794-2274.

Notes

Notes

Barbecue
Routes

Barbecue Routes

Interstate 40: Tennessee to Wilmington

Skeeter's BBQ House, Canton
Barbecue Inn, Asheville
Mountain Smoke House Barbecue, Asheville
Perry's BBQ, Black Mountain
Timberwood's Family Restaurant, Morganton
Bennett's Smokehouse and Saloon, Conover
Little Pigs Barbecue, Statesville
Carolina Bar-B-Que, Statesville
Deano's Barbecue, Mocksville
Little Richard's Lexington Bar-B-Que,
  Clemmons
Little Richard's Bar-B-Que, Winston-Salem
Hill's Lexington Barbecue, Winston-Salem
Stamey's Barbecue, Greensboro
Hursey's Barbecue, Burlington
Allen and Son Barbecue, Chapel Hill
Bon's Bar-B-Q, Carrboro
Bullock's Barbecue, Durham
Clyde Coopers Barbeque, Raleigh
Don Murray's Barbecue and Seafood, Raleigh
Stephenson's Barbecue, Willow Springs
Ralph's Barbecue, Angier
Ron's Barn, Coats
Eddie's Barbecue, Newton Grove
Smithfield's Chicken 'n Bar-B-Que, Newton
  Grove
Bland's Barbecue, Warsaw

Bland's Barbecue, Wallace
Cavenaughs Family Supper House, Wallace
Pink Supper House, Wallace
Wells Pork Products, Burgaw
Flip's Bar-B-Que, Wilmington

**Interstate 77: Lambsburg, VA to Rockhill,
  SC**

Wallace Brother's BBQ, Lambsburg, VA
Carolina Bar-B-Que, Statesville
Lancaster's BBQ, Mooresville
Bubba's Barbecue, Charlotte

Interstate 85: Charlotte to Wise

Bubba's Barbecue, Charlotte
Troutman's Bar-B-Q, Concord
Gary's Bar-B-Que, China Grove
Hendrix Barbecue, Salisbury
Richard's Bar-B-Que, Salisbury
Wink's Bar-B-Que and Seafood, Salisbury
Lexington Barbecue, Lexington
The Barbecue Center, Inc., Lexington
Jimmy's Barbecue, Lexington
Kepley's Bar-B-Q, High Point
Stamey's Barbecue, Greensboro
Hursey's Barbecue, Burlington
Allen and Son Barbecue, Chapel Hill

Bullock's Barbecue, Durham
Bob's Barbecue, Creedmoor
Evans Famous Barbecue and Chicken,
 Henderson
Gary's Barbecue, Henderson
Nunnery-Freeman Barbecue, Henderson
Skipper's Forsyth Barbecue, Henderson

**Interstate 95: Lumberton to Roanoke
 Rapids**

Village Inn Barbecue, Lumberton
Fuller's BBQ, Lumberton
Chason's Famous Buffet, Fayetteville
Cape Fear Bar-B-Q and Chicken, Fayetteville
Ernie's Barbecue, Dunn
Holt Lake Bar-B-Que and Seafood, Smithfield
White Swan Restaurant, Smithfield
Mitchell's Barbecue Wilson
Bill Ellis Barbecue, Wilson
Parker's Barbecue, Wilson
Gardner's Barbecue, Rocky Mount
Bob Melton's Barbecue, Rocky Mount
Parker's Barbecue, Rocky Mount
Ralph's Barbecue, Weldon

**U.S. Highway 421: Brooks Crossroads to
 Wilmington**

Doc's Deli, North Wilkesboro
Hall's BBQ Restaurant, Yadkinville
Little Richard's Bar-B-Que, Winston-Salem
Hill's Lexington Barbecue, Winston-Salem
Stamey's Barbecue, Greensboro
Bud's Place, Cumnock
Ron's Barn BBQ and Seafood, Sanford
Howard's Barbecue, Lillington

Ron's Barn, Coats
Ernie's Barbecue, Dunn
Farmhouse Restaurant, Clinton
Lewis Barbecue, Clinton
Southern Style BBQ and Chicken, Clinton
Flip's Bar-B-Que, Wilmington

U.S. Highway 158: Mocksville to Wise

Deano's Barbecue, Mocksville
Little Richard's Bar-B-Que, Winston-Salem
Hill's Lexington Barbecue, Winston-Salem
Short Sugar's Drive-In, Reidsville
Evans Famous Barbecue and Chicken,
 Henderson
Gary's Barbecue, Henderson
Nunnery-Freeman Barbecue, Henderson
Skipper's Forsyth Barbecue, Henderson

U.S. Highway 220: Madison to Rockingham

Fuzzy's, Madison
Stamey's Barbecue, Greensboro
Hop's Bar-B-Q, Asheboro
Henry James Barbecue, Asheboro
Hamilton's Barbecue, Biscoe

U.S. Highway 64: Manteo to Murphy

F.B. Duncan's Bar-B-Que, Manteo
Piggybacks BBQ, Creswell
Simp's Barbecue, Roper
Shaw's Barbecue House, Williamston
Abrams Barbecue, Tarboro
Parker's Barbecue, Rocky Mount
Bob Melton's Barbecue, Rocky Mount
Gardner's Barbecue, Rocky Mount

Knightdale Seafood and BBQ, Knightdale
Clyde Cooper's Barbecue, Raleigh
Don Murray's Barbecue and Seafood, Raleigh
Henry James Barbecue, Asheboro
Hop's Bar-B-Q, Asheboro
Jimmy's Barbecue, Lexington
The Barbecue Center, Inc., Lexington
Lexington Barbecue, Lexington
Deano's Barbecue, Mocksville
Little Pigs Barbecue, Statesville
Carolina Bar-B-Que, Statesville
Scotz BBQ and Diner, Taylorsville
Hannah's Bar-B-Que, Lenoir
Timberwood's Family Restaurant, Morganton
The Barbecue Place, Rutherfordton
Duncan's Barbecue, Chimney Rock
The Cajun Pig, Chimney Rock
Sam's Country Cook-Out, Edneyville
Old Hickory House, Brevard
Carolina Smokehouse, Cashiers
Fat Buddies Ribs and BBQ, Franklin
Rib Country, Hayesville
Herb's Pit BBQ, Murphy

U.S. Highway 52: Mt. Airy to Wadesboro

Snappy Lunch, Mt. Airy
Hill's Lexington Barbecue, Winston-Salem
Lexington Barbecue, Lexington
The Barbecue Center, Inc., Lexington
Jimmy's Barbecue, Lexington
Hendrix Barbeque, Salisbury
Richard's Bar-B-Que, Salisbury
Wink's Bar-B-Que and Seafood, Salisbury
M&K Barbecue and Country Cooking,
    Granite Quarry
Arey's Barbecue, Rockwell

Whispering Pines Barbecue, Albemarle
Log Cabin Barbecue, Albemarle

U.S. Highway 264: Raleigh to Manteo

Mitchell's Barbecue, Wilson
Cherry's Barbecue, Wilson
Bill Ellis Barbecue, Wilson
Parker's Barbecue, Wilson
B's Barbecue, Greenville
Skylight Inn, Ayden
Hog Heaven, Washington
Boss Hog Backyard Bar-B-Que, Washington
F.B. Duncan's Bar-B-Que, Manteo

U.S. Highway 70: Raleigh to New Bern

White Swan Restaurant, Smithfield
Holt Lake Bar-B-Que and Seafood, Smithfield
Wilber's Barbecue, Goldsboro
McCall's Barbecue and Seafood, Goldsboro
Ken's Grill, LaGrange
King's Restaurant, Kinston
Moore's Bar-B-Que, New Bern

U.S. Highway 1: Laurinburg to Wise

General McArthur's Original Pig Pickin',
    Laurinburg
John's Barbecue and Seafood, Southern
    Pines
Ron's Barn BBQ and Seafood, Sanford
Clyde Cooper's Barbeque, Raleigh
Don Murray's Barbecue and Seafood, Raleigh
Evans Famous Barbecue and Chicken,
    Henderson
Nunnery-Freeman Barbecue, Henderson

Skipper's Forsyth Barbecue, Henderson
Gary's Barbecue, Henderson

U.S. Highway 17: Elizabeth City to Shallotte

Tuck's Restaurant, Elizabeth City
Captain Bob's BBQ and Seafood Restaurant,
    Hertford
Lane's Family Barbecue and Seafood,
    Edenton
Bunn's Barbecue, Windsor
Shaw's Barbecue House, Williamston
Boss Hog Backyard Bar-B-Que, Washington
Hog Heaven, Washington
Moore's Bar-B-Que, New Bern
Fisherman's Wharf, Jacksonville
Flip's Bar-B-Que, Wilmington
Joe's Barbecue, Shallotte

U.S. Highway 74: Charlotte to Lake Lure

Bubba's Barbecue, Charlotte
R.O.'s Barbecue, Gastonia

Bridges Barbecue Lodge, Shelby
Alston Bridges Barbecue, Inc., Shelby
The Hickory Log Barbecue, Forest City
The Barbecue Place, Rutherfordton
Duncan Barbecue, Chimney Rock
The Cajun Pig, Chimney Rock

Recipes

Stamey

Scott

Melton

How To Cook
A Whole Hog

Assuming that you are a novice to the world of barbecuing pork and do not possess one of those large pork cookers that is towed behind a motor vehicle, we will start with the basics. You will need the following:

1. One of those large pork cookers that is towed behind a motor vehicle
2. A kettle-type charcoal grill (Webber is good) or No. 3 below
3. One fire bucket or small charcoal grill
4. Eighty pounds of hardwood charcoal (Kingsford is good)
5. A short-handled shovel
6. Four pairs of heavy rubber gloves
7. One sharp knife
8. Cutting board
9. Meat cleavers or chef knives
10. One stock pot (approximately 10-12 quarts)
11. Several rolls of paper towels
12. One Kitchen sized waste can with liners
13. A half-pound of salt
14. Charcoal lighter gel
15. Matches or some mechanical apparatus to light the charcoal
16. Two pieces of clean heavy gauge wire larger than the pig but slightly smaller than the inside of the cooker
17. A plastic water bottle with cap with holes (for fires)
18. Meat thermometer
19. Two to three quarts of barbecue sauce (recipes follow)
20. A #3 washtub filled with ice and beverages of choice
21. Lawn chairs for you and guest invited and those that simply show up when they smell your pig
22. A dozen good cigars (optional)
23. Three to four friends whose stories and company you enjoy
24. A clear day
25. A shed if No. 24 doesn't work out

PORK COOKER

If you do not own a large pork cooker or have a friend who does, you can rent one of these from most equipment rental companies. Look in the yellow pages or ask your local barbecue man or butcher. Most large pork cookers can be rented for approximately $75 per day. Cars, SUVs or trucks can easily tow these mobile pig cookers. Most are equipped for a two-inch ball. Most have standard four-prong lighting. Most are narrow enough that you can tow them without hooking up the lighting as long as the driver of the vehicle behind you can see your brake lights and turn signals. (Several rental agencies as well as the North Carolina State Highway Patrol confirmed this to me.) Be sure the pig cooker has at least two four-inch reflectors on the rear.

MEAT

You can purchase your whole hog from a meat-packing house or through a friendly barbecue place or a retail supermarket. Several weeks prior to purchasing your pig, I suggest you call and make your arrangements and find how much notice is necessary to order and pick up your meat. Also be sure that your source is open at the time you need your pig. A yardstick for as much pork, charcoal, gas, wood, etc. is as followed.

Weight of Pig	Charcoal	Amount of Gas	Wood	Cooker Temperature	Approx. Cooking Time
75 lbs.	60 lbs.	40 lb.	1/3 cord	225 – 250	6 to 7 hours
100 lbs.	70 lbs.	Cylinder	1/3 –1/2 cord	225 – 250	7 to 8 hours
125 lbs.	80 lbs.		1/2 cord	225 – 250	8 to 9 hours

A hog's weight is generally measured "on the hoof" which is the gross weight of the hog prior to being processed. This is the weight used as a yardstick by the pork producer for sale to the processor. When you purchase your hog retail or wholesale you will specify the size of the hog you desire in "dressed" weight. This term means the hog will have been processed and its carcass cleaned, scraped free of bristles and head removed. If your pig comes to you with hooves (trotters) on, simply cut them off above the dew claws (those little tabs on the "ankle") with a saw. I would also suggest using a knife and making a V incision and removing the tail. Without head, trotters and tail the carcass looks less like "Babe" did a belly flop on your grill. I would also suggest that you have your processor split the backbone so the pig will lie flatter on the grill. If you are working alone you may have the processor cut the pig in half lengthwise in order to make it easier for you to handle and turn.

When ordering a pig to cook most people allow for one and a half pounds of "dressed weight"

329

carcass per person. After you remove the skin, fat, bones, etc. a "dressed weight" carcass will render less than half its "dressed weight" in serving weight. The following is a guide to determine the size of "dressed" pig to produce the desired amount of cooked pork.

A Guide For Purchasing
     75 lbs. dressed pig = approximately 30 lbs. cooked, chopped pork
     100 lbs. dressed pig = approximately 40 lbs. cooked, chopped pork
     125 lbs. dressed pig = approximately 50 lbs. cooked, chopped pork
     14 lbs. uncooked Shoulder = 10 lbs. cooked 6-7 hours
     6-7 lbs. uncooked Boston Butt = 3 lbs. cooked 3-1/2 - 4 hours
     14 lbs. uncooked Ham = 6-7 lbs. cooked 6-7 hours

As most pig pickins' will be a social event attended by males and females, the following is a guide for the amount of "dressed weight" pig to buy for such an occasion.

Weight of Pig	Number of Couples	Number of Males	Number of Females
75 lbs.	25	35-40	60-65
100 lbs.	30	40-45	70-75
125 lbs.	40	45-50	80-85

If your group exceeds 40 couples, I do not suggest buying a larger pig. I would suggest perhaps a 125-pound pig and a 75-pound pig. Pigs much under 75 pounds have meat that tends to be fluffy. Pigs over a 125 pounds start to take on a grainer meat which generally does not render as good a serving product as pigs in the 75-125 pound range.

After you have arranged all of the necessary items to produce this feast place 20 pounds of charcoal on the inside of your pork cooker. Place dollops of charcoal lighter gel over the charcoal and ignite. Let the charcoal burn until it has attained the desired ash gray. Spread your coals evenly over the floor of the cooker so there are coals under the entire pig once it is placed on the grid.

Sprinkle salt into cavity and rub into flesh. With a sharp knife, score the inside fleshy part (not the outside skin) of the hams and shoulders to allow for more heat penetration. These cuts should run parallel to the bone not crosswise. Next place your clean heavy gauge wire over the grid on the cooker. With the wire in place, place your pig flat, skin side up on the wire surface. Close the lid of the cooker, then you are in business. Cook the pig at 225 degrees (no more at least for the first two hours of cooking). In your Webber kettle light another five pounds of charcoal so it will attain the desired ash gray 45 minutes after the pig was placed on the cooker, add additional charcoal layer under the hams and shoulders. You do not have to place additional charcoal under the pig between the hams and shoulders as this thinner area will not need additional heat. Adding coals under the

330

backbone rib area will cause overcooking and burn spots. After you have added your first five pounds of charcoal, wait a bit and start another five pounds so it will be covered with gray ash about 45 minutes from the time you last added additional charcoal. This process is repeated throughout the cooking for a period of approximately six hours. Check the ventilation doors on your pig cooker throughout the cooking process. Generally they should be left cracked open about an inch. Resist the temptation to open the cooker and look at your pig, this causes heat loss. Some when preparing barbecue increase the cooking temperature from 225 to 250 after the first two hours cooking. Others maintain 225 throughout the entire cooking process. Still others cook at 180 for a period of time then step up the temperature in increments finishing at 250 or better and cook for a longer period of time. For your first attempt, I suggest you follow the general guideline of cooking at 225 degrees for six hours. This temperature should remain constant throughout the cooking process. You will be able to ascertain this if your cooker has an external thermometer. If it does not, one of the rules of thumb to determine if your cooker is too hot is to place your hand palm down several inches above the cooker's closed lid for five seconds without discomfort. Generally five seconds without discomfort indicates an interior temperature of approximately 225-275 degrees. Discomfort after two seconds indicates your internal temperature is approximately 375-400 degrees. If you find this yardstick to be like examining a horseshoe that has just been dipped, chances are your cooker is too hot. Also your cooking pig will drip fat on to the coals as it cooks. This will produce a hiss. This is good; however, if the smoke from the chimney on your pig cooker is continuous or there is too much dripping and hissing, your cooker is too hot. This can be remedied by simply closing the ventilation door for a few minutes until the internal temperature drops to a desired level.

About six hours after you first place your pig on the cooker, it is time to turn the pig skin side down. The six-hour number mentioned here is assuming that you are cooking a 75-pound dress weight pig. However if your pig is larger, this time will be longer. See the chart above for 100- and 125-pound pigs. When it is time to turn the pig, open your cooker and place your second clean heavy gauge wire grid on top of the pig so that the pig is "sandwiched" between the two wire grids. If you have help (preferably three other persons), have each person wear heavy rubber gloves and grab the corners of the grid. On a given count, turn the pig so the skin side is now on the grid of the pig cooker. I suggest you turn the pig inwardly so that (heaven forbid) if the pig should come out of your wire sandwich, it will fall inside the lid and not on the ground. If you only have one helper, you and your helper, again wearing heavy rubber gloves, should stand at each end of the pig and grab the ends of the legs. On a count, lift the pig and roll it towards the back of the cooker. This rolling will allow the pig to "fold" like a pocket sandwich. Then scoot the pig back toward the center of the cooker and unfold it so the skin side is on the grid and the meat side is facing upward. If you are going to be cooking the pig by yourself, I suggest you have the processor split the pig lengthwise along the back to make the process described above easier for one person.

After having turned the pig, light another 10 pounds of charcoal in your auxiliary grill. During

the time it takes for this last batch of charcoal to reach ash gray, brush the exposed surface of the pig with melted margarine or marinade. Baste the entire carcass with your choice of barbecue sauce. Pour sauce into the rib cavity to a depth of approximately one inch. Now scatter the last 10 pounds of charcoal over the entire floor of the cooker as you did in the first process. This last batch should be under the entire pig not just the hams and shoulders. This final stage is to "finish" the pig producing the wonderful golden brown skin and cooking the meat to the desired internal temperature of 170 degrees. The meat should cook during this last phase for approximately two additional hours (total cooking time seven to eight hours). Before serving, the internal temperature of the thickest part of your pig should be 170 degrees (do not let the thermometer touch bone) and there should be no pink meat visible when the hams and shoulders are cut.

I suggest that, in addition to the prescribed cooking time, you allow yourself an additional two hours from the estimated time of cooking to the time you intend to serve. This "margin of comfort" will allow you to cook the pig some more if you find your pig is not completely done, that there was an emergency that disrupted your cooking, or your fire simply dropped below the desired 225-degree constant cooking temperature. This is a fun cooking experience to be shared with friends. There is no reason to plan it too tightly and "jam" yourself at the time of the arrival of your first guest. Enjoy.

COOKING PORK SHOULDERS LEXINGTON STYLE

Assuming that you are a novice to the world of barbecuing pork and do not possess a charcoal grill, we will start with the basics. You will need the following:

1. A kettle-type charcoal grill (Weber is good)
2. One fire bucket or small charcoal grill
3. Fifteen pounds of hardwood charcoal (Kingsford is good)
4. One bag of hickory wood chunks
5. One small shovel or scoop
6. One pair of barbecue tongs
7. One pair of heavy rubber gloves
8. One sharp knife
9. One cutting board
10. One or two meat cleavers or chef knives
11. One stock pot (approx. 10-12 quart)
12. One roll of paper towels
13. One kitchen size waste can
14. One cup of salt

15. Charcoal lighter gel
16. A plastic water bottle with cap with holes (for fires)
17. A meat thermometer
18. One and a half quarts of barbecue sauce (recipes follow)
19. A #3 washtub filed with ice and beverages of choice
20. Lawn chairs for you and guests invited and those that simply show up when they smell your pig
21. A dozen good cigars (optional)
22. Three to four friends whose stories and company you enjoy
23. A clear day
24. A carport if number 23 doesn't work out

MEAT

Have your butcher prepare you an eight-to-nine-pound fresh pork shoulder Boston Butt.

PREP.

Rub the exposed side of the meat (not skin side) with a fair amount of salt. Set aside at room temperature. Place approximately half of a 10-pound bag of charcoal in a charcoal chimney, add dollop of ligher gel and light. Do not use lighter fluid, gas or other substance that might impart flavor to the charcoal. When the charcoal briquettes are lit and covered with light gray ash, transfer to kettle cooker. Arrange seven or eight briquettes in a circle at the center of the grill around the grate in the bottom and equally divide the remaining briquettes into piles positioned on opposing sides of the grill. Place several hickory wood chunks on top of each pile of briquettes. Arranging the briquettes in this fashion is the same principle employed by my grandfather and taught to me as a child. He called it "banking your fire." It is the same principle of slow cooking meat with the fire around the edges that James Kirby imparted to Eddie Mitchell (Wilson). The wood chunks will soon begin to smoke. Put the cooking rack on the kettle (be sure the rack has been wire brushed, well cleaned and oiled with vegetable oil and dried). Set the pork butt, skin side up on the center of the grill above the circle of coals. Place the lid on the grill and leave the vent holes top and bottom open. Light another dozen or so briquettes in the charcoal chimney. When the briquettes in the chimney are covered with ash, add five or six briquettes to each pile on either side of the kettle grill. You do not have to replenish the circle of briquettes during the cooking process. Place a couple of hickory wood chunks on each of the two piles of charcoal. This process is repeated every 30 minutes from the time you initially place the meat on the grill. Try to replace the kettle grill lid quickly each time you

333

add additional coals and wood to prevent the cooking fire from cooling. You do not need to check the meat between replenishing the charcoal briquettes and hickory chunks. After meat has cooked for six-and-a-half to seven hours, turn the meat skin side down on the grill. If meat is cooking too quickly, only add four or five briquettes plus wood chunks to each side of the kettle grill each half hour for the next two-hour cooking period. If meat does not appear to brown, continue with adding six briquettes plus wood chunks every half-hour for the next two-hour cooking period. Cook meat skin side down for two hours. Entire cooking time should be eight to nine hours. At this point if you are Phil Schenck (pit master at Bridges Barbecue Lodge) and have been cooking 60-90 shoulders per night, six nights a week for 19 years you can simply look at the meat, mash on it with a finger and know if it is cooked to perfection. Some people at this point wearing heavy rubber gloves, grasp the meat with both hands and squeeze it firmly. The meat should "give" if it is sufficiently done. I prefer to use a meat thermometer. The meat should have 170 degree internal temperature. If you do not feel "give" or the meat has not attained an internal temperature of 170 degrees, replace the meat on the grill, cook for another hour and try again. If you have kept your fire at a constant cooking temperature the meat should be done the first time you squeeze it or check with a meat thermometer. When the meat is done remove from the grill to the cutting board, remove skin, and trim away any fat. The meat is now ready to be pulled from the bone in chunks and chopped. After removing the meat from the bone, use cleaver(s) or sharp chef knives to chop the pork into the consistency you like. (I prefer coarsely chopped). You may wish to finely chop a tiny bit of fat (no gristle) and some crisp pork skin and mix with your chopped meat. Either or both of these additions add great flavor to your offering. Dowse meat lightly with sauce or dip and turn until all meat has some exposure to the sauce or dip. Do not over-sauce at this point. Guests can add additional sauce to suit their particular tastes. If you are not ready to serve at this point, place the meat in a warm stockpot and cover with heavy foil, keeping airtight. Do not set the stockpot on the grill, as the meat will continue to cook and the meat in the bottom of the pot will scorch.

The preceding instructions for buying, prepping and cooking a whole hog and shoulder were shared by and reprinted with permission from the North Carolina Pork Council, Inc., The Kansas City Barbeque Society and various friends. I have provided information from my own cooking experiences that I thought would be helpful to the reader.

BARBECUE SAUCES

The following are several of many good basic recipes for vinegar-base barbecue sauce, tomato-base barbecue dip and side dishes shared by and reprinted with permission from the North Carolina Pork Council, Inc. Also included are some ingredients you may want to add to create your own "secret recipe." When you barbecue your own meat the following should add zest to your celebration. Enjoy your "pretty pig!"

BASIC
VINEGAR-BASE SAUCE

2 quarts apple-cider vinegar
2 ounces crushed red pepper
2 tablespoons salt
1 tablespoons black pepper

Mix all ingredients well. After basting pig, pour remaining sauce in small jars to serve with cooked pig. Yield: two quarts.

BASIC
TOMATO-BASE DIP

3-1/2 cups apple-cider vinegar
1/2 cups brown sugar
1/2 cup ketchup
2-1/2 tablespoons Texas Pete Hot Sauce
1/2 teaspoon salt
1 teaspoon black pepper
1 teaspoon Worcestershire Sauce
1 teaspoon onion powder
2 teaspoons Kitchen Bouquet Browning Sauce

Combine all ingredients in a medium pot; simmer over medium heat, stir until sugar melts. Set aside for two hours before serving.

PIEDMONT
LEXINGTON-STYLE DIP

1-1/2 cups distilled white or cider vinegar
10 tablespoons tomato catsup
Salt to taste, if desired
1/2 teaspoon cayenne pepper
Pinch of crushed hot red pepper flakes
1 tablespoon sugar
1/2 cup water
Freshly ground pepper to taste

Combine all ingredients in a small saucepan and bring to a simmer. Cook, stirring, until the sugar dissolves. Remove from the heat and let stand until cool. Spoon a small amount of the sauce over barbecued meats. Yield: three cups.

EASTERN
PIG PICKIN' SAUCE

1 gallon vinegar
3/4 cup salt
2 tablespoons red pepper
3 tablespoons red pepper flakes
1 cup firmly packed brown sugar or 1/2 cup molasses

Combine all ingredients; mix well. Allow to stand four hours before using. Yield: about one gallon.

WESTERN
CATSUP-BASE BARBECUE SAUCE

1 cup tomato catsup
1 cup brown sugar
1/2 cup lemon juice
1/2 stick butter
1/4 cup minced onion
1 teaspoon liquid hot pepper sauce
1 teaspoon Worcestershire sauce

Place all ingredients in heavy saucepan and bring to a boil. Reduce heat and simmer for 30

minutes. Yield: three cups.

The following are some ingredients to make your barbecue sauce suit your own particular taste:

Sweet – sugar, both brown and white, honey, molasses, catsup, sherry
Sour – vinegar or lemon juice
Hot – Chili sauce, Tabasco, cayenne pepper, crushed red pepper, black pepper, hot pepper sauce
Spicy – mustard, onion, garlic, ginger, cloves, Worcestershire sauce
Salty – salt or soy sauce
Note: As a rule of thumb, allow two quarts of barbecue sauce per 75 pounds of pork.

SIDE DISHES

EASTERN-STYLE SLAW

6 medium heads cabbage (about 36 cups) finely shredded
1-1/2 cups green onion, sliced
1-1/2 quarts mayonnaise or salad dressing
3/4 cup sugar
3/4 cup vinegar
2 to 4 tablespoons celery seed
2 tablespoons salt (or to taste)

In large bowl, combine cabbage and onion. In small bowl, blend mayonnaise, sugar, vinegar, celery seed and salt. Mix well. Drizzle mayonnaise mixture over cabbage mixture in bowl. Toss lightly to mix well. Refrigerate until serving. Yield: 50 servings.

PIEDMONT-STYLE SLAW
(Red Slaw)

Using the basic recipe above omitting green onions and celery seed, add approximately a quarter cup plus catsup enough of the Lexington-style Barbecue sauce to taste, mixing well.

POTATO SALAD

10 to 12 pounds potatoes
24 hard cooked eggs, chopped

337

2 large bunches celery, chopped

1 quart salad pickles, chopped

5 small cans pimiento, chopped

3 medium onions, chopped

3-4 green peppers, chopped

1/4 cup salt

1 tablespoon pepper

1 quart mayonnaise

1 jar (6 ounces mustard)

Wash potatoes. Cook covered with water for 30 to 40 minutes or until tender. Remove potatoes from water and cool. Peel and dice. Add next 6 ingredients. Add salt and pepper. Mix. Blend mayonnaise and mustard. Add to potato mixture and mix well. Chill at least an hour to permit flavors to blend. Yield: 50 servings.

LONG AND LEAN HUSHPUPPIES

3-1/2 cups water

2 cups cornmeal

1 teaspoon baking powder

1 tablespoon sugar

1 teaspoon salt

1 medium onion, finely chopped

1/4 cup butter, softened, or lard

Bring water to a boil. Combine cornmeal, baking powder, sugar, salt and onion; slowly add to boiling water, stirring constantly until mixture is smooth. Remove from heat; add butter, stirring until melted. Cool mixture 10 minutes.

Shape batter into 2 x 1-inch oblong rolls. Deep fry in hot oil (375 degrees) cooking only a few at a time. Fry until hushpuppies are golden brown. Drain well on paper towels. Serve hot. Yield: About 40.

ROUND AND FLUFFY PUPPIES

5 lbs. self-rising corn meal

1/2 cup self-rising flour

2 tablespoons sugar

2-1/2 quarts (or more) water and buttermilk (or 2-1/2 quarts of either)

1/2 cup shortening, melted (optional)

338

3 tablespoons onion, minced (optional

4 eggs (optional)

Stir liquid into dry ingredients, making a thick batter. (Addition of shortening improves texture. Onion adds flavor. Eggs improve texture and flavor.) Drop from spoon into fat that has been heated to 350 – 375 degrees F. Fry to a golden brown. Yield: 125 to 150 hushpuppies.

JIM EARLY'S BANANA PUDDING

4 quarts Half-n-half (milk)

12 tablespoons (level) cornstarch

4-1/4 cups white sugar

16 eggs

4 teaspoons vanilla extract

1 pinch of salt

6-7 fully ripe, firm bananas, sliced

1 box Nabisco Nilla Wafers

Separate the whites and yolks of six eggs. Set the six egg whites aside. In a large bowl combine your dry ingredients, cornstarch, four cups sugar and salt together. In another large bowl whisk your ten whole eggs and the yolks from six eggs until the mixture is well blended. Continuing to stir, pour in milk. Then continuing to stir add dry ingredients at point of stirring to prevent lumps. When your liquid is satin smooth pour into double boiler and cook, uncovered over hot almost boiling water stirring constantly. When your custard begins to thicken (approximately 20 minutes or when it will coat a wooden spoon) remove from heat and add vanilla extract. Set custard aside to cool some while you prepare your baking dish.

Line bottom and sides of a 9x13 or larger baking dish with Nilla wafers; cover the bottom layer of Nilla wafers with sliced bananas. Pour a small amount of custard over your first layer of wafers and bananas and repeat until the dish is full with the top layer being custard. Do not fill to the top but allow approximately 1/2 inch for meringue. Whisk the remaining egg whites, stiff but not dry. Add 1/4 cup of sugar as you whisk and continue to whisk until mixture forms stiff peaks. Spread meringue on top of pudding covering entire top to each edge. Bake in preheated oven (425 degrees) for five minutes or until light golden brown.

Set pudding aside to cool for several hours and allow the Nilla wafers, bananas and custard to get to know one another. If the pudding is not to be eaten within 4-5 hours of completing, place toothpicks in the pudding to support aluminum foil, cover completely and refrigerate.

When serving later the pudding does not have to be reheated but simply brought out and allowed to rest at room temperature for an hour or so before serving. Serves 12-15.

NOTE: The custard used in this banana pudding dish is my grandmother's Eastern North Carolina Selzabub recipe kicked up a notch or two. This custard can be served in a cup medium to hot. Make a cross (x) with homemade fruit brandy, peach, apricot and apple are all good. I suggest one quarter to one-half jigger (to taste), you have Selzabub.

This custard can also be served as sweet cream with raspberries or other fresh fruit layered in a small parfait glass without liqueur (if preferred). Add a dollop of real whipped cream on top. Garnish with a few berries and a sprig of mint.

THE WORLD'S BEST BRUNSWICK STEW

12 – 28 oz. cans whole tomatoes
15 pounds white potatoes
5 – 11 oz. packages frozen baby lima beans
3 – 32 oz. packages frozen yellow corn
12 pounds of chicken breast (skin on)
12 pounds beef tips (or sirloin tips)
12 pounds T-bone pork chops (bone in)
1 ham hock or 1/4 pound fatback or streak of lean streak of fat
4 – 40 oz. bottles of Hunt's ketchup
2 – 15 oz. bottles of A-1 Sauce
1 – 15 oz. bottle Heinz 57 sauce
2 – 10 oz. bottles Lea and Perrin's Worcestershire Sauce
1 cup Texas Pete

Sea salt, black pepper, red pepper, chives, parsley flakes, celery salt, dill weed, dill seed, basil leaves, and bay leaves

1 pound creamery butter

Place 12 pounds beef tips in stockpot, cover well with water, season as follows:

1 tablespoon parsley flakes
1/3 tablespoon celery salt
1/2 tablespoon coarse ground black pepper
1 tablespoon dill weed
1/3 tablespoon celery seed

1 tablespoon crushed red pepper
2 tablespoons chives

Cook beef on medium heat (setting 5 or 4) for approximately 30 minutes, check doneness. Depending upon the size of your beef cubes, 30 minutes may be enough to achieve medium (light pink) or it may require another 10 to 15 minutes. You do not want to overcook the meat, as it will make it tough. Suggest that you stir the meat every five minutes so no pieces remain on the bottom and become scorched. When meat is cooked to desired doneness, remove meat from the stockpot with a strainer and place in aluminum foil pans to cool. Retain the stock for use later.

Place 12 pounds pork chops in a stockpot, cover well with water, season as follows:

1 tablespoon parsley flakes
1/3 tablespoon celery seed
1/2 tablespoon coarse ground black pepper
1 tablespoon dill weed
1/3 tablespoon celery salt
1 tablespoon crushed red pepper
12 bay leaves
2 tablespoons chives

Cook over medium heat for approximately two hours until tender to fork (meat should break easily when pierced with fork). Remove meat from stockpot onto large foil pan to cool. Retain stock for use later.

Plate 12 pounds chicken breasts (skin on) into stockpot, cover well with water, season as follows:

1 tablespoon parsley flakes
1/3 tablespoon celery salt
1/2 tablespoon coarse ground black pepper
1 tablespoon dill weed
1/3 tablespoon celery seed
2 tablespoon crushed red pepper
15 bay leaves
2 tablespoons chives

Cook over medium heat for approximately two hours until tender to fork (meat should break easily when pierced with fork). Remove meat from stockpot onto large foil pan to cool. Retain stock

for use later.

Stir the broth in each stockpot well so that it is thoroughly mixed. Retain approximately one-and-a-half quarts of broth from each meat. The rest may be packaged and frozen for stock for another day.

While the meat is cooling and the broth has been set aside, it is a good time to clean your stockpots for the next round of cooking.

Place five 11-ounce packages of frozen baby lima beans into a pot of sufficient size that they may be well covered with water. At this point, you may add a piece of ham hock about the size of softball or a 2x4-inch piece of streak of lean streak of fat to season the beans. This is discretionary. The liquor from the beans does not go into the stew. I prefer to add the ham hock as I think it gives the beans better flavor. Cook the beans on medium heat, stirring often, do not let the beans stick on the bottom of the pan and do not overcook the beans. The beans should be firm, barely done. The beans will not cook further in the stew so they need to be done and tender at this point. However, do not overcook and make the beans mushy or mealy. The beans can be cooked simultaneously with the meat if you have four surface units and your stockpots and the bean pot will all fit on the stove at one time. The lima beans and the beef take approximately the same time. The pork and chicken take much longer. If you cook the limas at the same time as the beef, pork and chicken, simply set the limas aside until needed.

Into a 30-quart stockpot, place 12 20-ounce cans of whole tomatoes. Cap the tomatoes with a paring knife before placing in the stockpot. This will permit the tomatoes to come apart much easier. Also, you do not want the crunchy cap section in your stew. After all the tomatoes are in the stockpot scrunch the tomatoes with your hands or mash them with a potato masher to break them up as much as possible. Add the juice from all the tomato cans to the stockpot. Add the three 32-ounce packages of yellow corn kernels. Cook over medium heat, stir often. If you do not stir the tomatoes and corn often, the corn kernels will settle to the bottom and get little brown scorch marks on them and they will look like black-eyed peas in your stew. While the tomatoes and corn are cooking down, peel and slice 15 pounds of white potatoes and place in a stockpot, cover with water, add 2 tablespoons of salt and cook until tender. When the potatoes are tender enough to mash easily against the side of the pot with a spoon, pour off the water, add one pound of creamery butter (four sticks) and mash with a potato masher. Do not whip or use a blender, as this will make the potatoes gummy. Mash the potatoes by hand with a hand masher until all the butter and potatoes are well blended.

When your tomatoes and corn have cooked down, approximately two hours, stir them until well mixed. Next, add your baby limas. Strain the limas from their liquor and add to the corn and tomatoes. Discard the lima-bean liquor. Give the ham hock to the birds as suet.

Stir your lima beans into your corn and tomatoes gently. Do not smush the lima beans here. Fold

them in gently.

Next, separate half of your tomatoes, corn and lima beans into a second 30-quart stockpot. You will then have half of your tomatoes, corn and lima beans in each of two 30-quart stockpots. While your corn and tomatoes are cooking down, as soon as your meat has cooled, remove all fat, gristle, bones and skin from the beef, pork and chicken. You may wish to keep the bone for stock. If so, package, label and freeze. At this point you can either hand shred the meat into the aluminum baking pan or use a Cuisinart Chopper. I prefer the Cuisinart Chopper. It saves a lot of time and I can detect no difference in the meat if the meat has been allowed to sufficiently cool so it does not mush when chopped. I suggest cooling the meat in the refrigerator as soon as it is removed from the stock. I use aluminum foil turkey pans that are inexpensive and hold this amount of meat well and cover with aluminum foil and place the meat in the refrigerator while I am cooking the vegetables. If the meat is sufficiently cooled, place a double handful in the Cuisinart with the chopper blade, press the pulse button in short bursts. You do not want to cut the meat any more finely than moderately coarse chop. (Think chopped barbecue for a sandwich.)

When the meat is all chopped, add half of your meat to one of the 30-quart stockpots with half of your tomatoes, corn and limas and half of your meat into the other 30-quart stockpot with the remaining vegetables. Divide your beef, pork and chicken one-half to each stockpot.

Stir the meat into the tomatoes, corn and limas. At this point, your stew will be so heavy that it will be difficult to stir. Take a quart of your beef broth and shake it well to be sure it is well mixed, pour half quart into each stockpot. Repeat with the pork broth and chicken broth. This should give you sufficient liquid to stir your stew until it is the right consistency.

Next, add half of your creamed potatoes to each stockpot. Fold the creamed potatoes into your stew gently and continue to stir. You stew will be very thick and the stirring will be difficult. You must mix all your ingredients well at this point. It just takes a lot of horsepower and stirring.

After you have thoroughly mixed all of your ingredients in each stockpot, rinse your palate and taste each stockpot. Next, add two 40-ounce bottles of Hunt's Ketchup to one stockpot, stir in well and taste. Then add one 15-ounce. bottle of A-1 Steak Sauce, stir in well and taste. Then add half of a 15-ounce bottle of Heinz 57 Sauce, stir in well and taste. Then add one 10-ounce bottle of Worcestershire Sauce, stir in well and taste. Then add a half cup of Texas Pete Hot Sauce, stir in well and taste. I suggest you do your tasting as one would a wine tasting. Rinse your mouth with water and taste again. You may wish to add less A-1 and Heinz 57 Sauce if you want the stew to taste sweeter. The Hunt's Ketchup will make the stew initially taste sweeter, the addition of the A-1, Heinz 57 Sauce and Worcestershire will change the complexion of the taste of the stew to a different flavor that is not quite as sweet. The addition of the Texas Pete will change the flavor of the stew again to a bit hotter but not more than mild to moderately hot. Each spice will change the taste of the stew. You will have to tune your stew as best suits your taste. The seasonings I have added will give the stew a rich, full, robust flavor that is mildly hot, enough to be interesting, but not so much so as to

be distasteful to those who do not like spicy foods. The stew should achieve a taste all its own like a good mixed drink. One should not be able to taste the component parts in a predominant manner. Of course, you will be able to taste the corn and the butter beans as they have different texture and size, otherwise the stew should have its own unique flavor.

Repeat the spices with the second 30-quart stockpot. Again, season, taste, season, taste, season, taste. Do not assume that the second stockpot will taste the same as the first. It will not. It may vary ever so slightly, but it will vary. The variance may not be sufficient to require changing the amounts of spices, but it will vary despite your best efforts to duplicate on every instance. Sometimes in dipping from one pot to the other to divide, we pick up a bit more moisture or a bit more vegetable. In any event, there will be miniscule variances in your two pots. This will not have any effect on your stew. Only a discriminating palate tasting both pots at the same temperature, one after another, could discern it.

This recipe will produce approximately 45 quarts of the best brunswick stew you or your guests have ever tasted. If you like your stew a bit hotter (as I do), add a few drops of Texas Pete to your bowl at the table. I suggest you not add more than a few drops of Texas Pete at a time, as it will not take much to raise this stew up a click. Also, effort has been made to make this stew low sodium. I have used spices to replace a lot of salt. With the spices, only a small amount of salt will change the stew dramatically. If you desire more of a fatty taste, add a hunk of butter to your stew at the table and stir in well. Again, the stew was designed with little fat to achieve the best possible taste with the least amount of cholesterol. The stew recipe is easily divided into half or fourths. I would not suggest making less than a fourth, the recipe is very time intensive.

I generally package my stew in Best Pack quart containers, leaving an inch room for expansion and then freeze. The stew will keep well for a year. It is a complete meal in itself and requires little more than a salad, bread and beverage. For breads, I like hushpuppies, cornsticks, cornbread, French bread or sourdough bread. The Eastern North Carolina beverage of choice is slow-brewed sweetened tea with lemon. It also goes well with your favorite red wine.

Tips From the Pit Masters

THE GRILL

- A warm grill is easier to clean. Use a wire brush. Always remove ashes after the grill has cooled. Removing ashes will prevent corrosion in the bottom of the grill and its early demise.
- Hot coals are barely covered with a gray ash. Medium coals glow through the layer of gray ash. Low coals are covered with at thick layer of gray ash. Know your fire.
- When grilling thicker cuts of meat on a gas grill, light one side of the unit and place the meat over a drip pan on the other side.
- If using wooden skewers for shish kebob, soak skewers in water for 30 minutes before using to prevent burning while grilling.
- Always wash hands, countertops, cutting boards, knives and transporting utensils used in preparing any kind of raw meat before they come in contact with other raw or uncooked foods. This is particularly true of chicken and pork but should be adhered to with beef as well.
- If your fire is too hot, shut the dampers, mist with water, raise the cooking grill and close cover or lid to reduce the amount of oxygen available.
- To cook with direct heat, evenly distribute coals over the bottom of the grill. To cook with indirect heat, move coals to one side and place a foil drip pan under the meat in the middle area between the coals. The indirect cooking method is slower and better for thick or large pieces of meat.
- Do not turn meat with a fork, turn with tongs or a spatula to prevent juices from escaping.
- To prevent meat rimmed with fat from curling, slice through the fat to the meat at one-inch intervals.
- As a rule of thumb, it generally takes 30 to 45 minutes for charcoal to obtain the proper gray ash desired to start cooking.
- Charcoal is ready for grilling when it is more than 80 percent ashed over.
- Dry wood burns faster than green wood. Hickory burns twice as fast as oak. Apple, peach and pecan wood imparts a sweeter smoke.
- After cleaning the grill and before cooking, coat the grill rack with olive oil or spray with non-stick cooking spray before using.
- Marinating or a rub before cooking greatly enhances the flavor of any meat. After applying marinade or rub, let meat stand at room temperature for up to 15 minutes or marinate in refrigerator covered for up to 24 hours. Marinade or rub can be stored in an airtight container in a cool place.

- Cleanliness may not be next to godliness but it certainly is the rule when cooking raw meats indoors or out. Never use containers that contained raw meat to receive cooked meat. Wash everything you use after each use. An ounce of prevention is worth a pound of cure.
- If you are going to serve leftover marinade with your cooked meat, be sure to boil the marinade to kill any microorganisms before serving.
- Some advocate raising the smoker to 300 degrees Fahrenheit before placing meat on grill to sear meat. Then reducing temperature for cooking to 200 degrees Fahrenheit to 220 degrees Fahrenheit. Others advocate not permitting the cooking temperature to exceed 220 degrees Fahrenheit for the first two hours of cooking. Some advocate cooking at 200 degrees Fahrenheit to 220 degrees Fahrenheit others advocate a constant 225 degree Fahrenheit while others advocate cooking at 225 degrees Fahrenheit to 250 degrees Fahrenheit. This is largely a matter of choice and knowing your fire. Of course if you cook at a lower temperature, you will have to cook a bit longer. All agree that the internal temperature of 170 degrees Fahrenheit must be reached regardless of cooking temperature or cooking time.

ABOUT PORK

- To tenderize ribs, pierce both sides of ribs between rib bones with meat fork before applying marinade or rub of choice. The ribs are done when the meat starts to pull away from the bone.
- To apply rub to ribs, remove the membrane from the backside of the ribs. Rub both sides of ribs with your rub of choice. Shake off excess.
- In addition to the flavors imparted by the wood of choice, fresh herbs such as bay leaves, marjoram, rosemary, thyme, oregano and sage may be moistened with water and sprinkled over the hot coals to impart additional flavors to the meat.
- If your marinade, rub or sauce does not contain sugar, you should apply to meat about every 45 minutes to an hour. This will prevent dryness during grilling or smoking. If your barbecue marinade, rub or sauce contains sugar, do not apply until you are at the last few minutes of grilling as the sugar will caramelize and cause black charred spots that most guest will not find attractive and they do not enhance the flavor of the meat.
- When making your sauce, cook without cover to accelerate reduction and achieve the desired consistency.
- As a rule of thumb, steaks and chops should be basted after being turned for the last time or on both sides during the last three minutes of grilling. Chicken should be basted during the last 10 minutes of grilling turning only once.

ABOUT POULTRY

- Chicken should be thawed in the refrigerator or in cold water. Allow 24 hours to thaw a four-pound chicken in the refrigerator. Allow three to nine hours to thaw chicken pieces depending upon thickness.
- As with pork, start chicken cooking on grill skin side up with smaller pieces at the edges to prevent overcooking.
- To feed four people, purchase a three-and-a-half to four-pound chicken. This will yield approximately three to three-and-a-half cups cooked chicken.
- To ensure doneness in chicken, the internal temperature should reach 180 degrees Fahrenheit, for a whole chicken, 170 degrees Fahrenheit for bone in pieces and 160 degrees Fahrenheit for boneless pieces.

ABOUT BEEF

- When purchasing beef brisket, the bigger the brisket the better for smoking. Buy thick briskets with a heavy layer of fat.
- Brisket fat should be trimmed to approximately a quarter inch. After coating the fat side with some of your sauce of choice, sprinkle with some of your barbecue seasoning. Turn brisket and repeat. Start cooking brisket fat side down, which is the reverse from cooking pork. Depending upon size of brisket cooking time will be eight to 12 hours. Turn brisket and sauce every four to six hours. Start brisket with the larger thicker portion toward the heat source. Rotate each time you baste.
- Indirect heat with a foil drip pan is, in the opinion of many, the better way to cook brisket.
- When purchasing steak, order one and a half-inch thick steak of choice. This thickness will permit proper cooking to achieve desired results. Cooking over medium coals nine to ten minutes per side should produce rare.
- Always turn steaks with tongs or spatula to prevent juices from escaping.
- If steak has an edge of fat, score the fat to the meat approximately every one to one-and-a-half inches to prevent curling. If steak does not have fat such as filets, wrap steak with bacon to prevent dryness. Apple cured bacon is a good choice.

Many of the Tips From the Pit Masters were shared and reprinted with permission from the Kansas City Barbeque Society, the world's largest organization of barbecue and grilling enthusiasts. My thanks to the society members and to the Executive Director, Carolyn S. Wells, Ph.B.

Pig Parties

April	-	Newport Pig Cooking Contest – Newport – North Carolina's largest whole hog pork barbecue contest, Newport Community Park – Jim Ferrell (252) 223-PIGS.
April	-	King's Mountain Fire Department Barbecue Cook-Off – Kings Mountain – Frank Barnes (704) 734-0555.
April	-	Garner Historic Festival – Garner – Lois Bartholow, PO Box 881, Garner 27529.
April	-	Hog Happen' – Kinston – Skip Palmer (252) 527-1131.
April-May	-	Spring Poultry/Pork Fest – Warsaw – Chamber of Commerce (910) 293-7804.
May	-	Smithfield Ham and Yam Festival – Smithfield – Troy Carter (919) 934-0887.
May	-	N.C. Strawberry Festival and Annual Pig Cookin' Off – Chadbourne – Ms. Bonnie Caines (910) 642-4677 or (910) 640-2422.
*May	-	Memphis in May World Championship Barbecue Cooking Contest - Memphis, TN – www.memphisinmay.org.
May	-	Gastonia's Beach Blues and Bar-B-Q – Gastonia – Larry Wood (704) 866-6860.
June	-	General William C. Lee Pig Cook-Off – Benson – Michael Hartley (919) 894-5635.

June	-	Blue Ridge Barbecue Festival, North Carolina State Championship - Tryon – Carl Wharton (704) 859-6236.
June	-	Hillsborough Hog Day – Hillsborough – Pat or Lois (919) 732-8156.
*Sept.	-	Annual Bubba Fest South Carolina State Championship – Duncan, SC – Chet Hoag (864) 949-8242.
*Oct.	-	Jack Daniel's World Championship – Lynchburg, TN – Tara Shupe (615) 279-4165.
Oct.	-	Lexington Barbecue Festival – Lexington – Kay Saintsing (336) 956-1880.
Nov.	-	7th Annual Homebuilders Hog Happen' – Shelby – Jerry Gardner (704) 482-4202.

Note(*) indicates event outside North Carolina
Note: Call in advance, dates change annually

James H. Early, Jr.

1320 Westgate Center Drive

Winston-Salem, NC 27103

Fold here

Information can be sent by e-mail to jearlyjratty@earthlink.net

Please cut out card, fill in back, fold where indicated, affix postage and mail.

Name and address of your favorite place:

1 _____

_____

_____

2 Phone (   ) _____

_____

_____

Phone (   ) _____

Senders name _____

Phone (   ) _____

Sender's name and phone number are optional

Please cut out, fold over, tape to seal and affix postage on other side.

Thank You.

Please print